OLIVI AND FRANCISCAN POVERTY

University of Pennsylvania Press
MIDDLE AGES SERIES
Edited by
EDWARD PETERS
Henry Charles Lea Professor
of Medieval History
University of Pennsylvania

A complete listing of the books in this series
appears at the back of this volume

OLIVI
and
FRANCISCAN
POVERTY

The Origins of the *Usus Pauper*
Controversy

DAVID BURR

upp

UNIVERSITY OF PENNSYLVANIA PRESS
Philadelphia

Library of Congress Cataloging-in-Publication Data

Burr, David, 1934–
  Olivi and Franciscan poverty: the origins of the usus pauper
controversy / David Burr.
    p.   cm. — (Middle Ages series)
  Bibliography: p.
  Includes index.
  ISBN 0-8122-8151-9
  1. Franciscans—History. 2. Poverty, Vow of—History. 3. Olivi,
Pierre Jean, 1248 or 9–1298. I. Title. II. Series.
BX3603.B87   1989
271'.3'009022—dc19   88-39056
                                                              CIP

CONTENTS

ABBREVIATIONS

AF	*Analecta franciscana*
AFH	*Archivum franciscanum historicum*
Archiv	Heinrich Denifle and Franz Ehrle, *Archiv für Literatur- und Kirchengeschichte des Mittelalters*
BF	*Bullarium franciscanum*
CF	*Collectanea franciscana*
FS	*Franciscan Studies*
Gen.	*Lectura super Genesim*
Isa.	*Lectura super Isaiam*
Job	*Lectura super Iob*
MF	*Miscellanea francescana*
Minor Prophets	*Lectura super prophetas minores*
Mtt.	*Lectura super Matthaeum*
Rev.	*Lectura super apocalypsim*
RSCI	*Rivista di storia della chiesa in Italia*
SF	*Studi francescani*

PREFACE

On May 7, 1318, in the marketplace at Marseilles, four Franciscans were burned at the stake. Their deaths were significant not only to themselves but to their entire order. For approximately four decades the Franciscans had been divided into warring factions. As late as 1312 these factions had been summoned by Pope Clement V to confront one another almost as equals, or at least as representing two opinions worthy of serious consideration. In 1316, however, the elections of Michael of Cesena as minister general and John XXII as pope had tipped the scales toward one group, and by early 1317 the other was being asked to concede or face the consequences. The four brothers who died at Marseilles chose the latter course. Others would soon follow.

Although the resulting persecution did not entirely succeed in crushing the dissidents, it did mark them as outside the limits of orthodoxy. Thus the fires of 1318 might be considered significant, not as the end of a movement but as the end of an era. If this era closed around 1318, when did it open? The answer obviously depends on what one sees as the basic issue separating these factions. In 1318, papal authority was the question which sent the four Franciscans to their deaths. In the fall of 1317, John XXII had promulgated the bull *Quorumdam exigit*, which ordered the spirituals (as the dissidents were termed by that date) to stop protesting and start obeying their superiors, even if they thought it meant compromising their standards. John's message was neatly summarized in a single line: "Poverty is great, but unity is greater; obedience is the greatest good of all if it is preserved intact."[1]

Shortly thereafter, Michael of Cesena had confronted a group of spirituals with two questions: would they comply with *Quorumdam exigit*, and did they believe the pope had the authority to make the demands contained in that bull? The four who died were part of a twenty-five-man group which had answered "no." All but the four had recanted, although some of them later recanted their recantations and became fugitives.

The question of papal authority was hardly a new one in 1318. Peter Olivi had already discussed the matter in his *Questions on Evangelical*

Perfection, and a group of brothers in the March of Ancona had been disciplined at least partly for their stand on it; yet it would be incorrect to explain the controversy as nothing more than an argument over the pope's power. The four brothers at Marseilles went to the stake not because they were willing to die for a theoretical position on papal authority but because they were unwilling to obey a specific papal command.

That command entailed compromising what they referred to as *usus pauper*, restricted use of goods, in specific areas such as food and clothing. John XXII and Michael of Cesena had ordered them to discard their "short, tight, unusual, and squalid habits" in favor of regulation garb as defined by their superiors, and to concur with the latter's decision to store wheat and wine. They had refused. This issue lies closer to the center of the controversy. One faction wanted to limit consumption through a strict interpretation of the Franciscan rule, while the other favored a flexible approach more in keeping with the phenomenal size attained by the order and more useful in discharging the new pastoral, educational, and administrative functions which Franciscans had assumed by that date.

Nevertheless, whatever importance the idea of restricted use may have assumed in the controversy, it was by no means the only issue involved. If it had been, then the *usus pauper* controversy might be said to have begun the first time one of the brothers asked for an extra piece of bread or a thicker habit. The question of more or less was as old as the order itself, but between approximately 1279 and 1318 it was debated in a very new context. If the four Franciscans at Marseilles were not dying to defend a thesis on papal authority, neither were they simply defending their right to live austerely should they wish to do so. They went to the stake because they felt they could not do otherwise, having vowed to obey the Franciscan rule. They were bound to *usus pauper* because they saw it as an essential part of the Franciscan vow. Their opponents disagreed, believing that their vow to observe the rule committed them to lack of personal or communal property but not to restricted use of other people's property.

Thus the distinguishing characteristic of the *usus pauper* controversy was that the long-term debate over the degree of restricted use suitable for a Franciscan was combined with another over the relationship between restricted use and the vow. For the modern historian, the latter debate surfaces in southern France in the writings of Peter Olivi. Shortly before the bull *Exiit qui seminat* was promulgated in August 1279, Olivi wrote two questions on poverty. The first was essentially a further installment in the secular-mendicant controversy, which had been in progress for over two decades. The second explicitly asked whether *usus pauper* was part of the vow and concluded that it was. It is impossible to say whether the latter question was the first to address this issue, although existing evidence makes it equally impossible to believe that the matter had received much attention before then. In any case, once Olivi's opinion began to circulate, the controversy escalated rapidly and soon caused serious trouble.

The debate in southern France was originally a battle among lectors about a relatively abstract point, but practical issues were also involved. The two positions on *usus pauper* were adopted by groups with notably different attitudes toward practice. Olivi's view was attractive to those who insisted on tighter standards of conduct, while his opponents' stance proved convenient for those who sought greater latitude. Nevertheless, the debate in its early stages was not tightly bound to such aims. There were other valid reasons for objecting to Olivi's formulation, and these reasons dominated at first. The question of rigor versus laxity entered the controversy only gradually, and it is not until the 1290s that one finds solid evidence of a serious problem on that issue in southern France.

There *is* evidence of such a problem in the 1270s, but it comes from Italy. By 1279 the question of practice had produced a deep rift between some Italian zealots and their leaders, but their argument did not encompass the theoretical question of whether *usus pauper* was part of the vow. Thus Italy seems to have been far ahead of southern France in one sphere and well behind it in another. During the following decades each area caught up with the other.

My major intent in this work is to investigate the first two decades of the *usus pauper* controversy, which are coterminous with the last two decades of Olivi's life. This is the period about which least has been said over the years. Franz Ehrle and others have published a number of sources for the period from 1308 on, and several contemporary historians have written extensively about it;[2] yet little has been printed about the controversy up to that point. As a result, scholars have tended to see the origins of the controversy in terms of the debate over it at the Council of Vienne. David Flood remarks that Ehrle's pioneering study of Olivi was inspired by his research on the Council of Vienne, and thus Ehrle had, "as he made his way through the busy traffic of council dispute, a rearview mirror image of the man."[3] Much the same could be said for subsequent investigations.

The sources necessary for a study of Olivi and his time have long been available in manuscript form and are now finally receiving the critical editions they deserve. I had hoped that, by the time this book was published, readers could verify my argument by checking it against editions of questions eight, nine, fifteen, and sixteen of Olivi's *Questions on Evangelical Perfection*, as well as of his *Treatise on Usus Pauper*. Unfortunately, while all but question fifteen are now essentially finished, only question sixteen is in print. More will follow, however.

There are, as always, too many people to thank. I am especially grateful to the National Endowment for the Humanities and the American Philosophical Society for grants that enabled me to work with the manuscripts and to the Bodleian Library, Oxford, for excellent service during the year spent there. Beyond that, I need only point to the list of manuscripts to suggest the complex pattern of debts I have incurred across western Europe. Finally, I am indebted to a series of excellent scholars, including E. R. Daniel, Charles Davis, Bernard McGinn, Robert Lerner, the late Decima Douie, Marjorie Reeves, David Flood, and many others for their advice and gentle correction.

Notes

1. *BF* (Rome, 1759–1904), 5:130.
2. Franz Ehrle, "Die Spiritualen, ihr Verhaltniss zum Franciscanerorden und zu den Fraticellen," in *Archiv* (Berlin, 1885–1900), 1:509–69; 2:106–64, 249–336; 3:553–623; 4:1–190; "Zur Vorgeschichte des Concils von Vienne," in *Archiv*, 2:353–416; 3:1–195. Two of the better contemporary studies are Malcolm Lambert, *Franciscan Poverty* (London, 1961), and Marino Damiata, *Guglielmo d'Ockham* (Florence, 1978), vol. 1.
3. David Flood, *Peter Olivi's Rule Commentary* (Wiesbaden, 1972), 6. For Ehrle's study of Olivi, see "Petrus Johannis Olivi, sein Leben und seine Schriften," in *Archiv*, 3:409–552.

CHAPTER 1

The Franciscan Order in 1279

Between around 1279 and 1318, the Franciscans were divided by a debate over whether their vow bound them merely to lack of ownership or to restricted use as well. Thus formulated, the question was a new one; yet disagreement over practice can be traced back to Francis's time, and even before the 1270s some friars had protested against purported decay in the order. The *usus pauper* controversy had roots.

Angry Letters

Shortly after becoming minister general in 1257, Saint Bonaventure wrote a letter to his new charges.[1] He began by observing that the order, which should function as a mirror of sanctity for all, was, for a variety of reasons, regarded with loathing and contempt. Money was "avidly sought, incautiously received and even more incautiously handled." Some of the brothers were guilty of idleness and many wandered about aimlessly, burdening those who supported them. There was so much begging that travelers avoided Franciscans as though they were highwaymen.

Nor did settling down make them less burdensome. The friars caused scandal through excessive familiarity with those outside the order. They alienated the parish clergy by pursuing legacies and burial rights. They belied their dedication to poverty through sumptuous living and frequent moves to better quarters. Leadership, too, left something to be desired. Franciscans were being promoted to office before they were ready for such responsibility.

Bonaventure's solution was simple: put the idle to work; tell the complainers to be quiet; give the overly familiar a bit of solitude; and above all, obey the existing statutes concerning burial, legacies, the examination of preachers, etc.

In 1266 Bonaventure wrote again, and his mood had not improved.[2]

He announced that the order, once so loved, was now considered by many to be "despicable, burdensome and hateful." The brothers, unwilling to live in poverty, pestered the laity with fund-raising and constructed sumptuous buildings. Competition for legacies and burials had alienated the parish clergy. The problem, he observed, was that the legislation promulgated in general chapters was ignored. The solution was to start observing that legislation.

If the message had been ineffective in 1257, it was no more efficacious in 1266, and in 1273 Bonaventure again found himself chiding the Franciscans. This time, in the apocalyptically oriented *Collationes in hexaemeron*, he compared his order with ancient Israel. Backsliding heirs of the promise, they were doomed to wander in the wilderness and be purified through tribulation before they could enter the promised land.[3]

That the situation continued to worry Bonaventure's successors is clear from a letter to the order written in 1279 by another minister general, Bonagratia of San Giovanni in Persiceto.[4] It was, in effect, a covering letter for the papal bull *Exiit qui seminat*, which attempted to defend the Franciscan rule from external criticism and clarify it for the Franciscans themselves. Bonagratia began by reporting Pope Nicholas III's threat that the Franciscan order "would be shaken right to the hair of our head if we were not more careful in the future, both in word and in deed." He went on to catalog areas in which caution should be exercised. The brothers should be more careful in handling money, avoid unnecessary travel, cease horseback riding, and stop promoting the unfit to office. Bonagratia ordered that ministers, custodians, and guardians be more zealous in demanding obedience of the statutes, "concerning which the brothers seem noticeably lukewarm, as experience shows."

A common thread runs through the Bonaventuran and Bonagratian letters. Both men saw notable slippage, but neither portrayed the problem as structural, the result of contradictions built into the order. Both described the basic difficulty as lack of attention to the statutes promulgated by general chapters and suggested that the solution was to observe these statutes.[5] Nevertheless, it would be dangerous to conclude from these writings that either man really thought the problem that simple. If they saw deeper causes, they could hardly have been expected to address them in hortatory letters to the entire order. Nor could Bonaventure have been expected to agonize over them in other works written to defend the Franciscans against outside criticism. In the latter, he acknowledged violations of poverty but was likely to underline that he was speaking of exceptions, an affliction which even the twelve disciples suffered.[6]

Some Explanations

This observation would have to be modified if Bonaventure were credited with authorship of the *Determinations of Questions Concerning the Rule*,[7] but most modern scholars prefer to assign them elsewhere.[8] The author of this work celebrates the legitimate prerogatives of the secular clergy but defends the Franciscans' right to preach and hear confessions despite clerical opposition, because there are pressing needs which the parish clergy are either unwilling or unprepared to fulfill. The possibility of excessive construction is acknowledged, but the writer explains in some detail why the Franciscan mission to society necessitates large building complexes in the heart of town.[9] Tall buildings may seem to be a departure from Franciscan poverty, but they are really just the opposite because otherwise the brothers would need more land. Stone buildings may seem extravagant, but they really save money because they protect books, liturgical ornaments, and so on from fire. Extensive grounds may seem undesirable, but they are necessary to protect the mental and physical health of those who devote their lives to spiritual perfection.[10]

These are, of course, rationalizations, but the total argument is quite consistent. The writer accepts the Franciscan mission as dictated by thirteenth-century popes. His brothers have important work to do and need the resources to do it. Nevertheless, he is often disarmingly frank about those same brothers' limitations. During occasional pauses to reflect on the dynamics of decline in a religious order, he offers three different types of explanation. First, there are explanations based on individual failings. Some people enter the order after a life of luxury and cannot tolerate extreme self-denial; some are less endowed with spiritual gifts than others; some are simply hypocrites.[11]

Second, there are explanations involving change within the institution itself. Greater numbers make spiritual direction more difficult and contribute to laxity. Increased wealth, greater contact with the world, and heavy involvement in practical tasks all take their toll. Frequent changes of leadership, though effective in weeding out bad superiors, are ultimately counterproductive because the new leaders hesitate to work for reform, knowing that the result would be a movement calling for their own ouster.[12]

Third, the author occasionally transcends such contingencies and posits something resembling a law of inevitable spiritual decline. Those who originally caused the fame of an order eventually die or, becoming old and weakened by years of self-discipline, can no longer provide a good example for newer members. If these older brothers are leaders, they hesitate to demand what they cannot themselves perform. Even if they are not leaders, they are still a problem because their superiors cannot hold them at a level of extreme austerity or they will perish and the young, seeing their fate, will avoid austerity. If superiors allow the older brothers a less arduous life, however, they will have to grant it to all in order to avoid complaints among the young and embarrassment among the old. Thus the young become used to relaxed discipline and, when leadership devolves upon them, they govern the order accordingly. Once such relaxations become accepted they are extremely hard to reverse. Even if leaders recognize them for what they are, the desire to live peacefully and avoid greater trouble will usually prevent them from doing much to reverse the situation.[13]

Whether or not these comments were produced by Bonaventure—and scholars tend to say that they were not—they are intriguing. They add up to a very tough-minded appraisal: all is not as it once was, but in view of time, increased numbers, altered function, and human fallibility, a certain amount of decline is inevitable.

Overall, the analysis is not a bad one. It anticipates much that has been said by modern historians. Time was certainly a factor. There is no way to institutionalize a dream, and a spiritual law of entropy seems apparent in the history of all religious reforms. The increased size of the order also had its impact. Around 1210 there were twelve Franciscans, but according to one recent estimate there may have been thirty thousand by mid-century, with one-third of that number in Italy.[14] If so, then by mid-century perhaps one in every thousand Italians was a Franciscan. Such an increase would surely produce a drop in quality. One out of every thousand people cannot be expected to emulate Saint Francis, even in Italy.

Expansion of the order also encouraged bureaucratization. Francis had called for leaders who, like the Son of Man, sought not to be served but to serve.[15] The very titles of office chosen by him are significant: *minister, custos,* and *guardianus* all reflect his ideal. The word *prior* was rejected.[16] There was to be discipline and even physical constraint if necessary, but these were to be exercised mercifully and with genuine pastoral concern.[17] Moreover, Francis expected such coercion to be exercised not only by the leaders but by the rank and file as well.[18] In fact, in the rule of 1221 the latter are to some extent given the task of overseeing the former. They are advised not only to withhold obedience if told to act in violation of the rules or their own souls but to study their superior's conduct carefully and, if they are not edified, to denounce him at the next general chapter meeting.[19] According to Théophile Desbonnets, this mutual surveillance reflects a fundamental element in early Franciscan spirituality. Obedience was primarily a matter of listening to the word of God and to the spirit; yet the privileged intermediary of that communication was not the abbot as in Benedictine monasticism but the brotherhood in a diffuse sense. The result was a substantial respect for individual liberty and responsibility.[20]

There is no way to describe in a few words how expansion compromised this vision of Franciscan governance, but some results seem obvious enough. Leaders had to be less concerned with cultivating personal, pastoral relationships and more concerned with enforcing regulations to protect general standards and preserve order. Subordinates inevitably lost some of the freedom and responsibility implied by the surveillance duties Francis had assigned them. Even by 1221 such duties must have seemed dangerous to those entrusted with governing the order. The 1223 rule, while continuing to promulgate the characteristically Franciscan ideal of the leader as loving servant, reduced the friars' supervisory powers, although it limited their obedience requirement to "those things which they have promised the Lord to observe and which are not against their souls or our rule."[21] A leadership class, based on education and clerical status, soon developed in the order.[22]

The same popularity which caused rapid expansion also resulted in the recruitment of Franciscans to occupy a rich variety of spiritual and secular offices. Popes encouraged friars to become teachers, preachers, pastors, inquisitors, bishops, and cardinals. Kings enlisted them in royal administration. City governments employed them in a variety of roles. Acceptance of these offices changed the order in several ways. First, it attracted people who were willing and even anxious to perform such functions. Recruits could now see the order not as a way of renouncing worldly success but as a means of achieving it. Franciscanism became a career opportunity. That fact becomes doubly significant when one reflects that those with such proclivities were precisely the people who might be expected to gain leadership positions within the order.

Second, the new offices gave Franciscans worldly power, and that in itself was problematic. Although Francis, in a reflective moment, might have been willing to acknowledge that he exercised an impressive amount of spiritual, charismatic authority over those outside the order, he tended to see juridical, coercive authority as something to which Franciscans should submit. The nature of the order he envisaged was implicit in its title: the *ordo fratrum minorum*. Francis wanted to be *minor* in the sense that he wanted to identify with what are now termed the marginal elements of society: the poor, the weak, the humble, and the despised. His ultimate aim was identification with Christ, who voluntarily became poor, weak, humble, and despised for mankind. Francis's notion of poverty emerged from that context. He saw it as one aspect of a self-emptying which involved the surrender not only of possessions but of prestige and power.[23]

Once the order began to exercise new functions, this goal was harder to attain. Many of the offices given to the Franciscans entailed coercive power over others, and such power might be disputed or at least resented. Franciscans were forced into a new relationship not only with those over whom they exercised this power but also with those who felt they themselves should be exercising it.

Here again there is no way to document this claim in a few words. In cases like the episcopacy or Inquisition, it seems to require no documentation. In other cases like teaching or pastoral ministry, the coercive power may seem less obvious, but it was there nonetheless. At any rate, exercise of the latter two offices involved the order in a prolonged and bitter power struggle with the secular clergy. This struggle seems at variance with the Francis's ideal of submission;[24] yet Franciscans were driven into it not merely by personal ambition but by a sense of mission. They had been assigned certain tasks by God through the pope, tasks they were admirably fitted to perform. The priest, bishop, or scholar who stood in their way was opposing not only the Franciscans but God and the pope as well.[25]

Third, the new offices enabled or even encouraged their holders to enjoy higher living standards. Indeed, the officeholder could occasionally argue that there was no escape from opulence if he wanted to perform his appointed task. It seemed sensible to some late thirteenth-century friars that the pomp and luxury which accompanied episcopal office should be viewed, not as a perquisite, but as a symbol without which the bishop's authority would be compromised. In other cases such an argument might have seemed less rationally satisfying, yet the connection between the office and its material rewards had gained something approaching inevitability through established practice. A Franciscan cardinal found himself in an ethos where there was nothing odd about being offered a retainer by some foreign power in the expectation that he would intervene benevolently at the opportune moment.[26] The conscientious friar could renounce such payments if he wished, but he would be defying custom in the process. In still other cases the office ostensibly offered no such rewards, but the Franciscan was nonetheless plunged into a situation that allowed him to prove Lord Acton's dictum about power. Inquisitorial office offered ample opportunity for corruption, and there is evidence that, when Franciscans were given that office, its temptations occasionally mastered them.[27]

The notion of new offices must not be overemphasized. In some ways the order was still doing precisely what Francis had envisaged. Its commitment to missionary activity among the heathen and evangelical preaching within Christendom remained strong.[28] Nevertheless, even the areas which reflect continuity also show significant change. In essence, Franciscans came to stand in a different relationship with one another and with the world.

The author of the *Determinations* did omit one important solvent of the early minorite ideal. Friars were called upon to play an important role in popular piety. This role was in some ways at variance with their own goals, yet it was probably the most pervasive result of their popularity. Most of the offices heaped upon Franciscans were held by a small elite, but their role in popular religion was shared by the order at large. This is such an important point that consideration of it will be reserved for a later, fuller discussion.

It can hardly have escaped the reader's attention that these developments endangered other aspects of the Franciscan vision besides poverty. The point is worth emphasizing because modern scholars have tended to regard poverty as the central issue in determining whether Franciscans remained true to their founder. This distortion is to some extent a legacy of late thirteenth- and early fourteenth-century reformers, who chose to argue about that particular element within the total apostolic life envisaged by Francis, thereby obscuring the fact that other elements were equally at risk. In reality, poverty was no more threatened than humility, and neither was in greater danger than the brotherly love that characterized early Franciscan life. In fact, one could maintain that in the later thirteenth century, poverty became a bit of high ground defended long after Francis's ideal had been defeated on other parts of the battlefield. *Maioritas* had been thrust upon the Franciscans in the form of new duties, offices, and honors. On the whole they had accepted it; yet they could still try to assure that, as the friar pursued his appointed task, he at least observed *minoritas* through restricted use of goods.

Legislation

How did the Franciscans attempt to assure their dedication to poverty? When ministers general decried laxity, they were likely to prescribe observance of the statutes as a remedy. Modern scholars are apt to regard this advice as itself evidence of laxity, since it implies a retreat from strict observance of the rule in favor of less demanding constitutions. Whether they are justified in this belief is another matter. There are a few negative witnesses. Jacopone da Todi writes of the statutes that "the first to propose them is the first to break them," and Salimbene reports that when leaders at the chapter of Metz in 1254 asked the minister general, John of Parma, for constitutions, he suggested that instead of multiplying them they ought to try keeping the ones they already had.[29] The general picture derived from Ubertino da Casale in the early fourteenth century is that of a community hell-bent on securing laxity through legislation yet unwilling to meet even these reduced standards. The reality seems a bit more complex. John of Parma may well have uttered the *bon mot* in question, but he also joined in creating new statutes.[30] Moreover, even if many Italian spirituals were skeptical about the constitutions,[31] French spirituals such as Olivi and Raymond Geoffroi showed confidence in them.

Much of the legislation between 1260 and 1279 suggests that their confidence was justified. The constitutions of Narbonne in 1260 represented the first major effort at codification.[32] Far from relaxing the rule, they tried to build a fence around it through prohibitions that specified and at times exceeded restrictions vaguely stated in the rule. For example, the rule tells Franciscans to observe *vilitas* in choosing their habits. The constitutions of Narbonne determine that this refers to color, size, and shape as well as cost; forbids completely black or white habits; and demands that the entire house including its leaders use the same commonly purchased wool, which must not be carded.

What the constitutions do for clothing they also attempt to do for food. Brothers must not eat meat unless required to do so by illness or debilitated condition. They must not arrange for meat meals outside the house. If some pious layman wants to provide them with a special treat (*pitancia*) in the cloister or at a chapter meeting, they should be content with one dish. When on business outside the cloister, they should not drink in town and should dine only with prelates, lords of the land or other religious. Some attempt is made to specify fasting regulations.[33]

Far from being relaxed, the constitutions of Narbonne were generally either left unchanged or tightened up by succeeding chapters at Paris (1266), Lyons (1274), Padua (1276), and Assisi (1279). It is of course dangerous to assume too great a correlation between surviving legislation and actual practice. The constitutions of Narbonne take a firm position against eating meat, and, if it were not for another document, we would never know that the same general chapter absolved lectors from that prohibition. Succeeding chapters provide even less information, but what is available indicates little obvious slackening.

There is some relaxation. The Narbonne prohibition against taking a *bursarius* or secular servant to carry money on trips was modified at Assisi by adding that, in the case of a long, necessary trip in a situation that precluded begging, the brothers' needs should be met through some honest *nuntius* to whom money was provided.[34] One suspects that the brothers had readmitted the forbidden practice through the simple expedient of renaming it. Even more interesting, perhaps, is the announcement at Strasbourg in 1282 that those who attend general chapter meetings should not bring servants *if they can do without them* and those who must bring them should share one for each province.[35] Given the size of the order and the distances traveled by Franciscans, one might well argue that these were acceptable relaxations, but they were relaxations nonetheless and invited more of the same. Provincial statutes of Aquitaine produced between 1280 and 1296 allowed first one *nuntius* for each custody at provincial chapter meetings, then two.[36]

Another significant relaxation was allowed at the 1279 Assisi general chapter meeting. Whereas the constitutions of Narbonne had limited *pitanciae* to one dish, the Assisi chapter gave guardians the power to do otherwise for rational cause. This change is noteworthy, not because the order was irrecovably corrupted by two-course dinners, but because it demonstrates an important element in Franciscan legislation during the following years. Anyone who has had much contact with large organizations knows that he who attempts to live entirely by statutes will probably die smothered in them. This is partly due to change—new situations seem to call for additional rules—but it also happens because life is very complex, and laws that seemed precise when promulgated have a way of appearing amorphous on further reflection.

This phenomenon is illustrated not only by the successive waves of Franciscan legislation but also by the *Explanations of the General Constitutions of Narbonne*, which are sometimes attributed to Bonaventure.[37] In this document, an anonymous friar seeks clarification. He has read the constitutions and he has a few questions. For example, the constitutions insist that brothers are to have only one tunic each, which may be patched. The questioner recognizes that patching is envisaged not simply as a way or repairing damage but as a method of fortifying strategic areas against the cold. Thus he asks whether he can wear two tunics sewn together, one of them being considered, in effect, a very large patch. If so, can he disassemble them and use them separately when the cold weather is over? If so, then in autumn, when the weather is changeable, can he sometimes wear one, sometimes both?

Again, the questioner knows he is supposed to sleep in his habit except when it is manifestly necessary to remove it. Does a wet habit constitute necessity? If so, is "manifest necessity" to be determined by the person alone or by others as well? In other words, must a friar wake people in the middle of the night to witness that his habit is wet?

Again, the questioner is concerned about the possibility of finding himself on the road and in need of a cart. He knows he can accept a ride only if it is necessary, but what if only he and his *socius* are present to make the judgment? If they can decide, then what should their criteria be? Are great fatigue and inclement weather sufficient reasons to climb aboard? What if his companion accepts an unnecessary ride, thus placing the questioner in a position where he will break the rules either by riding or by abandoning his companion?

In his odyssey through the constitutions, the questioner pauses again and again to demand elucidation of a specific word. Granting that the brothers should not customarily wear shoes, what does "customarily" mean? If they cannot ask money from *transeuntes*, does that word mean anyone passing through the city or foreigners only? On each occasion the respondent must provide a definition, and it takes little foresight to see that the definition itself will often call for further definition. As the questioner proceeds in what one can almost hear as an insistent, wheedling tone, his queries normally point toward relaxation. He is in search of loopholes. Nor does he fail to discover them. The harried respondent often grants him the extra room he seeks.

Despite the unintentionally humorous aspect of the *Explanations*, they point to a hard fact about organizations and the rules that govern them. If a group is to adopt standards and apply them, someone has to deal with specific cases. That can be done through legislation or by giving local officials the right to use their wits. The statutes did a surprising amount of the former, but they also did the latter. Franciscan leaders were realistic enough to see that provincial ministers, custodes, guardians, and even individual friars had to be granted a certain amount of discretionary power. In following this course, the leaders were simply acknowledging what the rule itself already presupposed. Nevertheless, it meant granting freedom that could be and sometimes was abused.

Perhaps the word *grant* is itself misleading. Whatever authority the minister general and general chapter might possess in theory, their control over local situations was quite limited. Even their knowledge had its limitations, although formal and informal channels were available. Throughout the period each province was required to send visitors to another before every general chapter meeting and report excesses to the general chapter. Custodes were supposed to visit their charges at least once a year. Provincial ministers could do so as well, but it was not required. There was also a mechanism by which each level (local, custodial, provincial) regularly investigated and reported on its own leaders.[38] Thus in theory provincial chapters were aware of local and custodial flaws, while general chapters were informed of provincial failings. Corrections could be attempted through exhortation, change of leaders, or visitation.

How well the system worked is impossible to say. Presumably, most abuses would have been noted at no higher level than the provincial. Those necessarily reported to the general chapter (for example, those uncovered through interprovincial visitation) would depend on the acuity and standards of the visitors for their very status as abuses. The only way a general minister could be confident of receiving a balanced picture was to send his own visitors on tour or visit the provinces himself. The former could not be done often without exhausting provincial patience, and ministers had little time for the latter even when the pope was not sending them off on other errands.

For the most part, the task of maintaining decent standards was in the hands of provincial ministers, custodes, and guardians. Thus in order to know what the order was like in the later thirteenth century, one must examine individual provinces and towns. The earliest extant provincial statutes probably tell us more about the first decade or so after the *usus pauper* controversy began than about the decade or so before, but they are instructive nonetheless. They present a picture of regional leaders responding to regional problems. They also offer a clearer picture of economic realities than does the legislation of general chapters. We find statutes that ponder the grim necessity of pawning books to cover expenses. We hear the guardians being admonished to make friars pay their debts, confiscating their books if necessary. We meet guardians arriving at the provincial chapter to report the annual income, yearly expenses, and current indebtedness of their convents.[39] We begin to see the texture of life in a Franciscan convent.

Local Entanglements

An even clearer picture of economic realities emerges at the local level. Wills can be enormously revealing in this respect. The use of books will serve as an example. Arlotto of Prato, writing as minister general in 1286, notes that laymen are free to give books to individuals or convents, but the provincial minister or custode can still decide who uses them.[40] His assertion seems generally supported by provincial constitutions.[41]

The bequests of Bolognese novices about to profess their vows seem to reflect a very different world. In 1297, one novice gives a confrere, Brother Bartholomeus, two books with a total value of 72 libri Bolognesi (hereafter represented as L.72) and an additional L.28 to buy more books. If Bartholomeus dies before the testator, the latter is to receive all the books, and upon his death they are to go to Brother Hugolinus. When Hugolinus dies, they are to be sold and the money is to be used to purchase a piece of land that will be held by the Clares with the income from it going annually to a specifically designated Franciscan house.[42] This is rather careful planning for a man who is technically about to flee the world, but the testator at least deals himself into the will only at a later date. In 1281 another novice leaves himself L.100 for books of which he is to have the use during his lifetime, and in 1284 other novices leave themselves sums of L.180, L.150, and L.200 for that purpose.[43] These are not trifling sums. One could have eked out an existence on L.15 per year.[44]

It is also instructive to note how Bolognese laymen treated the Franciscans in their wills. An example can be seen in the career of one Bonaventura de Gisso. He makes his debut in 1268 when his mother, Gualdina, desiring to be buried among the Franciscans, leaves L.6 for a *pitancia* to the Bologna convent and various small sums to individual friars. As executors she names her husband, Gandolphus, and her son Bonaventura, OFM, who is to receive L.50 upon Gandolphus's death.[45]

Bonaventura appears in four wills during the 1270s and 1280s, witnessing three and receiving money in two. During the 1290s he seems to have become one of Bologna's favorite friars, for he appears in seventeen wills and receives money in eight of them. In one of these, he is one of three Franciscans who each receive L.5 in a single payment and another 30 solidi annually for life.[46] In 1300 his star continued to ascend, for he appears in thirteen wills, receiving over L.11 for his own needs plus another L.32 to distribute at his discretion. Nor does Bonaventura bear away the prize as Bolognese friar with the highest income during this period. One Franciscan appears in a stunning seventy-eight wills between 1286 and 1300, averages around L.10 per annum in bequests during the 1290s, and receives over L.29 in 1300 alone.[47]

Such people are worth studying, not as examples of minorite decadence but as evidence of tendencies that made laxity difficult to control. Many of these friars were local products. It is difficult to move as a pilgrim and stranger through streets in which one has played as a child, streets one's own family may still control, often with extreme violence. When Bonaventura's mother wrote her will, it was only natural that her son should be named an executor, not to mention a beneficiary. Family solidarity thus extended into the cloister, making one degree more difficult that departure from worldly society presupposed by the Franciscan vocation.

Popular Piety

Nor were family members the only problem. Lay generosity toward the friars was motivated by religious assumptions that were in some ways antithetical to Franciscan rigor. For example, laymen knew that voluntary poverty was a good thing, but they also knew that feeding the poor was one of the seven acts of mercy and therefore meritorious. Whatever else the friars represented to the laity, they were the "poor of Christ"— even when that designation seemed ludicrously inexact—and they were treated accordingly. Thus King Louis IX and others not only fed individual Franciscans in their homes but provided sumptuous meals for whole groups of them.[48] Laymen often left substantial sums to individuals and to convents as a whole. In doing so, they were motivated by desire to help the friars and themselves. Refusal of their gifts thwarted their efforts at spiritual self-improvement.

Restitution of ill-gotten gains also played a role. Laymen acknowledged that they were supposed to restore them but did not always know precisely whom they had wronged. Thus they not only asked Franciscan and other executors to distribute money to known victims but left large sums to the "poor of Christ," who served as proxies for unknown victims. Sometimes the friars were designated as recipients. On other occasions they were simply asked to designate the recipient and, yielding to the obvious temptation, named themselves.[49]

Lay piety also put increasing stress on prayers and anniversary masses. People wanted to hasten their progress from purgatory to heaven by subsidizing those who could pray for them.[50] They left money to convents and individuals with precisely that stipulation, and sometimes the rich created whole convents for that purpose.

All of these elements come together in the 1292 will of Obizzo II d'Este, lord of Ferrara.[51] Obizzo says he wants a *locus religiosus* constructed just outside the gates of "our town," Rovigo. It will house fifty Franciscans, at least twelve of them priests. Every day, in a church which is to be "great, long, wide and spacious," a mass will be celebrated for Obizzo's soul and for the souls of those he has wronged. Since he leaves L.10,000 Venetian to cover construction costs, he can reasonably expect something special in the way of size. The friars are free to offer any other prayers they may consider fitting in the new church, but Obizzo must be included in them, too.

Having made his contribution to Franciscan architecture, Obizzo does some administrative reshuffling. The Franciscan convent already at Rovigo is to be joined with this one. It seems that the Rovigo convent is already committed to praying for another benefactor. Obizzo graciously allows it to continue. The new convent (or, as Obizzo keeps calling it, "our place") is to be included in the province of Bologna. It should have a *studium generale* to which each citramontane province will send one student.

The project must be initiated within two years and completed in five. If the Franciscans fail to meet these deadlines, the bequest will go to the Dominicans, and the Franciscans will be held accountable for any money already received. If the Dominicans, too, fail to measure up, the Templars are next in line.

Should the Franciscans lose this inheritance, they will drag the Clares down with them. Obizzo leaves to the Sisters Minor of Ferrara lands yielding an income of L.1,000 per annum plus L.3,000 with which they are to buy more land. The income from all this real estate will go to Obizzo's Franciscan convent, but the Clares can keep 10 percent. If the Sisters Minor of Ferrara prove to be negligent stewardesses, the land and 10 percent of its income will go to the Sisters of St. Anthony. If the Franciscans fall behind on the construction schedule and the Dominicans take over, the Sisters of St. Catherine will succeed the Clares. If the Sisters of St. Catherine turn out to be inept landlords, the Sisters of St. Barnabas will get their chance. Once the place is built, the Franciscans can still lose it by failing to fulfill their obligations, in which case the same order of succession will apply.

As executors of his will, Obizzo, ever cognizant of his own worth, designates the minister general of the Franciscan order, the provincial ministers of Lombardy and Treviso, and the guardians of Ferrara, Padua, and "our place." They will, of course, be changed accordingly if the Dominicans take over.

Having arranged for his new *locus religiosus*, Obizzo turns to the problem of ill-gotten gains. He leaves L.5000 to the Sisters Minor at Ferrara. They are to buy land with it, keep 10 percent of the profits, and give the rest to the "poor of Christ" in cities where the testator seems to have done evil. Obizzo specifies that by the "poor of Christ" he means those begging door-to-door. He wants one hundred of them clothed each year. All of these things are to be accomplished with the counsel of specifically designated Franciscans. Here again failure will result in another group taking over.

So much for *male ablata incerta*, wrongs against those who cannot be identified. Obizzo also leaves, this time to the executors, L.30,000 with which they are to buy land. The income from it will be used to redress wrongs against those who can prove their case. We are now in the realm of *male ablata certa*. Should L.30,000 prove inadequate to satisfy the flood of applicants Obizzo seems to anticipate, he creates a reserve fund of L.50,000. Should that, too, fail to suffice, the executors can sell some of his possessions. After five years, the claim period will end and all income from the land will go annually to the "poor of Christ" as designated by the executors or by specifically named local Franciscans. This time Obizzo notes that he does not want it to go to any religious order.

Of course, he wants to be buried in his new church. If it is completed by the time he dies—a touching bit of optimism on his part—he is to be placed there immediately. If not, he wants to lie with the Franciscans at Ferrara and be transferred to Rovigo as soon as possible.

One wonders how the Franciscan leadership reacted to this will. Obizzo was not so much contributing to a Franciscan convent as stocking a private chapel. To support it, he was setting up precisely the sort of annual revenue the Franciscans opposed elsewhere as violating the purity of their rule.[52] Only the dubious practice of laundering money through the Clares prevented the friars from being landowners as well. He was also involving the friars in those secular concerns inescapably connected with executing a will.[53] Then again, there was the family to consider. The will provides sanctions against any relatives who might offer "injury or molestation" to the beneficiaries, but these words must have been a chilling reminder to the executors that the family might not be entirely happy with Obizzo's project.

Nevertheless, one can understand why the Franciscans may have considered it an offer they could not afford to refuse. One thinks twice before offending a man who provides a small fortune to redress past victims who cannot be identified and an even larger amount to cover victims who can, then wonders if he has set aside enough. Even ignoring that element, however, there was the irreducible fact that Obizzo was an important leader with a network of allies. Those Franciscans who wanted to live humbly still had to depend on the generosity of others. Thus they had to avoid offending the laity, particularly the rich and powerful.[54] Moreover, in this particular case their refusal to accept Obizzo's conditions would deprive not only themselves but the Clares of support.

One might expect that, had the Franciscans attempted to preserve their virtue in the face of lay efforts to enrich them, they could have counted on support from their ultimate earthly protector, the pope; yet the supreme pontiff often proved strangely unsympathetic as he pursued his own ends. This is demonstrated by the lengthy battle over a Venetian will in which one Marcus Zianus gave land for a convent and arranged for six friars to be supported there so that they could perpetually say anniversary masses for him. The Franciscan provincial minister apparently decided that perpetual annuities violated the rule and ordered the Venetian friars not to accept the land. This might have been the course of least resistance in any case, because the will was disputed in court, but Innocent IV confirmed the bequest. In 1255 Alexander IV ordered the reluctant Franciscans to accept the land "any contradictions to your statutes or mandate notwithstanding." Four months later, in the same terms, he again commanded them to do so.[55]

In other words, however much Franciscan leaders might have wished to maintain strict standards, a host of factors militated against their doing so. The pope and laymen alike found the Franciscans useful, and the uses to which they were put undermined some of the same characteristics that made them admirable. Far from viewing this situation with alarm, many Franciscans undoubtedly found it comfortable. Others were undoubtedly less enthusiastic. The reader is especially advised to note the word *undoubtedly*. Even before any evidence is presented, one is inclined to assume that such must have been the case, since divergence of this sort is only natural. Thus one can simply accept the existence of differences concerning the proper level of poverty, turning to a more precise and more interesting question: is there any evidence whatsoever that by 1279 those who differed on this matter were already polarizing into two factions, a "proto-spiritual" group that demanded strict observance and a more easygoing faction that saw relaxation as necessary for performance of the roles newly acquired by the order?

Factionalism Before Bonaventure

Angelo Clareno says that relaxations encouraged by Crescentius of Iesi, provincial minister in the March of Ancona and then minister general (the latter from 1244 to 1247), were so painful to certain friars that they sent a delegation to Rome with the intention of complaining to the pope. Crescentius and his henchmen discovered their plan, got to the pope first, won him over, then ambushed the delegation en route and punished them severely.[56]

It is hard to decide how much weight this story should be given. Crescentius obviously did little to guard against relaxations and probably encouraged them.[57] Moreover, other sources attest that he had trouble with rebellious friars when he was minister in the March of Ancona. Thomas of Eccleston describes this trouble as existing on the eve of his election as minister general, and thus it is possible to imagine him continuing the battle after moving on to his new responsibilities. Pelegrino da Bologna, writing in 1305, says that, shortly after becoming provincial minister, Crescentius discovered "a sect of brothers who, . . . despising the institutions of the order and thinking themselves better than others, wanted to live as they wished and attributed all to the spirit, wearing cloaks so short that they came up to their buttocks."[58]

Pelegrino's story is intriguing but not very informative. What did these scantily attired Franciscans want? What did they complain against? Only Angelo seems to answer such questions, and he is writing nearly a century later. He says that pious brothers were scandalized by "the changes in location and building projects in the cities and towns, with scandal to the clergy and people;" by "the abandoning of solitary poor places and construction of sumptuous edifices;" by the struggle for legacies and burial rights, undercutting the rightful claims of the secular clergy; by neglect of prayer and preference for "the curious and sterile knowledge of Aristotle" over divine wisdom; and by the multiplication of schools devoted to worldly knowledge. This list of grievances neatly matches the one offered by fourteenth-century Italian spirituals, but we might think twice before accepting it as a mirror of conditions in Ancona during the 1240s.

Still another source, Salimbene, alludes to trouble in Germany in late 1245 or early 1246, roughly the same period when Crescentius was confronting his Italian problem: "Certain solemn brothers, showing contempt for the discipline of the order, did not wish to obey the ministers." They went to consult Philip, archbishop of Ravenna, who was serving as legate in Germany. Philip took them prisoner and handed them over to their ministers for punishment "as the statutes of the order required."[59] Here again, the anecdote is little more than suggestive.

Crescentius's successor, John of Parma (1247–57), is one of Angelo's major heroes. The question in his case is not whether he persecuted the rigorists but whether, as Angelo suggests, leaders of the order were split on the poverty issue in John's time and his fall was partly due to his rigorist leanings. There is little evidence for that notion. The diatribes Angelo attributes to John reflect Angelo's own preoccupations too neatly to inspire confidence. Salimbene, who seems a more trustworthy witness because he knew John during that period and had no ax to grind concerning poverty, suggests that John's fall stemmed from his commitment to Joachim of Fiore's apocalyptic speculation. He notes that John lived simply and grants that he had *aemulos*; yet he does not suggest that John had enemies because he advocated living simply, nor does he suggest that advocacy of restricted use was a factor in his fall.[60] Certainly John anticipated later spiritual Franciscan complaints in trying to limit the use of papal privileges and to prevent involvement in legal wrangling over wills and burial rights, but so did other leaders, including Bonaventure.

Hugh of Digne

It seems natural to progress from John of Parma to his friend Hugh of Digne. Hugh is often volunteered by modern historians as an early example of the spiritual Franciscan mentality, but there is reason to treat this claim cautiously. We learn about Hugh from what others say of him and from what he himself says in three works. From others (Salimbene and Joinville) we discover that he expected Franciscans to take their vocations seriously and, in a sermon before King Louis IX, castigated religious for hanging about the royal court;[61] yet on other occasions he was just as willing to roast the cardinals, "rating them like asses" as Salimbene says.[62] The total impression one gets from Salimbene and Joinville is that Hugh does not fit well into any notion of growing factional dispute. He was seen by contemporaries not as spokesman for a faction but as a latter-day prophet somewhat on the model of Saint Bernard, venerated and cultivated for his occasional diatribes, the sort of man whose eloquence wins him not persecution but dinner invitations.[63]

The picture changes somewhat when we turn from the man portrayed by Joinville and Salimbene to the one revealed in Hugh's own writings. Even here the general impression will vary slightly in accordance with the work one happens to inspect. In his *Rule Commentary*, Hugh establishes his place within the mainstream of thirteenth-century Franciscan history. He agrees with papal declarations and the *Commentary of the Four Masters* in arguing that the friars are bound by their vow only to observe those evangelical counsels expressed *praeceptorie vel inhibitorie* in the rule.[64]

Hugh recognizes that the basic distinction between precept and counsel cannot be tied to any simple verbal formula. Not every imperative in the rule can be considered a precept,[65] nor is every precept stated as an imperative.[66] Otherwise the brothers would not be required by their vow to wear a special habit or remain chaste. How, then, are we to determine what is included among the precepts? Hugh does not attempt to present a complete list. Instead, he speaks of those things which are "of the integrity of the vow," which a professor of the rule cannot lay aside (except for sufficient cause) without being considered an apostate. On these terms wearing the Franciscan habit, having nothing of one's own, saying the required office, not riding, and preaching only with permission are of the integrity of the vow, even if they are not demanded by precept in the rule, since a friar who violated any of them would unhesitatingly be branded a transgressor of his vow.[67] In effect, Hugh solves the problem by appealing to common sense.

On the whole, Hugh is less interested in apostasy than in laxity, less in mortal than in venial sin. He sees about him an order which, though it has not gone whoring after false gods, has nonetheless declined from the pristine purity of the early Franciscans. His work is filled with descriptions of the good old days, occasionally accompanied by invidious comparisons.[68] Among other things, he complains of excess in clothing and liturgical paraphernalia as well as hoarding of books. Nor is he happy about papal privileges. He remarks that "it is not safe for the brothers, because of a privilege, . . . to recede without urgent cause from the intention of the rule which they vow."[69] If Jacques Paul is correct in placing the commentary around 1253, Hugh is studiously avoiding an entire papal declaration, *Ordinem vestrum*. More precisely, he is carrying on an implicit debate with it without ever mentioning it by name.[70]

It is important not to make too much of such criticism, however. Bonaventure, too, saw decline around him. Hugh's complaints would be more significant if they were strikingly at odds with the views of Franciscan leaders, but they are not. He bemoans the same laxity which general chapters attempted to curb through legislation. Franciscan leaders, too, were loath to take advantage of *Ordinem vestrum*, and continued to avoid some aspects of it right through the 1270s. It is also important to note that Hugh's criticism of current events is founded on the rule, not on Francis's intention as revealed by his testament, by brother Leo, or by some other source. He acknowledges that the *Testament* is not binding[71] and, although he is willing to speak of Francis' intention on occasion, recognizes that ultimately "we are bound, not to blessed Francis's intention (which we do not know), but to a common rational understanding of the rule which we vow."[72] Even when Hugh feels that he knows Francis's intention, he does not necessarily consider it binding. He grants that Francis wanted everyone in the order to engage in manual labor, but dismisses this evidence with the observation that the order was then full of uneducated brothers who wanted to work.[73]

In the final analysis, one of the most striking things about Hugh is his willingness to grant that the order is legitimately in a different situation now than it was when Francis founded it. He accepts the concept of an order that lives from income processed through procurators, leaving the brothers free to pray, preach, and teach. Far from discouraging scholarship, he thinks that Franciscans are of all men most fitted to teach.[74] He feels that the days of wandering are over, for good order demands stable residence in convents.[75] He insists that Franciscan poverty entails not merely lack of possessions but restricted use of goods;[76] yet he thinks this use can extend beyond what is necessary for survival to encompass whatever is necessary for the tasks now being performed by the order. In none of these opinions can Hugh be said to differ from Bonaventure. On the contrary, he makes his point so emphatically and so entertainingly that Bonaventure pirated large sections of Hugh's *Rule Commentary* in his own *Letter on Three Questions*.[77]

Hugh's other two works, *On the Ends of Poverty* and *Dispute Between a Zealot for Poverty and His Domestic Enemy*, seem to display a slight shift in emphasis. It is so small in *On the Ends of Poverty* that scholars are apt to consider this work along with the *Rule Commentary*, distinguishing both from the *Dispute*.[78] *On the Ends of Poverty* is a tightly ordered statement concerning the practice of Franciscan poverty. It begins by alluding to the *insignia* of poverty, external signs of an inner quality. When there is no adequate correlation between internal and external reality, the result is superstition or hypocrisy. These *insignia*, already discussed by the *Rule Commentary* in more or less the same words found in *On the Ends of Poverty*, include the standard elements of vile clothing, bare feet, and avoidance of horseback riding.

Hugh then turns to a long discussion of dispensation. His message can be reduced to two very important assertions. First, "no man, whatever his authority and for whatever cause, can licitly dispense from a solemn vow of continence or poverty."[79] Second, he who vows Franciscan poverty binds himself to the *insignia* of poverty, since they are "of the integrity of the vow."[80] This is to state very starkly what Hugh, for all his scholarly rigor, manages to blur at the edges. For example, he does grant at one point that superiors can dispense "for rational cause," yet this idea is lost along the way and plays no part in his conclusion. Again, the two major assertions are juxtaposed but never completely merged, since, when he finally offers a concrete application of the first, he speaks of the superior's inability to dispense a Franciscan from lack of property, not from restricted use; yet anyone can follow the argument to its logical conclusion, which is that restricted use is included in the vow and is therefore outside the legitimate scope of dispensation.

None of this can be said to contradict the *Rule Commentary*, in which

Hugh clearly sees lack of property and restricted use as two complementary aspects of Franciscan poverty and takes a negative view of dispensations. Nevertheless, in the *Rule Commentary* he does not focus attention on the limits of authority. In a brief acknowledgment of Francis's words, "ordering nothing against the soul or our rule,"[81] he remarks that "leaders do not have to command nor subjects obey" such orders,[82] but his major emphasis is on the fact that these are the only limits placed on obedience. In fact, he discusses obedience at length in the *Rule Commentary*, and his major intent is to praise and enjoin it, not to undermine it.[83]

A further shift occurs in the *Dispute*. Here Hugh creates a dialogue between two Franciscans, one an exponent of limited use (Hugh's "zealot") and the other a spokesman for laxity (the "domestic enemy"). The domestic enemy offers a series of arguments which were destined to have a long and distinguished career. In the first place, he insists on two different occasions that internal attitude is the important thing, not external actions.[84] The zealot concedes that true poverty does indeed lie in the heart, and that one cannot infallibly deduce from good actions that the heart is right. Nevertheless, bad actions certainly show that the heart is wrong. Thus the *insignia* of poverty do not guarantee internal poverty, but their absence insures that it, too, is absent.

Second, the enemy asserts that he is free to live expansively as long as he has his superior's permission, because leaders have discretionary power in matters of use.[85] The zealot replies that leaders can dispense only when there is reasonable cause to do so. He is aware that notions of "reasonable cause" and "necessity" are dangerously malleable when placed in the service of human greed. The enemy, in turn, is confident that he can provide the required apologia for relaxation, and launches an argument that luxurious buildings are desirable because they attract people to the order, making it easier for them to leave all they have and follow Christ. This is especially true of nobles, who are used to having lovely houses.[86] When the zealot objects that such buildings attract people for the wrong reasons and work against their being good Franciscans when they do enter, the enemy tries another tack, arguing that liturgical splendor is useful in glorifying God.[87] The zealot replies that "he would be foolish indeed who violated his vow to God in order to honor God."

Finally, the enemy argues that choosing high-quality goods results in greater efficiency and is in the long run more economical. A fine, warm tunic makes it easier to spend long nights praying in cold churches. It may cost a bit more, but it will also last longer.[88] The zealot offers a double-barrelled reply. He begins by making it clear that in such matters the ultimate appeal must be to the rule, not to prudence. Having established this point, he proceeds to challenge the enemy's optimism about savings, observing that those who buy expensive goods also seem to replace them more frequently.

Here again, Hugh is arguing that superfluity is forbidden by the vow.[89] As in *On the Ends of Poverty*, he defines superfluity as "that which, when taken away, leaves enough to suffice."[90] He recognizes that inclusion of restricted use in the vow of poverty makes transgression of that vow harder to determine than in the case of chastity or obedience, but he does not pursue the matter.[91] Here as elsewhere, Hugh criticizes essentially the same types of excess combated by Franciscan legislation. He attacks superfluity in buildings, clothes, food, books, and liturgical ornaments. Nor do the standards implied in his criticism vary wildly from those established in the legislation.[92]

On the other hand, there are moments when the zealot seems to break sharply with the mainstream of Franciscan development. For example, when the enemy cites Solomon's temple as a justification of sumptuous churches, the zealot replies that he would not care much if a rich noble unencumbered by the vow of poverty should wish to honor God by building something along those lines. This seems straightforward enough, but Hugh does not stop there. Such behavior, he says, "seems to fit that state and people [i.e., Solomon's time] more than the modern age," for they were "carnal, rude and sensual, and consequently more prone to idolatry." Thus God gave them a beautiful temple to woo them away from wicked cults. Later, however, in the fullness of time, Christ came and taught us to despise external, visible things.[93]

The zealot soon finds himself discussing clothes. He cites Bernard's observation that soft vestments suggest a soft soul,[94] then quotes with approval Gregory the Great's suggestion that John the Baptist dressed as he did to show that those who seek softness and luxury "serve the earthly and not the heavenly kingdom."[95] If one could desire such things without sin, then Christ would not have praised John's attire and Peter would not have warned against desire for expensive clothing.[96]

In each case, Hugh could have argued that splendor is sinful only for those who have chosen the higher way, or at least he could have limited the discussion to that group. Instead he suggests that it is unfortunate in any case and therefore *a fortiori* wrong for Franciscans. By taking this position he inevitably sharpens an implication most Franciscan spokesmen preferred to avoid, namely that praise of the Franciscan life consti-

tuted an implicit negative judgment on other lives. Franciscan authors
were eager to recall the distinction between gospel precepts and counsels,
arguing that other ways of living were less perfect without being absolutely sinful; yet the implication was hard to erase completely. Hugh does
not even try to do so. In this respect he is not entirely different from his
continuing inspiration, Bernard of Clairvaux, but the direction of his
thought is significant nonetheless, since it anticipates Olivi's occasional
tendency to offer Franciscan poverty as a pattern for the entire church.

Equally significant are Hugh's scattered suggestions that the order is
moving in the wrong direction. When the enemy begs the zealot to "flee
singularity and be content with the community," the zealot acknowledges
that he is indeed singular, but only because the community has deviated
from the rule.[97] Later, when his exhausted enemy, seeking a final refuge
in sarcasm, advises the zealot to see his superior "and perhaps you'll
reform the order," the zealot replies that "the superiors are responsible
for all the aforesaid abuses . . . and it would be pointless to talk with
them, since many not only refuse to listen but cruelly persecute those who
speak." He normally speaks of these matters "only with lovers of poverty," although occasionally, inspired by the Holy Spirit, he opens his
heart to others.[98] The domestic enemy is presumably an unfortunate vic-
tim of just this phenomenon.

Hugh's assessment seems a grim one, yet the dialogue closes on a note
of optimism. The zealot states his faith that God will not be mocked. The
order will be reformed by precisely those complainers whom the domestic enemy and his kind try to repress and destroy.

Who are the superiors on whom Hugh blames the decay? If the work
was written after *Ordinem vestrum* (1243) but before John of Parma's
election as minister general (1247) as Alessandra Sisto contends,[99] his
words might constitute evidence that persecution of the Anconan zealots
under Crescentius of Jesi was widely known and criticized in the order or
even that Crescentius's generalate saw an extension of that persecution
to other localities, a possibility offered some support by Salimbene's reference to the fate of the "solemn brothers" in Germany. Nevertheless,
one cannot unhesitatingly assume that Hugh intends to place blame at
the highest levels. He may be thinking primarily of local or regional superiors, in which case his work could have been written at any time, even
at the beginning of his friend John of Parma's generalate. John was an
indefatigable traveler and the *Dispute* might have encouraged him to
look around southern France.

On the other hand, perhaps Hugh's description of the zealot as *iuvenis* should be taken seriously, and the *Dispute* should be seen as a work of youthful idealism and enthusiasm (as well as youthful intolerance, which often accompanies the other two). In that case it would be the earliest of the three writings[100] and the progression implied in this presentation would be reversed. Instead of seeing a man become progressively more disenchanted with current practice, we would see an angry young man eventually develop into the respectable yet prophetic figure encountered in the pages of Joinville and the *Rule Commentary*. Such a transformation would hardly be unique.

The difference between these two Hughs is largely their variant attitudes toward Franciscan leadership. Perhaps one could reconcile his indictment in the *Dispute* with his heavy emphasis on order and obedience in the *Rule Commentary*, but it would take some explaining. The difference in emphasis seems great enough to suggest a difference in attitude. Nevertheless, it is hard to push even this point too far, since the works were produced with diverse ends in mind.

Factionalism Under Bonaventure

Unlike Crescentius and John, Bonaventure left a substantial body of writings. Thus we can ask not only whether he was seen by other authors as involved in a struggle between lax and rigorist factions but whether he saw himself as somehow mediating between these factions. No such view is suggested in the letters examined earlier. Bonaventure sees himself as defending the order against external critics on the one hand and lax brothers on the other. He is not preoccupied with any serious threat from Franciscan zealots. The last thing in the world he seems to worry about is excessive zeal in pursuing poverty. He does, by implication, choose a mediating position insofar as he takes Franciscan poverty seriously yet recognizes that its original rigors must be somewhat modified if the order is to fulfill the mission entrusted to it by the church and if it is to pay any attention to the realities of human nature; yet the conflict implied here seems to stem from the concrete Franciscan situation, not from the claims of rival factions.

These observations are particularly important because so much good modern scholarship has emphasized Bonaventure's role as guardian of the *via media*. His generalate is seen as a sustained effort to hold together two extreme factions. After him, the deluge. Nor is this an entirely modern view. Dante portrays a beatified Bonaventure as acknowledging that a few Franciscans still maintain the old standards within a decadent order,

But not at Casale or Aquasparta, where
they come to our rule in such a way that
one flees it while the other constricts it.[101]

It is much harder to argue that Bonaventure saw himself in these terms. He did apply the notion of the *medium virtutis* to poverty but, given his own interest in the notion of *medium* and the popularity of Aristotle's ethics in his time, it would have been amazing if he had not. It is how he did so that is significant.

The idea of virtue as a mean was an important one for Franciscans, because it was only too easy for secular critics to argue that mendicant poverty was wrong precisely because it represented an extreme. In his *Defense of Poverty*, Bonaventure raises this problem and settles it by distinguishing between various types of mean in the handling of goods. Those who live in the world and shoulder its economic burdens can indulge in *largitas politica*, which involves moderate enjoyment and pious dispensation of justly acquired goods. This obviously applies to barons and merchants, but it is also fitting for the church, which must own goods in order to provide for the needs of its flock. Thus heretics err in asserting that the church fell from grace when rulers endowed it with possessions.

Evangelical poverty, however, has its own mean inasmuch as it renounces possession but retains use, and limits use without rejecting necessities. This was the mean practiced by Christ the mediator and the one followed by Paul when he followed the naked Christ. Thus those who complain that Franciscan poverty violates the *medium* of virtue are ascribing vicious excess to Christ and the apostles.[102]

In other words, it does not occur to Bonaventure that the Aristotelian mean demands a compromise between two sorts of demand within his order, much less two factions within that order. True poverty need not be compromised by involvement in teaching and pastoral duties, for Franciscan poverty is not to be measured by any absolute standard, even by the example of Francis. It is defined by the role one is called upon to perform, and it requires taking only what is necessary for the fulfillment of that role. On this point, Bonaventure and Olivi were in substantial agreement.

Lacking any clear indication from Bonaventure himself that he is contending with a nascent spiritual faction, scholars sometimes read it into his works as a hidden interpretive key. Thus his reference to Francis as angel of the sixth seal becomes a subtle attempt to neutralize or at least moderate spiritual apocalyptic excesses, as if he could never have proclaimed such a notion simply because he happened to accept it himself; or the *Letter Concerning Three Questions* is interpreted as a reply to one seduced by zealot criticism of Franciscan practice, although the work is clearly directed at criticism from outside the order. When such hypotheses are eliminated, there is nothing left in Bonaventure's writings to suggest such a faction.

If Bonaventure gives no indication that he is struggling to rein in a proto-spiritual faction, neither is there much evidence of such a faction opposing him. The three major spiritual spokesmen offer mixed testimony. Olivi was in the order during most of Bonaventure's generalate and had some personal contact with him at Paris. His comments are respectful though realistic. Probably writing in the early 1280s, in a passage which I will later quote at length, he acknowledges that others are citing the deceased Bonaventure's laxity as precedent for their own. Olivi replies that Bonaventure, though perhaps a bit self-indulgent, was nonetheless a reformer who opposed recent decay in the order.[103]

Ubertino da Casale, who entered the order within a year of Bonaventure's death, is at worst ambivalent. Writing over three decades later, he relies heavily on Bonaventure as a devotional writer yet suggests that the *Legenda maior* suppressed certain elements of tradition so as to avoid highlighting Franciscan decadence in Bonaventure's own time.[104]

Angelo Clareno probably entered the order less than a decade before Bonaventure's death and seems to have had no direct contact with him; yet his hostility toward Bonaventure is remarkable. One can deduce from various sources[105] that John of Parma was told to resign because of his Joachism, that he was later called to some sort of reckoning on this score, and that Bonaventure, as minister general, participated in the hearing; yet only Angelo writes of Bonaventure's duplicity in the hearing, his hostility toward John, and his fall from sanctity on that account.[106] Moreover, it is Angelo who provides the famous story of James of Massa's vision, in which James saw Bonaventure refuse the full measure of Franciscan poverty and then attack John of Parma.[107] This vision seems to suggest that a vein of hostility toward Bonaventure already existed among Italian zealots at the time Angelo joined the order. Angelo says he heard about the vision from James himself after joining and that the vision occurred early in John of Parma's generalate. Thus if Angelo and James were both telling the truth, there was hostility at least by the early 1270s; yet that hostility was based, not simply on what Bonaventure did after becoming minister general, but on a vision purportedly experienced long before his generalate even began, a vision recounted around a quarter-century later to someone who recorded it at least a half-century after that. Such a situation cannot fail to make modern historians uneasy.[108]

Perhaps the best one can say of this story is that it suggests some dissatisfaction with Bonaventure among zealots in the March of Ancona. Is there any evidence that such dissatisfaction existed elsewhere? The so-called "Leo sources" suggest a degree of disillusionment with Franciscan leadership, but when? Rosiland Brooke suggests that the *Verba Leonis* were written by Brother Leo around 1257–60, when John of Parma's fall produced a crisis of confidence.[109] It seems credible that John's decline would have produced such a crisis. Perhaps we see it reflected in both the "Leo sources" and the story of James of Massa's vision. It does not automatically follow that tension continued to build.

The evidence so far proves little about attitudes toward Bonaventure in his own day, but it shows that some friars in each camp later saw him as a defender of relaxation. Before leaving Bonaventure we should at least ask whether his behavior *should* have inspired such charges. Probably not. Few historians today would take seriously Angelo's implication that a fateful change of direction occurred when John of Parma stepped down. Most would grant that John and Bonaventure both sought an observance compatible with new Franciscan duties; tried to impose reform from the top; and were frustrated by resistance at the provincial and local levels. Undoubtedly policy changed somewhat under Bonaventure, since he was a different person and came to power in a much different situation; yet the fundamental continuities are striking.[110]

Factionalism Immediately After Bonaventure

However difficult it may be to show that there was controversy during Bonaventure's generalate, there is ample evidence of trouble immediately after his death. Angelo Clareno writes that, during the Council of Lyons in 1274, a rumor spread through the March of Ancona that the pope was about to make the Franciscans accept property.[111] Most of the brothers decided that they would obey such an order, but a few promised resistance. The basic issue was whether one should obey one's vows or the pope when the two seemed at odds. The rumor proved false, but the controversy continued to smoulder and eventually embraced other issues. Here we encounter what would eventually become major elements in the litany of Italian spiritual complaints against the order: establishment of friaries in the heart of the city; heavy commitment to worldly learning; and the scramble for burial rights, legacies, and privileges.

According to Angelo, some of the more insistent brothers were finally condemned to life imprisonment as "heretics and destroyers of the order." They were denied the sacraments, and their jailers were forbidden to talk to them. Their sentence was to be read weekly in local chapter meetings. When, upon hearing the sentence, a friar criticized it, he was shackled with irons and placed in a foul prison. When he became ill they ignored his condition, and when he died they threw his body in a ditch and covered it with dirt to avoid scandalizing the laity. The zealot leaders were more fortunate. They remained in confinement until Raymond Geoffroi ordered their release after becoming minister general in 1289.

It is impossible to say how long their incarceration lasted because we do not know how long after the Council of Lyons it began. Angelo's casual references to the passage of time suggest a substantial delay. He says opponents of the zealots called for action against them "at their first [provincial] chapter meeting celebrated after the council." There was an inquiry, and "the following year they called [the outstanding zealots] to their chapter meeting again." Thanks to the intervention of a canny old friar who spoke for them, nothing happened to them at that chapter, and thus "after three years the question of their penance was settled." The argument continued, however, "and within a few years [the zealots] so multiplied that the other brothers began to fear they would convert the majority to their views and way of life." Finally, five provincial ministers met in secret and decided on a course of action. "At the next provincial chapter meeting" the zealot leaders were sentenced to prison.[112] Thus the incarceration did not commence before 1278 and could have begun substantially later.

Angelo was writing close to a half-century after the fact and has a flair for historically questionable anecdotes, but he was a participant in the Anconan crisis and we have little reason to question his general description of it. Two things should be noted, however. First, whatever the conflict was about, it does not seem to have been about the issue that divided southern French friars from 1279 on, the question of whether *usus pauper* was an essential part of the Franciscan vow. It concerned the relative importance of papal decrees and religious vows, which would indeed later become an important question but probably was not debated by Olivi and his opponents; and it was eventually about the virtue of Franciscan involvement in urban living and higher learning, both of which were questioned by many Italian brothers but were not explicitly attacked by Olivi.

The second thing to note is that even within Italy the quarrel seems to have been relatively localized. Most of the evidence suggests that it involved a few friars in a single province. Angelo writes that action against the group was decided upon at a secret meeting of five provincial ministers. Thus one-third of the provinces in Italy were represented at the gathering. Moreover, he claims that they decided to act because the number of zealots was growing and the leaders feared that they would eventually convince a majority of the brothers. Nevertheless, when Angelo goes on to describe the action taken, he is back at the provincial level: legal proceedings were carried out during the next provincial chapter. Nor does his narrative imply that the imprisonment became a cause célèbre in the order. According to Angelo, Raymond Geoffroi became familiar with the documents of the case when he came through the March of Ancona in the process of general visitation. It seems safest to conclude that, insofar as we are justified in forming any hypothesis at all concerning Italian difficulties in the 1270s, we should view them as essentially an Anconan problem. That problem was serious enough to justify consultation by five provincial ministers in the area, but the five were probably deliberating on how the province of Ancona should put its house in order, not how to stop a conflagration already raging across Italy.[113]

The view of these difficulties as limited in scope seems consistent with Bonagratia's letter, described earlier in this chapter. Although written at the beginning of the *usus pauper* controversy and eventually cited by the contestants, it does not even hint that such a contest is under way. Here again the real problems are outside criticism and internal laxity. Bonagratia's message is that the pope, in promulgating *Exiit qui seminat*, has warded off external attack, and it is now up to the Franciscans to put their lives in order.

Conclusion

On the whole, the evidence suggests that, though the practice of poverty was an issue in the decades preceding 1279, it is anachronistic to speak as if the "spiritual/community" polarization so evident around 1300 already existed during those years. Some people undoubtedly wanted stricter observance than others did, and there was unquestionably trouble during the generalate of Crescentius, but the issues involved are hardly obvious. Only from the March of Ancona is there any hard evidence that factions were crystallizing and serious trouble ensuing. Even there, the most trustworthy evidence comes from 1274 on.

Hugh's *Dispute* informs us that Franciscans were arguing about poverty in southern France, too. It also displays a feeling that leaders are to blame for decay, an awareness that dissidents are being punished, and an expectation that the currently persecuted minority will eventually reform the order, all of which seems to anticipate the later spirituals.[114] Unfortunately, it does not indicate which leaders are to blame or where people are being punished. The *Dispute* might be read as a call for the minister general to do something about decay at the regional or local level.

It is noteworthy how little of the evidence mentioned so far comes from the seventeen-year period of Bonaventure's ascendancy, or even from John of Parma's ten-year generalate. Angelo does suggest that the continuing debate over poverty led to John's fall, and it is at least theoretically possible that Hugh's *Dispute* could have been written during John's generalate; yet Angelo's portrait of John does not inspire great confidence, and the *Dispute* may have been written earlier. The silence under Bonaventure is even more striking. Despite Angelo's antipathy, his *History* accelerates rapidly after John of Parma's trial. The next horrors to interest him are from the generalate of Bonaventure's successor. No one else says much, either. If there had been any serious strife, there is reason to assume that we would have heard about it, particularly from Angelo.

Of course, there must have been some who felt that Bonaventure was not enforcing a sufficiently stringent level of poverty, just as there must have been some who wanted greater laxity. Of course, Bonaventure must have acted in the knowledge that such variant opinions existed. This is merely to suggest, however, that certain constants in Franciscan history were probably also operative between 1257 and 1274. One is still left with a significant lack of evidence for them, particularly when compared with the clouds of witness for trouble after that period. Add to that the decade under John of Parma and we have over a quarter-century of comparative silence preceding 1274. Even in the later 1270s, when there was obviously trouble, it seems to have been quite localized.

Notes

1. *Epistola* I in *Opera* (Quaracchi, 1891), 8:468f.
2. *Epistola* II in ibid., 8:470f.
3. *Collationes in hexaemeron*, 9:8, 20:30, and 22:23, as published in *Opera*, 5:373f., 431f., 441.
4. Published in Luke Wadding, *Annales minorum* (Rome, 1732), 5:75.
5. For the same advice by another minister general see Jerome of Ascoli's 1274 letter to the entire order, published by Giuseppe Abate, "Memoriali, statuti ed atti di capitoli generali dei fratri minori," *MF* 33 (1933): 21–23.
6. *Epistola de tribus quaestionibus*, in *Opera*, 8:331–33.
7. *Determinationes quaestionum*, in ibid., 8:337–74.
8. See Ignatius Brady, "The Writings of Saint Bonaventure regarding the Franciscan Order," *MF* 75 (1975): 107. For the sake of convenience I

shall refer to "the author" in the singular, although there may be more than one.

9. *Determinationes quaestionum,* 340–42, 367–68, 349–351.
10. Ibid., 341–42.
11. Ibid., 343–44, 347–48.
12. Ibid., 349–51.
13. Ibid., 342–44, 348–51.
14. See Luigi Pellegrini, "Gli insediamenti francescani nella evoluzione storica degli agglomerati umani e delle circoscrizioni territoriali dell'Italia del secolo XIII," in *Chiesa e società dal secolo IV ai nostri giorni* (Rome, 1979), 197f., and his more recent *Insediamenti Francescani nell'Italia del duecento* (Rome, 1984), 185 note 58. Rosalind Brooke, *Early Franciscan Government* (Cambridge, 1959), 378, suggests a smaller number.
15. *Regula non bullata,* c. 4, citing Matt. 20:28; *Admonitio 4.* All citations from Francis's writings are from *Opuscula* (Grottaferrata, 1978).
16. *Regula non bullata,* c. 6. When the word *minister* is used, its literal meaning is normally underscored by linking it with the word *servant.* See *Regula non bullata,* cc. 4–5; *Regula,* cc. 8 and 10. The Franciscan terminology is not entirely novel. See Cajetan Esser, *Origins of the Franciscan Order* (Chicago, 1970), 117 note 58.
17. See especially the *Epistola ad quemdam ministrum.* The *Epistola ad fideles* (recensio posterior), n. 28, and *Regula non bullata,* cc. 4 and 6 invoke the golden rule in this connection.
18. See especially *Testamentum,* nn. 31–33 and *Epistola ad quemdam ministrum,* nn. 15–16.
19. *Regula non bullata,* c. 5. In *Admonitio 3,* Francis says that those who refuse to obey orders harmful to their souls should humbly submit to any resultant persecution rather than separate themselves from their brothers.
20. Théophile Desbonnets, *De intuition à l'institution* (Paris, 1983), 60–63.
21. *Regula,* c. 10.
22. On clericalization see Lawrence Landini, *The Causes of the Clericalization of the Order of the Friars Minor* (Chicago, 1968). Landini altered his stance in a series of articles in the early 1980s, but I find his earlier presentation convincing. On Franciscan education see H. Felder, *Geschichte des wissenschaftlichen Studien im Franziskanerorden bis um die Mitte des 13. Jahrhunderts* (Freiburg im Br., 1904), and the shorter treatment by Dieter Berg, *Armut und Wissenschaft* (Dusseldorf, 1977).
23. See especially the *Regula non bullata,* c. 9. See also the comments by Thomas of Celano in I Celano, n. 38, in *AF,* 10:30; and Jacques de Vitry in *Historia orientalis,* c. 32, in *Testimonia minora saeculi XIII de S. Francisco Assisiensi* (Quaracchi, 1926), 81.
24. For example, in *Regula non bullata,* c. 14 (echoing Matt. 5:19); *Regula,* c. 9; *Testamentum,* nos. 7, 25–26.
25. On the friars' right to preach and hear confessions see *Quare fratres minores praedicent et confessiones audiant* in Bonaventure, *Opera,* 8:375–81, and the rule commentary in ibid., 8:428. The authorship of the former is unsettled, but the latter is probably by Pecham. See Conrad Harkins, "The Authorship of a Commentary on the Franciscan Rule Published

Among the Works of St. Bonaventure," *FS* 29 (1969): 157–248. On their right to teach see Hugo de Digna, *Rule Commentary* (Grottaferrata, 1979), 187. On their right to be bishops see Salimbene da Parma, *Cronica* (Bari, 1966), 247. Even if the Franciscan prelate tried to avoid pomp, he might still find himself embroiled in money problems. For an example of financial embroilments accompanying the mitre see Decima Douie, *Archbishop Pecham* (Oxford, 1952), 49.

26. See T. S. R. Boase, *Boniface VIII* (London, 1933), 205, regarding Matthew of Aquasparta.

27. See, for example, Gerolamo Biscaro, "Eretici ed inquisitori nella marca trevisana (1280–1308)," *Archivio veneto* 62 (1932): 148–72. On Franciscan inquisitors see Mariano d'Alatri, *L'Inquisizione francescana nell'Italia centrale nel secolo XIII* (Rome, 1954), and d'Alatri's subsequent articles now published as *Eretici e inquisitori in Italia* (Rome, 1986–87).

28. See E. Randolph Daniel, *The Franciscan Concept of Mission in the High Middle Ages* (Lexington, 1975); D. L. d'Avray, *The Preaching of the Friars* (Oxford, 1985).

29. Jacopone da Todi, *Laude*, lauda 91; Salimbene, *Cronica*, 438f.

30. Brooke, *Early Franciscan Government*, 255–72.

31. At the Council of Vienne the community continually maintained that the statutes were more strict than the rule, while Ubertino da Casale continually implied the opposite.

32. Michael Bihl, "Statuta generalia ordinis edita in capitulis generalibus celebratis Narbonae an. 1260, Assisii an. 1279 atque Parisiis an. 1292," *AFH* 34 (1941): 13–94, 284–358. Bihl lists general chapter meetings and editions of their legislation (pp. 32–34).

33. Limitations were also placed on excessive size, width, or height in church buildings. *Curiositas* in pictures, windows, and the like was prohibited.

34. Bihl, "Statuta generalia," 66.

35. Geroldus Fussenegger, "Definitiones capituli generalis Argentinae celebrati anno 1282," *AFH* 26 (1933): 137.

36. A. G. Little, "Statuta provincialia provinciarum Aquitaniae et Franciae (saec. XIII–XIV)," *AFH* 7 (1914): 476f.

37. Ferdinand Delorme, "Explanationes constitutionum generalium Narbonensium," *AFH* 18 (1925): 511–24.

38. Cesare Cenci, "Le costituzioni padovane del 1310," *AFH* 76 (1983): 551–59, 571–78.

39. Little, "Statuta provincialia provinciarum Aquitaniae et Franciae," 472; Little, "Statuta provincialia provinciae Franciae et marchiae tervisinae (saec. XIII)," *AFH* 7 (1914): 462, 464; Abate, "Memoriali, statuti ed atti di capitoli generali dei frati minori," *MF* 33 (1933): 26; 34 (1934): 253.

40. *Epistola statutoria*, in *Chronologia historico-legalis* (Naples, 1650), 1 : 34; yet Arlotto permits the custom according to which books of one custody will not be assigned to another except when "necessity or pious utility" requires it. For earlier statements on control over books Hugo de Digna's assertion in *Rule Commentary*, 147 that a father who gives books to his Franciscan son is not violating the rule, because the books could be taken away by the minister at any time (an argument later appropriated by Bon-

aventure in *Epistola de tribus quaestionibus*, in *Opera*, 8:333f.); the 1260 Constitutions of Narbonne in Bihl, "Statuta generalia," 73f., which forbid individuals to have books without permission of the provincial minister and provide not only for the return of those books to the brother's home province on his death but for their routine collection and redistribution when the provincial minister visits (a statute still in effect in 1310, according to Cenci, "Le costituzioni," 535). Nevertheless, Hugh also complains in *Rule Commentary*, 157, about brothers who hoard books.

41. The constitutions of Aquitaine in Little, "Statuta provincialia provinciarum Aquitaniae et Franciae," 476, 481, provide for redistribution of the dead brother's books and specify that no book is to be assigned to a brother's use for over a year unless it is of small value. The 1300 Umbrian statutes acknowledge that brothers routinely purchase books from one another, but stipulate that the books of dead brothers are to be returned to the provincial chapter, which will ascertain their value. Then they will be sold to other friars, but in such a way as to hinder any single friar from amassing a large collection. See Cesare Cenci, "Ordinazioni dei capitoli provinciali umbri dal 1300 al 1305," *CF* 55 (1985): 16. See also Ferdinand Delorme, "Constitutiones provinciae Provinciae (saec. XIII–XIV)," *AFH* 14 (1921): 424. Nevertheless, at Rieti in 1289 Pope Nicholas IV, himself a Franciscan, limited provincial prerogative by announcing that, although the provincial minister perhaps had the power to take away books given to some convent by a secular who wished to join the order, he should not do so. See Abate, "Memoriali," *MF* 35 (1935): 105.

42. Bonaventura Giordani, *Acta franciscana e tabulariis bononiensibus deprompta*, in *AF*, 9:385–87. The distribution scheme is more complex than I have indicated, and a codicil adds further refinements.

43. Ibid., *Acta*, 107f. In the case of the first novice the books will be divided on his death between the Bologna convent and the one where he dies, providing the latter is in the same province.

44. In ibid., 415f., a father leaves L.15 per year to his daughter, a Clare, remarking that this sum should cover her necessities, clothing, and medical expenses while allowing her to give alms for the sake of her father's soul. John Larner, *The Lords of Romagna* (Ithaca, 1965), xv–xvi, basing his estimate on figures used in papal taxation of the clergy (1291), suggests that L.15 "was the uncomfortable minimum upon which a single man with no responsibilities could live." In Cenci, "Ordinazioni," 21, the 1300 Umbrian statutes demand that L.70 Ravenna be provided to each student from the province studying at Paris to be a lector. Provinces or custodies were to pay for students' books. Responsibility for clothing them seems to have been a bone of contention. See Cenci's article for a summary of legislation.

45. *Acta*, 36.

46. Ibid., 314. Annual incomes are given in other wills to other friars. For example, in ibid., 234, a father leaves a piece of land to his wife with the instruction that the income from it should go annually to his son, a Franciscan.

47. The friar in question is Gandulfinus de Mutina. Another, Philippus de

Marcegonibus, appears in thirty-nine wills between 1270 and 1300 and is awarded L.11 in 1293 alone. In 1300 he receives L.15 for himself, L.180 to disperse to whomever he thinks worthy, and the power to name the "poor of Christ," who will receive L.10 per year for ten years.

48. Salimbene, *Cronica*, 322, presents the menu of a meal provided by Louis IX for a provincial chapter meeting. On the reduction of mendicant poverty to a cliche see Herve Martin, *Les Ordres mendiants en Bretagne* (Paris, 1975), 185f.

49. For example, *Acta*, 109.

50. The first century of Franciscan history also witnessed the increasing interest in Purgatory described by Jacques Le Goff, *La Naissance du purgatoire* (Paris, 1981).

51. *Acta*, 256–63.

52. They did so unsuccessfully in Venice, as we will see; yet Martin, *Les Ordres mendiants en Bretagne*, 180, gives an example of success.

53. In 1293, after Obizzo's death, the guardians of Padua and Ferrara began the process of calling in assets from his creditors. See *Acta*, 283–85.

54. The constitutions of Narbonne list "lords of the land" as the only laymen with whom Franciscans can dine outside the cloister; the statutes of the French province announce that only travelers or "noble friends of the brothers" can dine within the convent. Status is undoubtedly one factor implied when the constitutions of Narbonne tell the brothers to bury on Franciscan grounds no one who can be refused "without notable scandal," a criterion explicitly included in the 1303 provincial statutes of upper Germany, which limit burial to those deemed "of such sanctity *or dignity* as to merit it." Bihl, "Statuta generalia," 48 and 56; Little, "Statuta provincialia provinciae Franciae et marchiae tervisinae," 451; Geroldus Fussenegger, "Statuta provinciae Alemaniae superioris annis 1303, 1309 et 1341 condita," *AFH* 53 (1960): 233–75.

55. *BF*, 2:47f.; ibid., 159. Alexander and Innocent challenged Franciscan integrity in other ways. For example, in 1257 Alexander reissued *Ordinem vestrum*, which the order had been avoiding for years (ibid., 196); and in 1253 Innocent told the Franciscan charged with constructing the basilica of St. Francis at Assisi to collect and spend money for that purpose "notwithstanding any contradiction to the Franciscan statutes or any contrary instructions by the general minister, provincial minister, custode or guardian" (ibid., 666). Within a week, in similar words, he ordered the collection for Francis' tomb.

56. *Historia septem tribulationum* in *Archiv*, 2:256–62.

57. This conclusion is reached by Lambert, *Franciscan Poverty*, as well as Brooke, *Early Franciscan Government*.

58. Thomas of Eccleston, *De adventu fratrum minorum in Angliam* (Paris, 1909), c. 12; Pelegrino da Bologna, *Chronicon abbreviatum de successione ministrorum*, published as Appendix II of Eccleston's *De adventu*, 142f. Pelegrino's comment is repeated in the *Chronica XXIV generalium*, in *AF*, 3:261.

59. *Cronica*, 574.

60. Angelo, *Historia septem tribulationum*, 271–77 and 283; Salimbene,

Cronica, 332 and 449f. Pelegrino da Bologna, *Chronicon*, 144, also mentions enemies.

61. Jean de Joinville, *Histoire de Saint Louis* (Paris, 1874), 362f.
62. *Cronica*, 325.
63. Commenting on Hugh's preaching style as seen in Joinville, Jacques Paul, "Hugues de Digne," in *Franciscans d'Oc* (Toulouse, 1975), 80, characterizes it as traditional truths audaciously delivered. It was, he says, "this mixture of conformity in ideas and virulence in form" that made Hugh a successful preacher.
64. Hugo, *Rule Commentary*, 95. Ibid., 139, offers a threefold distinction of those things expressed *praeceptorie, monitorie,* and *informatorie. Expositio quatuor magistrorum super regulam fratrum minorum* (Rome, 1950), 125f. does not use the term *praeceptorie vel inhibitorie,* but explicitly accepts the passage from *Quo elongati* (in *BF*, 1:68) which does use it. On this issue see Chapter 6 below.
65. Ibid., 96, 120.
66. Ibid., 103, 107.
67. Ibid., 103.
68. For example, ibid., 95–97, 106.
69. Ibid., 116.
70. Jacques Paul, "Le commentaire de Hugues de Digne sur la règle franciscaine," *Revue d'histoire de l'église de France* 61 (1975): 231–41. See David Flood's discussion of the Paul thesis in his introduction to Hugh's *Rule Commentary*, 59–64.
71. *Rule Commentary*, 97.
72. Ibid., 189.
73. Ibid., 140. On the role of *intentio* see Antonio Volpato, "Gli spirituali e l'*intentio* di S. Francesco," *RSCI* 33 (1979): 118–53.
74. *Rule Commentary*, 186–88.
75. Ibid., 158.
76. Ibid., 159, 164.
77. See Kajetan Esser, "Zu der 'Epistola de tribus quaestionibus' des hl. Bonaventura," *Franziskanische Studien* 27 (1940): 149–59.
78. See, for example, Alessandra Sisto, *Figure del primo francescanesimo in Provenza* (Rome, 1975), ch. 6. Sisto publishes all three works. I shall cite from her editions of *De finibus paupertatis* and *Disputatio inter zelatorem paupertatis et inimicum domesticum eius.*
79. *De finibus*, 331. The idea is repeated on p. 336.
80. Ibid., 332f. His description of the *insignia* in ibid., 330, matches almost verbatim the one found in *Rule Commentary*, 163f., and his explanation of what is *de integritate voti* in *De finibus*, 332f. echoes that found in *Rule Commentary*, 103.
81. *Regula*, ch. 10.
82. *Rule Commentary*, 180.
83. Ibid., 106f., 180.
84. *Disputatio*, 349–51. He cites Matt. 5:3, "Blessed are the poor in spirit."
85. Ibid., 351, 361–65.
86. Ibid., 351f.

87. Ibid., 355.
88. Ibid., 358–61.
89. Ibid., 366.
90. Ibid., 364; *De finibus*, 339.
91. *Disputatio*, 348.
92. For example, ibid., 351, 354.
93. Ibid., 357f.
94. Bernardus Claravallensis, *Apologia*, in *Opera* (Rome, 1957–1963), 1:102. Hugh and his zealot enjoy quoting Bernard and do so to great effect.
95. Gregory, *Homiliarum in evangelia* I, in J.-P. Migne, *Patrologiae cursus completus, series latina* (Paris, 1844–66), 76:1097.
96. Luke 7:25f.; 1 Pet. 3:3.
97. *Disputatio*, 347.
98. Ibid., 367.
99. Sisto, *Figure del primo francescanesimo in Provenza*, 99–101. Hugh died before John of Parma's resignation in 1257. See Flood's introduction to the *Rule Commentary*, 50.
100. Jerome Poulenc, "Hugues de Digne," in *Dictionnaire de spiritualité* (Paris, 1932–69), 7.1:876–79, so dates it. The domestic enemy sees his antagonist as a presumptuous, self-righteous, and tiresome young troublemaker. Is Hugh painting a wry self-portrait?
101. *Paradiso* XII.
102. *Apologia pauperum*, cap. 12, nn. 18–20 in *Opera*, 8:322f.
103. See Chapter 3 below for the entire passage.
104. *Arbor vitae* (Venice, 1485 ed. rpt. Torino, 1961), 437, 445, 449. Frédégand Callaey, *L'Idéalisme franciscain spirituel au XIVe siècle* (Louvain, 1911), 2 and 19, favors 1273 as the date of Ubertino's entry into the order, but the relevant passage from Ubertino seems to make 1274 equally likely.
105. Salimbene, Thomas of Eccleston, Pellegrino da Bologna, and the *Chronica XXIV generalium* as in notes 58 and 60 above. They do not all give precisely this story, but it seems convincing nonetheless.
106. *Historia septem tribulationum*, 271–87.
107. Ibid., 279–81. It is also in *Fioretti*, c. 48, but the latter seems to get it from Angelo. See Giacinto Pagnani, *I fioretti di San Francesco* (Rome, 1959), 227 note 168. It is repeated later by the *Chronica XXIV generalium*, 283f.
108. The dates of James's death and Angelo's entrance into the order could not have been very far apart, but each is just undetermined enough to keep us from rejecting the story out of hand.
109. Rosiland Brooke, ed., *Scripta Leonis* (Oxford, 1970), 62f.
110. For the continuity see Brooke, *Early Franciscan Government*, 258–84, and Lambert, *Franciscan Poverty*, 110–24. For an example of how the new situation may have influenced policy see Mariano d'Alatri, "San Bonaventura, l'eresia e l'inquisizione," *MF* 75 (1975): 305–22.
111. *Historia septem tribulationum*, 301–5. For the basic chronology of this debate see Antonio Franchi, "Il concilio di Lione II (1274) e la contestazione dei Francescani delle Marche," *Picenum seraphicum* 11 (1974): 53–75; Lydia von Auw, *Angelo Clareno et les spirituels italiens* (Rome, 1979), 11–22.

112. *Historia septem tribulationum*, 302f.
113. This conclusion might seem questionable in view of Lydia von Auw's suggestion in *Angelo Clareno*, 18, that the long list of imprisonments given
by Angelo in a letter of 1317 published in *Epistole*, in *Angeli Clareni
Opera*, vol. 1 (Rome, 1980), 180f., should be seen as referring to this period; yet her suggestion is hard to accept. Angelo's list, which covers Italy
from the Marches to Sicily and claims incarceration "in every [Franciscan]
house between Rome and Ancona," seems to summarize the accomplishments of a lifetime. Even if the suggestion were accepted, it would not
necessarily change the conclusion much. It would imply that the trouble
was more widely spread, but only in the sense that the Anconan zealots
were being arrested in more places.
114. Hugh even uses the term, informing the enemy at one point (p. 353) that
"experience would teach you this if you were *spiritualis*."

CHAPTER 2

The Developing Controversy: Chronology and Sources

Early in 1279, Petrus Iohannis Olivi wrote his *Question on Usus Pauper*, the ninth of his *Questions on Evangelical Perfection*. He argued that *usus pauper*, or restricted use of goods, was an essential part of the Franciscan vow. It was a point he would spend the rest of his life trying to prove.

Olivi's Early Career

Before that time, Olivi's career had alternated between success and humiliation. Born in 1247 or 1248 at Serignan, just outside Béziers in southern France, he had entered the Franciscan order in 1259 or 1260 at the age of twelve. He was a student in Paris by the later 1260s,[1] but probably never taught there as a bachelor and certainly never became a master. He was back in southern France by the mid-1270s, teaching in the order *studium* at Narbonne or Montpellier, possibly both.[2] This in itself was hardly an ominous sign. Olivi was still young, and a few years of such activity offered a perfectly respectable way of proceeding toward the *magisterium*.

Why should one assume that Olivi was destined for the *magisterium*? The opportunity to become either bachelor or master of theology at Paris was severely limited. Most friars sent there in Olivi's time were expected to return to their provinces and become lectors before attaining either rank, and what little we know about the succession of masters at Paris suggests that few scholars from Olivi's province did stay on. Nevertheless, Olivi himself seems to have thought he was one of the chosen few. He later explained in a letter that his progress toward the *magisterium* had been blocked by doubts concerning his orthodoxy.[3]

These doubts began early. Angelo Clareno says that some of Olivi's confreres took issue with questions he had written on the Virgin Mary and submitted them to the minister general, Jerome of Ascoli, who in turn ordered them burned. Olivi's views on marriage were also challenged during Jerome's generalate, which extended from 1274 to 1279.[4]

If Olivi was subjected to close scrutiny in the 1270s, he was hardly stripped of all prestige and responsibility. He continued to teach, wrote prodigiously, and was considered important enough to be consulted when deliberations concerning the bull *Exiit qui seminat* were in progress. In recent years, as increased interest in Olivi has produced escalated appraisals of his importance, some historians have gratuitously appointed him to the commission that met at Soriano in the summer of 1279 to advise Pope Nicholas III in preparing the bull, and a few have seen its publication as a triumph for Olivi's position. In reality, little can be said of his involvement beyond what he himself tells us, namely that he was asked by his provincial minister to contribute something during the time the commission met.[5] His contribution was on the subject of whether the Franciscan rule excluded all ownership of property, not on the question of *usus pauper*.[6] It is possible that Olivi happened to be in Italy at the time anyway, since the general chapter was held at Assisi in the spring of 1279 and Olivi seems to have developed some familiarity with Italian Franciscans by at least the early 1280s.[7]

The Dispute with Brother Ar

In any case, Olivi was now around thirty-one, a recognized scholar, and still not really behind schedule for the *magisterium*. Richard of Middleton, who was born one year after Olivi and progressed without notable academic embarrassments, did not become a master until 1284. Olivi, too, might have attained that goal in the next few years despite his earlier difficulties had he not stumbled into a protracted controversy with some of his brethren. Olivi's major adversary was another Franciscan lector. In a letter to someone whom we will simply call "R," he describes his opponent as "Brother Ar."[8] This shadowy figure was probably Arnold Galhardi (Gaillard?), but it makes little difference, since all we know of Arnold is his name.[9] The important thing is that another document, a series of thirty-two articles which we will call the *Attack*,[10] can be identified with what the letter describes as "the explication of those things which I wrote against Brother Ar." The letter itself responds to nineteen charges against Olivi's own thought. Thus we have some insight into the scope of the quarrel at that stage. Both the letter and the *Attack* show that it involved not only poverty but a broad range of theological and philosophical issues.

Apparently the minister general received from Olivi's foes a list of nineteen suspect Olivian positions. He sent the list to Olivi's provincial minister and called for an investigation.[11] The provincial minister ordered Olivi to explain himself. Olivi had already compiled a list of Ar's erroneous views. Now he used this list as a basis for the *Attack*,[12] which he sent to the provincial minister along with his explanation of the nineteen articles.[13] He hoped that his superiors, having examined both sides, would see what seemed so obvious to Olivi himself. They did not. When Olivi wrote to R, his reply was in the hands of the minister general, but Olivi himself was in dire straits. The road to scholarly advancement had been blocked by his minister and Olivi had been "deprived of all things, including my writings."[14] Worse news was on the way.

When did all this occur? Infuriatingly enough, Olivi dates the letter to R four days before Easter but mentions no year. One can safely assume that it was sent before Olivi's censure in 1283, which we will examine shortly.[15] Raymond of Fronsac, writing close to three decades later, alludes to two letters written by Bonagratia di S. Giovanni in Persiceto, minister general from 1279 to 1283, against Olivi's errors, and affirms that Bonagratia "conducted various processes" against Olivi's views and supporters.[16] Presumably the events described above occurred within that period.

Joseph Koch suggests[17] that the letter to R was written four days before Easter 1282, since the *Chronicle of the Twenty-four Generals* notes that "in the year of our Lord 1283 this general [Bonagratia], according to the decision (*definitionem*) of the Strasbourg chapter, came to Paris visiting and, collecting all those things in the doctrine of Brother Peter which seemed to ring poorly, submitted them for determination and examination."[18] The *definitiones* of the general chapter held in Strasbourg at Pentecost 1282 contain only one relevant item: "The general chapter commands all ministers to notify the minister general if they have any brothers in their provinces who pertinaciously defend unsound opinions, also conveying the opinions and the arguments advanced in their favor."[19]

If this is the relevant *definitio*, then in what sense could Bonagratia have been acting in accordance with it? Obviously, if the letter to R was written by Easter 1282, neither Bonagratia's activities nor those of Olivi's provincial minister could have been completely inspired by this particular *definitio*, because the chapter was held at Pentecost and Olivi had been deprived of his works by Easter. Any inspiration would have been in the other direction. Discussion of Olivi's case at Strasbourg would have contributed to the promulgation of general rules for dealing with such matters. Nevertheless, by 1282 the order was alerted to other varieties of unsound opinion such as heterodox Aristotelianism and even Thomism. The 1279 chapter at Assisi had aligned itself with the Paris condemnation of 1277 by prohibiting opinions rejected "by the bishop and the Paris masters,"[20] and the Strasbourg chapter limited the reading of Aquinas to the more educated brethren, who were to peruse it with the aid of William de la Mare's corrections.[21] Thus, even if the Strasbourg chapter had Olivi in mind when it produced the decree in question, it may have been thinking of a good deal else as well.

We are still left with an odd delay. If Olivi's case was discussed at Strasbourg in the spring of 1282 and a standard procedure for dealing with such perils was formulated there, why did Bonagratia procrastinate until 1283 before taking the next step and submitting Olivi's writings to a Parisian commission? Presumably he needed little time to collect them, since Olivi's letter to R announces that they already have been confiscated. One can surmise that as minister general Bonagratia had other things to do or that he was waiting for a time when he himself was in Paris, but the delay is curious nonetheless.

Perhaps the solution is that Olivi's letter to R was written around Easter 1283, close to a year after the Strasbourg chapter. If so, then the *Chronicle of the Twenty-four Generals* can be taken quite literally. The Strasbourg chapter produced a general *definitio* rather than a specific course of action regarding Olivi. Bonagratia later applied that *definitio* to Olivi's case. He collected those Olivian writings which seemed to offend—if he was working through the provincial minister, this process would have taken some time—and eventually brought them to Paris, where he selected a commission and set it to work. By Easter 1283 Olivi had surrendered his writings and was waiting for the next step, which came that summer when the commission returned a negative verdict.

There are two problems with this scenario. First, Olivi's letter to R says nothing about a commission, but perhaps by that time he knew only that the matter was in Bonagratia's hands, not what the minister general would do with it. Presumably that part of the process was not settled upon at Strasbourg. The other problem is that the nineteen articles defended in the letter to R are not the same as those censured by the Parisian commission. This is understandable, however. The nineteen articles convinced people that Olivi's writings needed examination, but Bonagratia was not content to submit these articles to the commission. He wanted a more objective and more thorough examination. In stating that he collected those things "which seemed to ring poorly," the *Chronicle of the Twenty-four Generals* may give the impression that he gave the commission excerpts, but Olivi himself seems to say that he gave them entire works from which the commission itself excerpted offending passages.[22] Three extant manuscripts apparently used by the commission[23] corroborate Olivi's report. The commission studied entire *quaestiones*. Bonagratia may have exercised a prior selection by deciding which *quaestiones* were to be judged, but once the commission set to work it was free to choose the passages it thought worthy of censure. Thus it is not surprising that the list it settled upon should differ from the nineteen articles.

The discerning reader may have noticed an unsettling lack of reference to poverty in the preceding discussion. The sources we have been considering tell us little about the role it played in the controversy with Brother Ar. The *Attack* mentions it only in the opening sentence: "It having been shown that the first article contrary to evangelical poverty is erroneous and against the decretal of Pope Nicholas, the following ones should be touched upon briefly."[24] Thus Olivi's original list of suspect opinions held by Brother Ar began with one on poverty, and the *Attack* began with a lengthy refutation of that opinion. Does that refutation still exist? Koch thinks so, but the matter must wait for a moment. The important point for now is that the *Attack* as we have it deals with other matters.

The letter to R, too, deals with other matters and does not even mention poverty. If the "R" in question was Raymond Geoffroi or anyone else who agreed with Olivi on the subject, this silence is explicable. Olivi was responding to a letter R and his friends had written to him. They had heard of his difficulties and wanted to help, but they needed information. Probably they were disturbed by some of the accusations against him and sought reassurance. Thus they asked him to comment on the charges and he obliged. They did not ask nor did he provide any defense of his stand on poverty because it was an issue on which he and his correspondents knew they agreed.

In short, little in the material examined so far suggests that the poverty question was an element in the debate. Evidence that it was in fact a central issue comes from a completely different set of documents, the Olivian writings dealing with *usus pauper*. It is to these that we must now turn.

The Questions on Evangelical Perfection

It is possible that the *usus pauper* controversy was spawned by one of Olivi's most impressive projects, his *Questions on Evangelical Perfection*. As now employed, that title refers to a group of seventeen questions found in their entirety in manuscript Vat. lat. 4986 and in part elsewhere. The number and order of the questions varies in different manuscripts, and it is difficult to say which arrangement represents Olivi's final redaction.[25] It is also hard to say what the original order of composition may have been, or even whether the various questions were originally conceived as a single work. These are, happily, questions which will be discussed elsewhere.[26] Here we will simply employ the numeration of Vat. lat. 4986.

Taken in the order found there, these questions are more than a treatise on poverty. They offer a vision of the Christian life as Olivi aspired to achieve it, and they deal with poverty as a part of that totality. The first two deal with contemplation, the third and fourth with study, and the next seven with vows. Of the latter, question five discusses vows in general; questions six and seven the vow of chastity; questions eight through ten that of poverty; and question eleven that of obedience. Question twelve asks whether the pope should always be obeyed in matters of faith and morals, while question thirteen defends the legitimacy of papal resignation. Question fourteen examines whether a pope can dispense from vows, particularly evangelical vows. Questions fifteen and sixteen attack certain questionable means of support open to Franciscans, such as income from prebends. Question seventeen asks whether one vowing to observe the gospel or some rule sins mortally in failing to obey any part of it.

It is impossible to say when Olivi began writing these questions. Considering his youth, some scholars have been inclined to rule out a date earlier than around 1275; yet he himself tells us that some of his writings date from "before the time of brother Jerome,"[27] who became minister general in 1274. The important thing for our purposes is that questions eight and nine, the point at which he turns to poverty, were written before August 1279, when Nicholas III published the bull *Exiit qui seminat*, but not substantially earlier.[28]

Question Eight

Question eight lays the groundwork for question nine by asking whether the state of the highest poverty is better than that of wealth. Olivi decides, of course, that it is. His argument for that conclusion belongs in a familiar genre of Franciscan literature. It is a late installment in the secular-mendicant controversy, relying heavily upon the same arguments and proof texts encountered in works like Bonaventure's *Apologia pauperum* or Pecham's *Tractatus pauperis*. Olivi's use of these texts suggests that he had access to a set of citations composed by Franciscans for use in the secular-mendicant controversy but was very familiar with Pecham's work and influenced in his choice by what he found there.[29] His argument can also be seen as a mild contribution to another battle that was gaining momentum at that time, the *correctorium* controversy, which pitted the two major mendicant orders against each other. In some of his replies to opposing arguments, Olivi seems to be addressing the same passages from Aquinas which the *correctorium* literature found objectionable.[30] We would launch an even more direct attack shortly thereafter in the Matthew commentary.

Although question eight does not deal explicitly with the problem of *usus pauper*, it is important enough to merit close examination. Olivi divides his argument into five parts. In the first, he defends evangelical poverty by showing how it contributes to the achievement of various ends such as humility, sobriety, chastity, trustworthiness, liberality, social harmony, fortitude, faith, hope, love, and contemplation. In this section he might almost be described as studying the social and psychological impact of wealth, since he shows how the bonds uniting social structures like families, parishes, and monasteries are rent by acquisitiveness and how the rich are treated in a way that insulates them from a realistic view of their world or even themselves.

In the second part, Olivi shows how poverty conforms with the human will considered in its natural rectitude. In the third, borrowing a spatial metaphor, he describes the "dimensions" of poverty, speaking of its sublimity, width, length, and depth. In these early sections Olivi attempts to link a rich variety of phenomena with the poverty question. He neatly transfers the argument for poverty into the domain of faith by asserting that almost all the theological errors treasured by heretics and unbelievers stemmed from an overvaluation of sensible things. Although Aristotelian philosophy, Judaism, Islam, and the Arian heresy might seem wildly diverse phenomena to the casual observer, Olivi insists that they all proceeded from the same basic error. Conversely, the truth of Christianity rises or falls on acceptance of the proposition that God calls us to an end which is spiritual rather than material. Christ's career makes sense only if that proposition makes sense. If it does not, then he was not the messiah and the Jews were correct when, interpreting the Old Testament prophecies carnally, they rejected him and continued to seek a messiah who would bring them wealth and power.

In the fourth section Olivi argues the value of evangelical poverty by examining its founder, Christ. Drawing heavily on the Franciscan arsenal of biblical and patristic proof-texts, he traces Christ's progress from birth (in a stable because of his parents' poverty) to death (when his own poverty kept him from leaving anything to his mother). Olivi then uses the same arsenal to argue that Christ imposed poverty on his disciples through a vow and that the apostles took that vow.

In the fifth and final section, Olivi turns from the founding of evangelical poverty to its renewal in his own time. His argument has a double focus. He is intent on portraying Francis as *alter Christus*, but he is even more interested in sketching a theology of history which will make sense of the Franciscan movement. As for the first, Francis is to Christ as the wax figure is to the seal in which it was stamped. There is nothing excellent in Christ that was not somehow represented in Francis. He is in no sense Christ's rival, however. Like John the Baptist, he points to Christ.[31]

The parallel with John the Baptist is worth pondering. Although Olivi does not explicitly say so, it would hardly distort his meaning to say that, just as John was a prophet but more than a prophet, so Francis was a saint but more than just another saint. Here we arrive at the second element in this section, Olivi's theology of history. Many of the apocalyptic themes that would echo through his writings for the rest of his life are already present in this question, but consideration of them must be postponed until a later chapter. For the moment, it will suffice to say that Francis and his rule are seen as heralding a new, higher stage in church history. The church has been maturing over the preceding centuries and is now ready to experience "a clarification of faith, an inundation of divine delights, and a banishing of all errors insofar as such is possible in this life."[32] These are weighty claims. We must eventually look very closely at them.

Question Nine

Olivi parted with tradition by dividing his material into two questions, one defending poverty and the other specifically arguing that the poverty envisaged by the Franciscan vow involves *usus pauper* as well as lack of possessions. This double focus had some precedent, since Hugh of Digne, the *Commentary of the Four Masters*, Bonaventure, Nicholas III, and others spoke of Franciscan poverty as involving two elements: lack of possessions and using only what was necessary. Olivi's approach was unique in that, by allotting a separate question to the issue of *usus pauper* and the vow, he concentrated scholarly attention on a problem that had lain dormant throughout the secular-mendicant controversy and, once aroused, would give his order a great deal of trouble during the next four decades.

Question nine inquires "whether *usus pauper* is included in the counsel or vow of evangelical poverty in such a way that it is a substantial and integral part of that vow." Olivi replies that it is, and his argument for that position is based on question eight in the sense that it follows the same structure. Olivi tries to show that the argument for poverty presented there is valid only if one accepts *usus pauper* as an essential part of the vow. He goes through the same ends discussed in the first section of question eight, then rehearses the other four sections making the same point. Here again he relies heavily on the Franciscan treasury of biblical and patristic *auctoritates*. There are notable shifts of emphasis, though, particularly in the fifth section where attention shifts away from Francis's apocalyptic significance and centers on the rule.[33]

Moreover, the most important part of this response has no relation to question eight. It is the final section in which Olivi asks what *usus pauper* means and how it is included in the vow. Here he faces what may have been the core of Franciscan doubts about the wisdom of including *usus pauper* in the vow. The rule was under attack by both secular masters and Dominicans, and one element in that attack was the suggestion that the rule was dangerous to those who vowed it. Linking the vow with *usus pauper* seemed to confirm that accusation. It seemed to make the rule physically dangerous by denying Franciscans the right to plan prudently for the future, and also to make it spiritually dangerous by binding friars to a standard that could not be objectively determined. In a world of varying needs and shifting circumstances, who could say precisely what was allowable? Olivi's answer to that question would reverberate through the rest of the controversy.

Having said all this, Olivi is still only halfway through question nine. He next considers how *usus pauper* limits Franciscans in their use of money, clothing, shoes, and horses. These investigations give the question a specificity lacking in the earlier part. They also indicate how Olivi viewed current practices in his order.

Question Fifteen

Olivi's views on *usus pauper* were soon countered by some of his confreres in southern France. He returned to the issue in what is now considered the fifteenth of the *Questions on Evangelical Perfection*, written soon after August 1279.[34] Here the question is whether Franciscans can live from regular sources of income as long as proprietary rights are not involved. In his response, Olivi observes that those who defend the affirmative position are encouraged to do so by their belief that limited use is not required by the Franciscan vow, which demands only abdication of property rights.

Olivi recites nine arguments offered for this conviction.[35] It would be tedious to recite them in detail, but some general observations are in order. First, they are strikingly different from the ones cited in question nine. Of the eight arguments cited in question nine only one is still in evidence, and even it has been modified. Second, the opposing arguments in question fifteen assume the existence of Olivi's own arguments in question nine. The one modified argument demonstrates this point neatly. In question nine, Olivi pictures his opponents as arguing that *usus pauper* cannot be part of the vow because there is no way to determine the point at which violation would occur. He counters that objection with a distinction between determinate and indeterminate obligation. In question fifteen, Olivi's adversaries offer the same objection but now insist that it is valid even if the obligation is taken indeterminately.

Another argument in question seventeen suggests that an indeterminate obligation would lead to transgression and discord. Still another seeks to show that what Olivi offered in question nine as an unacceptable implication of the opposing view—the possibility of a higher vow than that of evangelical poverty—is in fact quite acceptable. Still another responds to Olivi's evocation of Franciscan tradition in question nine. In short, someone has responded to Olivi's earlier work, and Olivi is now responding in turn.

The Matthew Commentary

Olivi was obviously very much involved in the *usus pauper* debate by the time he wrote question fifteen, but it was hardly the only thing he had to do. He was a lector, and as such he was supposed to exposit various books of the Bible. At least three of his most important Bible commentaries, those on Matthew, Job, and Isaiah, stem from this period. Of these, only the Matthew commentary refers explicitly to the *usus pauper* controversy. The reference is brief, but it has its own importance.

In this commentary, which probably dates from between fall 1279 and late spring 1280, Olivi cites and energetically refutes two passages from Aquinas's *Summa Theologiae*.[36] In the first, Aquinas argues that Christ's instruction to the disciples in Matthew 10:9f., "Provide yourselves with neither gold nor silver nor copper in your belts, nor purse," and so on, can be interpreted in two ways. Either it was not an order but a concession allowing the disciples to accept sustenance from those to whom they preached, or it was a temporary order rescinded just before the passion. In the second passage Aquinas insists that common possessions can sometimes enhance the perfection of a religious order instead of detracting from it. An order formed to fight or offer hospitality can justify abundant wealth, and even one dedicated entirely to contemplation should have sufficient possessions to avoid solicitude for the morrow. Aquinas cites the case of Christ, who had a purse. "Poverty," Aquinas concludes, "is not a perfection but an instrument of perfection, and the least of the three principal instruments of perfection."

Olivi extracts seven main errors from Aquinas's words and attacks them in order, but we need not follow the assault, since his efforts have little to do with the *usus pauper* controversy. The main issue is possession, not use. Of the two passages from Aquinas, only the first bears any implications for the *usus pauper* conflict, and Olivi manages to refute Aquinas without exploring these implications.

Having dispensed with Thomas, Olivi notes that four other points need to be made concerning Matthew 10:9f., the passage he is currently expositing.[37] First, it may seem to some that the passage so absolutely prohibits carrying money, purse, shoes, staff, or extra tunic that any apostle transgressing this order would sin mortally. Second, some people have said that those who vow the highest poverty are bound to such things only *de congruo*. Third, some say that these prohibitions are no longer relevant because the material circumstances of the church have changed dramatically since Christ's day. Fourth, some people say that the apostles could licitly accept abundant support from those to whom they preached. Christ says, "Eat and drink whatever is set before you," a thought echoed by Francis in the rule. Olivi corrects all four errors, but directs his heaviest fire at the fourth.

The anonymous, misguided *quidam* cannot be identified solely with Olivi's opponents in the *usus pauper* controversy,[38] but Olivi's way of responding to the first and fourth views makes it clear that he has those opponents in mind. The passage hardly constitutes a major event in the debate. Its major significance is that it is the only point in the three commentaries at which Olivi explicitly alludes to the controversy. He must have been troubled by the burgeoning debate, but he was hardly obsessed by it.

The Treatise on *Usus Pauper*

The next evidence of the *usus pauper* controversy is a work written after October 1279 and probably before Easter 1283. We need only read the opening sentence to see that the debate has progressed significantly. Consciously echoing the words of Nicholas III in *Exiit qui seminat*, Olivi announces that he has taken pen in hand "because the serpentine cunning of the Old Adversary continues, as in the past, to stir up trouble against evangelical poverty, which has been renewed and revealed more clearly in these last days through Francis, the seraphic confessor of Christ."[39] He goes on to explain that said Adversary first attacked by inciting certain secular masters to stigmatize the mendicant life as dangerous and detrimental. Then he inspired "certain pseudo-religious . . . girded with teaching and preaching authority" (Olivi has Dominican critics in mind) to say that the Franciscan rule is neither evangelical, apostolic, nor perfect, but rather dangerous, unobservable, and blameworthy. Now, worst of all, he has sent "certain pseudo-apostles, professors of that very rule, who dare to state and teach publicly, as well as solemnly determine in the schools, that poor or moderate use in no way falls under the vow and profession of our rule." Neither, they insist, did Christ impose it on his disciples by precept or vow. In saying these things, they render the Franciscan vow and rule ridiculous as well as almost entirely useless. At the same time, they openly blaspheme against the life and gospel of Christ.

Obviously the rhetoric has escalated. Olivi's opponents are now seen as demonically inspired and the challenge to *usus pauper*, placed within a history of Satan's long chain of abuses, is portrayed as blasphemy even before Olivi gets down to specifics. He acknowledges, however, that his opponents carry some academic weight and that the battle is being waged within the Franciscan educational system.

Olivi goes on to say that, since the moment this view appeared, he has opposed it "in questions written earlier." Perhaps his use of the plural can be taken as evidence that both the ninth and the fifteenth of his *Questions on Evangelical Perfection* were directed against an existent faction, but that may be putting too fine a point on his words. At any rate, because the simpler brethren are now endangered by his opponents' deceitful claims, Olivi proposes to refute them once more. The resultant polemic, which I shall call the *Treatise on Usus Pauper*, is Olivi's most important work on the subject.

By what date did the controversy reach this point? Joseph Koch argues for a very early one, based on the opening sentence of the *Attack*: "It having been shown that the first article contrary to evangelical poverty is erroneous and against the decretal of Pope Nicholas, the following ones should be touched upon briefly." Where is this lengthy refutation of the first article? Koch thinks it is the *Treatise on Usus Pauper*, because both the *Treatise* and the *Attack* assail someone's teachings and the *Treatise* cites Nicholas.[40]

Such an argument seems less than airtight. Question fifteen also assails someone's teachings and cites Nicholas. Moreover, the *Treatise* could not have been written especially for the occasion. Its target is an anonymous "they," not an individual as is the case throughout the *Attack*.[41] It is hard to believe that this polemic could have taken shape as an attempt to explain at greater length what Olivi had said in the first of a series of articles previously aimed at Brother Ar. Of course, Koch never said that it did. He suggests that the *Treatise* was written earlier to convince Bonagratia and was well received, because Bonagratia already shared Olivi's thoughts on the subject. Seeing that Olivi had won the first round, Ar counterattacked on the theological front where Olivi was demonstrably vulnerable, having had his difficulties there in the past. Olivi retaliated with a list of thirty-one suspect articles aimed at Ar. Thus, for Koch, the original problem was *usus pauper*. The philosophical and theological charges were introduced as a flanking movement.

This scenario is at least possible, but there is little evidence for it. The *Treatise* bears no traces of having been directed to the minister general. Nor was it necessarily written before the *Attack*, much less before the nineteen articles eventually explained by Olivi in the letter to R. Olivi's opening statement in the *Attack* suggests that he already had written something that claimed Nicholas III's authority in disputing an erroneous view regarding evangelical poverty, but it does not say that the view concerned *usus pauper* as part of the vow. Even if such were the case, Olivi's opening remark would have been equally applicable if he had been thinking not of the *Treatise* but of what had been said in questions nine and fifteen combined, or even in fifteen alone.

Nor is it clear how thoroughly Bonagratia agreed with Olivi on the subject of *usus pauper*. In the *Treatise* Olivi quotes a letter from him demanding moderate use, but it does not say that such use is demanded by the vow. To be sure, Ubertino da Casale, writing in 1311, insists that Bonagratia agreed with Olivi on *usus pauper*. Ubertino bases his assertion on a letter written by Bonagratia shortly after the general chapter at Strasbourg in 1282, but his citations from the letter leave one wondering what it really said. At one point he quotes Bonagratia as saying that Franciscans are bound to *usus pauper* "by our profession." At another it is "from the perfection, that is, the vow of our rule." At still another it is simply "from our perfection." Elsewhere he says Bonagratia's letter contained "the same opinion" held by Olivi, "although in different words." The letter seems to have stated that Franciscans were more tightly bound to *usus pauper* than other orders; yet it was ambiguous enough for both sides to claim allegiance to it at the Council of Vienne, and Ubertino himself describes it as containing "many problems."[42] Since, as we will see, at least some of Olivi's opponents considered *usus pauper* to be very important and yet not part of the vow, one can see how Bonagratia's acknowledgment that the Franciscans were bound to *usus pauper* might not place him entirely in Olivi's camp. In any case, if Ubertino and his adversaries had the letter but were unable to agree on how it squared with Olivi's opinion, it seems unlikely that modern historians can decide much without it.

There is another problem with Koch's thesis. The *Treatise* was certainly written after October 1279, since it quotes the letter written by Bonagratia during that month and would in any case be hard to fit in before then; yet it is not mentioned in any document before early 1285.[43] If it was mentioned in 1285, it must have been written before Olivi's 1283 censure and subsequent disgrace. Why, then, did no one notice it when the commission set to work in 1283? We will see that the members the commission censured Olivi's view of *usus pauper* on the basis of what they found in question nine. It is hard to believe that they would have read the *Treatise* without seeing anything to criticize. Thus Bonagratia had not sent it to them, which means that even if it had been written by that time, it probably had not been in existence long enough to be inserted into the welter of charges and countercharges noted earlier.

Notes

1. On Olivi's biography see my *Persecution of Peter Olivi* (Philadelphia, 1976), esp. 5f. and 35–44.
2. Olivi was a lector in southern France by 1274, when Jerome of Ascoli became minister general. See his *Letter to R* in *Quodlibeta* (Venice, 1509), 51(63)v and 52(64)r. The *Letter to R*, 51(63)v, which was probably written in 1282 or 1283, places Olivi in Montpellier; yet the *Quaestiones in secundum librum sententiarum* (Quaracchi, 1921–26), 1:633 (q. 36), written before Olivi's censure in 1283, assumes that he is writing from Narbonne.
3. According to the 1260 statutes in Bihl, "Statuta generalia," 72, a student was normally to spend at least four years at Paris. For a summary of later legislation see Cenci, "Ordinazioni dei capitoli provinciali umbri," 20. On the succession of masters at Paris see Palémon Glorieux, "Maîtres francis-

cains régents à Paris," *Recherches de théologie ancienne et médiévale* 18 (1951): 321–32. For Olivi's comment see *Letter to R*, 51(63)v.

4. Angelo, *Historia septem tribulationum*, 288; *Series condemnationum factarum de erroribus quos frater Petrus Iohannis docuit*, a fourteenth-century document published in Leo Amorós, "Series condemnationum et processuum contra doctrinam et sequaces Petri Ioannis Olivi," *AFH* 24 (1931): 502, which says that some of Olivi's errors were condemned at a meeting called in Montpellier by Jerome; *Responsio quam fecit P. Ioannis ad litteram magistrorum praesentatam sibi in Avinione*, in Damasus Laberge, "Fr. Petri Ioannis Olivi, O.F.M., tria scripta sui ipsius apologetica annorum 1283 et 1285," *AFH* 28 (1935–36): 127, regarding marriage. *Letter to R*, 51(63)v and 52(64)r may also suggest difficulties concerning baptism and the relationship of existence to essence.

5. Flood, *Olivi's Rule Commentary*, 159.

6. The comments in *Rule Commentary* suggest that the work submitted was the treatise *Quod regula fratrum minorum excludit omnem proprietatem*, published in *Firmamentum trium ordinum* (Paris, 1511), 4:107vb–111rb.

7. In *Lectura super Mattheum* (hereafter *Mtt.*), MS Oxford, New College 49, 155rb–va, which was written by early 1283 and probably by early 1280, Olivi is aware of the vision concerning Francis's future resurrection to which he later returns in *Lectura super apocalypsim*, MS Rome, Bibl. Ang. 382 (hereafter *Rev.*), 55rb, a vision explicitly assigned to Conrad of Offida by Ubertino da Casale, *Arbor vitae*, 437.

8. *Letter to R*, 52(64)r. In this edition the letter is addressed to "R. de Camliaco and his associates," but MS Paris Bibliothèque Nationale Nouv. acq. 774, 94r, says "R.do and dearest associates" and is preceded by a note identifying R.do with Raymond Geoffroi, who later became minister general and was a spokesman for the spirituals at the Council of Vienne. Pierre Péano, "Raymond Geoffroi, ministre général et défenseur des spirituels," *Picenum seraphicum* 11 (1974): 192, combines both alternatives, suggesting that "Camliaco" was Raymond Geoffroi's birthplace, but he cannot identify that name with any location. I will avoid the problem by calling this document "the letter to R."

9. A fourteenth-century document, Raymundus de Fronciacho's *Sol ortus*, in *Archiv*, 3:16, says "frater Petrus Iohannis litigia suscitavit contra fratrem Arnaldum Galhardi et plurimos alios bonos fratres, qui dicta erronea impugnabant." Arlotto of Prato and Arnold of Roquefeuil also have been suggested. See J. H. Sbaralea, *Supplementum ad scriptores trium ordinum S. Francisci* (Rome, 1908–36), 3:597; Ehrle, "Petrus Johannis Olivi," 478. Arlotto would have been an inconvenient adversary. He sat on the commission that judged Olivi's works in 1283 and became minister general two years later; yet there is no good reason for choosing him. Arnold of Roquefeuil seems a better choice. Raymond of Fronsac, *Sol ortus*, 14, says that when Arnold was Olivi's provincial minister he joined with thirty-five other friars from the province in a document attacking Olivi; yet Gratien de Paris, "Une lettre inédite de Pierre de Jean Olivi," *Etudes franciscaines* 29 (1913): 419, notes that in the Paris manuscript of the letter Olivi refers to "Brother Ar" as *bone memorie*, yet Arnold of Roque-

feuil was alive as late as 1300. See Pierre Péano, "Ministres provinciaux de Provence et spirituels," in *Franciscains d'Oc: Les Spirituels, 1280–1324* (Toulouse, 1975), 41–68. Nevertheless, in "Raymond Geoffroi," 201, Péano refers to "Arnaud Gaillard de Roquefeuil." See also Péano, "Les Ministres provinciaux de la primitive province de Provence (1217–1517)," *AFH* 79 (1986): 27.

10. *Impugnatio*, in *Quodlibeta*, 42r–53r. It is directed against a single person but followed by five articles aimed at some of the person's associates. The five articles seem to be the only extant part of a longer work.
11. *Letter to R*, 52(64)v.
12. *Impugnatio*, 42r.
13. *Letter to R*, 51(53)v.
14. Ibid., 53(65)r.
15. Ehrle, "Petrus Johannis Olivi," 426f., dates it between the censure and 1285, but there is little to recommend this theory except Olivi's lack of his writings. Moreover, the charges countered in the letter to R are not identical with those in the censure of 1283. Most important, the letter to R assumes the existence of a minister general, but there was none between October 1283 and May 1285.
16. Raymondus, *Sol ortus*, 13; Raymondus de Fronciacho and Bonagratia de Bergamo, *Infrascripta dant*, in *Archiv*, 3:156.
17. Joseph Koch, "Die Verurteilung Olivis auf dem Konzil von Vienne und ihre Vorgeschichte," *Scholastik* 5 (1930): 489–522.
18. *Chronica XXIV generalium*, 374f.
19. Fussenegger, "Definitiones," 137.
20. Bihl, "Statuta generalia," 80. It also censured the notion that one who corrects a brother in secret according to the form of the gospel is not also required to report that brother's error to a superior, a problem important enough for the masters at the chapter to have discussed and passed judgment on it.
21. Fussenegger, "Definitiones," 139.
22. Olivi seems to say as much in *Responsio P. Ioannis ad aliqua dicta per quosdam magistros Parisienses de suis quaestionibus excerpta* (hereafter *Responsio II*), in Damasus Laberge, "Fr. Petri Ioannis Olivi, O.F.M, tria scripta sui ipsius apologetica annorum 1283 et 1285" (hereafter "Tria scripta"), *AFH* 28 (1935–36): 132.
23. They are MSS Vat. Borgh. 46, 322, and 358. See Koch, "Verurteilung," 505, and Annaliese Maier, "Per la storia del processo contro l'Olivi," *RSCI* 5 (1951): 330.
24. *Impugnatio*, 42r: "Ostenso quod primus articulus paupertati evangelice contrarius est erroneus et contra decretalem domini N. tangendum est aliquid breviter de subsequentibus." MS Vat. Borgh. 54, 120r, says *ostendo* rather than *ostenso*.
25. Ehrle, "Petrus Johannis Olivi," 502 prefers the arrangement in Vat. lat. 4986. Dionisio Pacetti, in the introduction to his edition of Olivi's *Quaestiones quatuor de domina* (Quaracchi, 1954), *21, chooses Vat. Borgh. 357.
26. See my forthcoming edition of *De perfectione evangelica*, q. 9, and the *Tractatus de usu paupere*. Internal evidence shows that all seventeen ques-

tions included in Vat. lat. 4986 except 13 (composed after Celestine V's resignation in 1294) and perhaps 16 were written by 1283, when Olivi was censured, in roughly the order seen in that manuscript.

27. *Letter to R*, 51(63)v and 52(64)r.

28. Q. 15, MS Florence Bibl. Laur. 448, 96vb, says q. 9 was written before *Exiit*, but q. 9, MS Vat. Burgh 357, 87va, announces that a particular topic will be discussed in the course of his commentary on the gospels. Olivi commented first on Matthew, since the Mark commentary, MS Vat. Ottob. lat. 3302, 1r, says he first commented on Matthew and John, then Mark and Luke, while the John commentary, MS Florence Laur. Plut. 10 dext. 8, 13rb, cites the Matthew commentary. The latter was probably delivered during the 1279–80 school year. Q. 9 is so closely dependent upon q. 8 that it was probably written immediately after. Q. 8 refers to a work that can probably be identified as Olivi's treatise *Quod regula fratrum minorum excludit omnem proprietatem*, which was written in the summer of 1279, shortly before *Exiit* was published; yet the absence of this reference in Vat. Burgh. 358, the earliest manuscript of q. 8, suggests that Olivi could have added it in an early redaction.

29. The lengthy citations from Bonaventure's *Apologia pauperum* now found in questions eight and nine are absent from Vat. Borgh. 358. They were added later to strengthen the argument.

30. See his response to the idea of poverty as an instrument of perfection in his reply to the twenty-seventh argument for wealth, or his response to the suggestion (in the sixteenth argument for common possessions) that Luke 10:4 should be seen as permission rather than precept. Here he seems to be responding to the *Summa theologiae*, IIa IIae, q. 185, a. 1, and q. 186, a. 2. These are only two of at least eight places where Olivi seems to be thinking of Aquinas.

31. Bibl. Laur. 448, 29ra.

32. Ibid., 33ra: "Non plene apparet Dei condescensio et magnificatio circa ecclesiam suam, si saltem in uno tempore eius non fieret clarificatio fidei et inundatio divinarum deliciarum et evacuatio omnium errorum, prout est possibile in hac vita."

33. There is little apocalyptic interest of any sort. Q. 9 dismisses in four lines what was, in q. 8, a substantial section dealing with that subject.

34. Q. 15 cites *Exiit* and notes that it appeared after he wrote q. 9; yet the opposing arguments cited in q. 15 suggest that his adversaries were not yet using *Exiit*, as they were by the time Olivi wrote the *Tractatus de usu paupere*. Was q. 15 originally a separate question or part of q. 10? Only in Vat. lat. 4980 is it found as a separate question. In four manuscripts (including Vat. Burgh. 358, apparently used by the commission in 1283) it is part of q. 10; yet internal evidence suggests that, if 15 was originally part of 10, Olivi wrote a series of questions on poverty consisting of 8, 9, 10/15, and 11 but wrote 12 and 14 during roughly the same period.

35. MS Florence, Bibl. Laur. 448, 95va–96va.

36. The section of the *Postilla in Matthaeum* criticizing Thomas has been edited (with some omissions) by Marie-Thérèse d'Alvernay, "Un Adversaire

de St. Thomas: Petrus Johannis Olivi," *St. Thomas Aquinas, 1274–1974* (Toronto, 1974), 2:179–218. The two passages from the *Summa Theologiae* are Ia IIae, q. 108, a. 2 ad 3, and IIa IIae, q. 188, a. 7. On the Matthew commentary see Decima Douie, "Olivi's Postilla super Matthaeum," *FS* 35 (1975): 66–92. In Burr, "The Date of Petrus Iohannis Olivi's Commentary on Matthew," *CF* 46 (1976): 131–38, I argue that the Matthew, Job, and Isaiah commentaries must have been delivered during 1279–80 or 1280–81, probably the latter. They could also have been written in 1281–82 if the letter to R was written around Easter 1283 instead of 1282 as Koch contends. Yet Olivi's reference to the Matthew commentary in q. 9 (see note 28 above) suggests 1279–80, since it is easy to imagine Olivi, as he wrote question nine sometime before August 1279, anticipating lectures he would begin that fall, but hard to imagine him looking forward to lectures he would deliver more than a year later.

37. *Mtt.*, 81ra–va.
38. Here as elsewhere there are echoes of the secular-mendicant and *correctorium* controversies.
39. *Tractatus*, 10ra: "Quoniam contra paupertatem evangelicam per seraphicum Christi confessorem Franciscum in novissimis temporibus plenius et clarius renovatam et revelatam antiqui hostis serpentina astucia quibusdam tortuosis anfractibus varios suscitavit et suscitare non cessat, primo quidem contra eam mittens clericorum precipuos magistrali scientia et auctoritate fulcitos, qui ausi sunt docere et dogmatizare quod status mendicantium evangelicorum et eorum mendicitas est mortifera et dampnosa; secundo vero pseudoreligiosos et precipue quosdam scientia magistrali et predicationis officio circumcinctos qui ausi sunt dicere regulam Francisci ac paupertatem in ipsa contentam non esse evangelicam aut apostolicam nec summe perfectam, sed potius periculosam inobservabilem calumpniabilem stultam et imperfectam; novissime vero diebus istis quod omnium est abhominabilius et intolerabilius mittere incipit quosdam novos pseudoapostolos eiusdem predicte regule professores qui audent publice astruere et dogmatizare et in scolis suis sollempniter determinare quod usus pauper seu moderatus nullo modo cadit sub professione et voto regule nostre, ita quod nec generaliter nec specialiter includitur in aliquo regule predicte precepto aut voto, nec est aliquo modo de substantia regule nostre, sed est solum sibi accidentalis, superaddentes quod Christus suis apostolis et specialibus sectatoribus pauperem usum nullatenus imposuit sub precepto aut voto, quod non est aliud quam professionem nostre paupertatis et regule ridiculosam et fere omnino inutilem reddere, et cum hoc aperte Christi vitam et evangelium blasphemare, et statum apostolicum a sua altitudine deprimere. . . . Quia autem eorum sermo non more apostolice tube intonat, nec instar evangelice aquile in altum volat, sed potius iuxta illud apostoli eorum sermo sicut cancer serpit ac per hoc simplicium animos quibusdam serpentinis suggestionibus et blandis delusionibus et dolosis verborum intortionibus possent circumvenire, seducere et intoxicare nisi spiritu Christi de suis flexuosis latebris tortuosus coluber quasi obstetracante manu domini Iesu celerius educatur, idcirco succincte aliquid

disserendo prefatis simplicibus intendo habundantem fidem facere de predicto." See *Exiit qui seminat*, in *Corpus iuris canonici* (Graz, 1959),
2:1110.

40. "Verurteilung," 500f.
41. In the *Attack*, Olivi says things like, "I have heard from trustworthy people
that he has determined in the schools that . . ."; "he said, according to
these people, that . . ."; "he said, with me present, that . . ."; and so on.
42. *Sanctitati apostolicae*, in *Archiv*, 2:385, 387, 400; *Sanctitas vestra*, in
Archiv, 3:82. See also Raymond of Fronsac, *Sol ortus*, 13f.
43. It is mentioned in *Responsio* II, 386.

CHAPTER 3

The Developing Controversy: Issues

The preceding chapter investigated the chronology of the *usus pauper* controversy to 1283. This one must explore a more delicate matter, the basic issues involved. Its greater delicacy stems not from any lack of evidence—there is more material to work with in describing the issues than in outlining the chronology—but from the difficulty of ordering that evidence into a coherent presentation. Olivi addressed the problem in four different works between 1279 and 1283. In each, he presented a slightly different set of arguments for his own view and refuted a slightly different set of arguments purportedly offered by his opponents. The following attempt at synthesis will inevitably belie the kaleidoscopic nature of the developing controversy. Belie it we must, however, since the alternative would be long and tedious.

Olivi's Position

Olivi insisted that *usus pauper*, restricted use, was a part of the vow. How did he support that claim? The easiest way of answering is to follow the order established by Olivi in his *Treatise on Usus Pauper*. There he announces that he will defend his position (1) through the words of Franciscan fathers and masters; (2) through pronouncements of popes; (3) through Christ's gospel and its elucidation by the fathers; (4) through the rule; (5) through some arguments offered elsewhere by Olivi himself; (6) by citing and demolishing the opposing arguments; and (7) by demonstrating the dangers of the opposing view.[1]

The Franciscan Tradition

Olivi devotes more than a third of the *Treatise* to placing the Franciscan tradition on his side. In the process he cites Francis, Bonaventure,

Pecham, Bonagratia of San Giovanni in Persiceto, general constitutions, general chapters, Bernard of Clairvaux, Jerome, and Hugh of Saint Victor. The last three might seem odd in an argument supposedly devoted to Franciscan sources. Their role is to show that every monastic group since the early anchorites has restricted its members' use to some extent, even if, as in the case of the Cistercian rule, no such limitation is explicitly demanded.

The Franciscan sources are most germane. Little is said about Francis, and consideration of him can be delayed until we look at the rule. Pecham is cited at length in the *Treatise*, as indeed he is in question nine.[2] Of course, Olivi cannot hope to hear Pecham saying that *usus pauper* is an essential part of the vow. To expect that much would be equivalent to demanding the gift of prophecy, because Pecham antedated both the controversy and much of its terminology. Nevertheless, Olivi does find him saying that, because Franciscans profess indigence (*profitentur egestatem*), they must avoid whatever suggests wealth or luxury. Again, he says that "many buildings of our order are monsters of our profession" (*monstra professionis*).[3] The operative words here are *profitentur* and *professio*, which Olivi takes to imply a vow, "for to profess indigence is nothing else than solemnly to vow poor and beggarly use."

Apparently Olivi was not the only one impressed by these passages. His opponents thought them important enough to explain away. "Some of these people," Olivi observes in the *Treatise*, "gloss the words *profess indigence*, saying, 'that is, the state which indigence follows.'" He dismisses their reading as "a ridiculous twisting of the words."

This is the most he can get from Pecham. Other citations prove that Pecham took *usus pauper* seriously and thought Franciscans ought to observe it, but do not imply that the obligation stems from their vow. Thus if Olivi's antagonists saw *usus pauper* as important though not part of the vow, such passages could be construed as affirming the common ground held by both positions without really siding with either. If Olivi's opponents actually devalued the importance of restricted use, however, Pecham could be seen as supporting Olivi against them. We will see that is no easy matter to decide which of these views they held.

Olivi's opponents also cited Pecham. Olivi reports elsewhere in the *Treatise* that they bolster their case with a statement by Pecham that Franciscans are held to moderate use—as well as to some other things not dictated in the rule through precept or something similar—only by approved custom.[4] Olivi protests that they are misreading Pecham, whose point is made more clearly elsewhere when he says that nothing in the rule is presented as an obligation unless the word *precept* or some equivalent is employed. Olivi is primarily interested in the words *some equivalent* and proceeds to race through Pecham's treatise uncovering cases where statements in the rule are taken as obligatory even though the word *precept* is not used. Richly satisfying as this exercise may prove on a short-term basis, its wider implications are more unsettling. It points to a major way in which Olivi broke with Franciscan tradition.

Bonaventure is cited at greater length than Pecham.[5] Olivi's attention to Bonaventure in the *Treatise* is understandable. He knows that later he will have to deal with his opponents' evocation of the Seraphic Doctor as an example of easy living. In the *Treatise*, as in question nine, most of Olivi's citations from Bonaventure demonstrate the latter's love for poverty rather than his identification of *usus pauper* with the vow; yet even this much is valuable as an antidote to the picture of him that will emerge as part of the opposing argument.

Olivi does manage to uncover a few nuggets. He quotes Bonaventure's observation that the form of poverty by which one possesses nothing and lives in the greatest want of things was prescribed (*precepta*) to the apostles and observed by them.[6] As the *usus pauper* controversy progressed, the word *preceptum* acquired a technical significance that placed it alongside *vow* and *profession* as a term the opposition would prefer to avoid.

Again, he quotes Bonaventure's affirmation that "evangelical poverty ... perfectly convinces those professing it that at all times they should strip themselves in the realm of desire and ownership and, in the realm of use, be content with enough to satisfy their necessities."[7] This passage comes as close to endorsing Olivi's position as one could expect from an author who had never heard of the *usus pauper* controversy. It suggests that evangelical poverty includes concrete practice as well as lack of desire and abdication of ownership, thus forestalling any attempt to identify it entirely with the latter. It even uses the words *usus* and *necessitas*. Moreover, it implies that all these things are entailed through the Franciscan *professio*, a term Olivi rightly identifies with the vow[8] and one his opponents considered dangerous enough to explain away when they encountered it in Pecham.

Olivi discovers more treasure in the first letter Bonaventure wrote to the order after becoming minister general.[9] The new leader offers a catalog of current malpractices, many of them involving excessive use. Sumptuous buildings and inflated operating budgets are prominently mentioned. He exhorts the brothers not only to avoid such behavior

themselves but to resist it in their brethren because it is harming the order. These pernicious practices must be eliminated, he says, "because the
profession of our perfection requires it." Bonaventure insists that he does
not intend to weigh his brothers down with a new set of chains, but his
conscience compels him to oppose these abuses with all his strength. He
feels required to do so by "the rule which we vow." Although it is possible to construe these words in such a way as to avoid the conclusion
that Bonaventure considered *usus pauper* a part of the vow, the interpretation would be a subtle one indeed.[10] Nor is it easy to evade the significance of another letter cited by Olivi in which Bonaventure announces
that "it is a filthy, profane lie to describe oneself as having professed
poverty if one does not wish to experience a lack of things."[11] Here again,
he clearly sees *usus pauper* as a part of the highest poverty and as involved in the Franciscan *professio*.

Olivi also cites the first letter to the order written by Bonagratia di San
Giovanni in Persiceto after he became minister general in 1279.[12] Unlike
the writings of Pecham and Bonaventure, this source was written when
the *usus pauper* controversy was under way; yet it is disappointingly un-
helpful not only to Olivi in making his case but to the historian in trying
to discover where Bonagratia stood on the issue. He says nothing that
would place him on either side, thus strengthening the suspicion that at
that date the controversy was still at most a local affair involving a few
southern French lectors and their adherents. Bonagratia admonishes the
brothers to follow the intention of Saint Francis and the declaration of
Pope Nicholas III, making sure that "in buildings, clothing, food and
other matters in which poverty should be reflected, you solicitously avoid
sumptuosity, curiosity and superfluity, which detract from poverty, lest it
be claimed by observers that, not knowing the virtue of poverty, we glory
in its name alone." Clearly Bonagratia assumes that *usus pauper* is a part
of evangelical poverty, but it is hard to go much farther, partly because
of the way he places the feared negative judgment in the mouths of
anonymous witnesses. Olivi works very hard on this passage, drawing
from it no less than seven points in his favor, but much of what he says
depends on his assumption that Nicholas III, Francis, and the rule all
support his position.

Olivi also recurs to the general constitutions of the order and defini-
tions of the chapters of Narbonne (1260) and Assisi (1279).[13] Here again
he finds little to aid him beyond an interest in correcting excesses and a
recognition that Franciscan poverty should involve *usus pauper* as well
as lack of ownership.

Papal Pronouncements

In question nine, Olivi quotes the words of Gregory IX in *Quo elongati*: "The order may have the use of those things which are licit for them, that is, those things which do not exceed the standard of poverty."[14] Question fifteen marks the first time he is able to appeal to Nicholas III and *Exiit qui seminat*, and he performs the task with gusto.[15] The total effect is impressive. Although there are moments when Olivi is obviously squeezing too much out of *Exiit*, there are others when it says just what he wants to hear.

As for the first category, Olivi quotes several passages in which Nicholas III insists that the rule allows Franciscans use of what is necessary to preserve their lives and perform their proper functions. Nicholas considered it necessary to make this point because, as Olivi himself recognizes, some detractors of the rule had challenged it on precisely such grounds. Having noted Nicholas's assurances, Olivi draws one valid and one questionable inference. He reasonably observes that such criticism shows how strictly the rule speaks about use, then less justifiably insists that, in arguing the legality of necessary use, Nicholas implies that all other use is illicit.

Olivi also goes beyond the limits of inference in generalizing from Nicholas's comment that, although the rule limits brothers to two tunics, ministers and custodians can decide such matters according to necessity. If (Olivi rhetorically inquires) Nicholas feels that the rule allows only necessary use in clothing, how much more is this true of other, less essential things? Olivi is generalizing from an area in which the rule explicitly limits use to other areas in which it does not. His opponents could just as easily reverse the argument, asking why the rule would bother to prohibit superfluity in clothing if it prohibited all superfluity. In fact, that is precisely what they later asked.[16]

Having remarked on Olivi's excesses, we can turn to what he legitimately infers from *Exiit*. He quotes a long passage in which Nicholas says that Franciscans are to receive no utensils or other things beyond what is necessary, nor should they lay up treasures on the pretext that they are providing for future needs. Their conduct should consistently reflect abdication of property rights and use according to necessity. Such matters should be determined by the ministers and custodians according to local circumstances "in such a way that holy poverty is reflected in them and in their acts, as is found to be proclaimed (*indicta*) to them in their rule." Obviously one can conclude from this passage that, according to Nicholas, the rule enjoins *usus pauper* as well as abdication of property rights. One can conclude that the *usus pauper* celebrated there limits Franciscans to what is necessary for physical health and the performance of their duties. One can conclude that Nicholas would not be pleased with a definition of poverty which considered *usus pauper* to be accidental.[17] Beyond that, there is the problem of how to interpret the word *indicta*, a matter which Olivi explores in the *Treatise*.

In the *Treatise* he offers an expanded version of the interpretation already found in question fifteen. In fact, the first half of his treatment in the *Treatise* consists of everything he said in question fifteen repeated almost verbatim, an unusual practice for him. The result is a convincing argument that, according to Nicholas III, the poverty demanded by the Franciscan rule includes restricted use, and the restriction involved limits Franciscans to what is necessary. He finds it easy to demonstrate the contradiction between *Exiit* and what we will see as his opponents' tendency to limit obligation to what is prescribed in the rule with words like *precipio* and *teneantur*. He even tries his hand at reading a comprehensive injunction to *usus pauper* into *Exiit* by showing that, according to medieval grammarians, the word *indicta* (which is used by Nicholas) is equivalent to *precepta* (which is not).

In the *Treatise* Olivi also goes beyond question fifteen in quoting some passages from *Exiit* which seem to suggest a different position than his own, although he never acknowledges as much. Expositing the rule, Nicholas says that Franciscans "promise to observe the gospel under this modification, namely living in obedience without personal property and in chastity."[18] Olivi neatly sidesteps the apparent limitation of poverty to lack of property by remarking that the poverty vowed is of the evangelical variety, which includes *usus pauper*, as the rest of *Exiit* clearly indicates.

Again, he quotes Nicholas's assertion that "in professing this rule, the brothers are held by precept only to those counsels expressed in the same rule by precept, prohibition or equivalent words." Olivi offers the "equivalent words" as a refutation of his opponents' concentration on words of precept like *precipio* and *teneantur*, but he ignores the larger question: is Nicholas's limitation of obligation to a specific number of things explicitly demanded and prohibited by the rule actually consistent with Olivi's own assumption of a general obligation to use only what is necessary? The problem here is the same one raised by Olivi's reaction to the passage from Pecham quoted by his opponents. Here again we are dealing with the important way in which Olivi was at odds with Franciscan tradition, a matter which must eventually be examined at length. The discussion can be postponed until later because Olivi does not face the problem in these works either, and his failure to do so says something about his approach to Nicholas. He simply cites a few passages. He makes no effort to analyze these passages carefully, much less to discuss *Exiit* as a whole, asking what it really says or whether it presents a coherent position at all. His behavior reflects the relative importance of *Exiit* at this stage of the controversy. In contrast to the situation thirty years later at the Council of Vienne, when *Exiit* would be seen as the critical document from which all arguments must proceed, Olivi and his adversaries simply saw it as one authority among many to be cited in building their cases.

However limited Olivi's involvement with *Exiit* may have been, his treatment of it suggests that he was more interested in it at this stage than were his enemies. He could cite it without having to counter any strong opposing interpretation. Nicholas is mentioned twice in the opposing arguments of the *Tractatus*, and on both occasions Olivi manages to respond to the argument without even mentioning *Exiit*. Of course this may be due at least partly to the order of the *Tractatus*. By the time Olivi reviews the opposing arguments in chapter six, he already has discussed *Exiit* in chapter two. Thus he may not see any reason to refute his opponents' view of *Exiit* at length in the latter chapter, having implicitly done so in the former one.

Christ and the Apostles

In tracing the New Testament roots of evangelical poverty, Olivi helps himself to the mass of biblical and patristic citations assembled by his predecessors for use in the secular-mendicant controversy.[19] Since he does so in both question nine and the *Treatise*, one might expect him to reproduce in the *Treatise* those citations already assembled in question nine, much as he reproduced question fifteen on the subject of *Exiit*. Instead, the two works differ notably, and only some references are the same.

However different the citations, we find here the same Christ glimpsed in question eight, one who chose to be born in a stable to parents so poor that his mother scarcely had a single tunic to warm her and his father could not afford to offer a lamb; who begged as a child along with the other poor; who had to sleep outside Jerusalem during passion week because no one would give him a room in the city; and so on. Olivi's presentation is directed toward showing that, in describing the poverty of Christ, his disciples, and the apostles, the *sancti* always allude more expressly to *usus pauper* than to lack of property rights, and thus they portray restricted use as an essential part of evangelical poverty. The sig-

nificance of this fact for Olivi stems from his assumption, shared by
Nicholas III and even by his opponents, that the poverty espoused by the
Franciscan order is identical with that of Christ and his disciples. It also
stems from his conviction (unhappily unsupported by his evidence) that
usus pauper was imposed by Christ upon the disciples through a vow.
His lack of success in proving this point probably had little effect on the
controversy because, if Olivi can be accepted as a sufficient witness to
what his antagonists were saying, they made only minimal effort to bolster their case with biblical exegesis. Only the arguments reported in question nine and the Matthew commentary show any interest in doing so.

The Franciscan Rule

Olivi still must investigate what the rule actually says about *usus pauper*.[20] The question seems an important one, yet Olivi devotes surprisingly little space to answering it, less than 6 percent of question nine and
less than 10 percent of the *Treatise*. The reason is that the rule offers him
strikingly little to build on. Much of what he says depends on ideas smug-
gled in from other aspects of his argument. He contends that the rule
must demand *usus pauper* because Franciscans are called to observe
evangelical poverty, and we know that the disciples vowed *usus pauper*;
because they are called to the highest poverty, and we know that it could
not be such without *usus pauper*; and because the rule says that such
poverty aids in attaining the virtues, and we know that only poverty
which includes *usus pauper* can do so. In each case, the crucial point is
not so much derived from the rule as imposed on it.

Olivi makes some effort to deal with the troublesome opening passage
of the rule, which says, "The rule and life of the brothers minor is this:
to observe the holy gospel of our lord Jesus Christ, living in obedience,
without personal property and in chastity." He notes that "living" as it
is used here suggests actual behavior involving both interior and exterior
acts. Thus if "living without personal property" signifies the highest
poverty—as is suggested by the preceding words, "to observe the gospel
of our lord Jesus Christ"—it must imply *usus pauper*. Moreover, Francis
certainly did not intend the poverty recommended here to be less exalted
than chastity and obedience, which he expected to be strictly observed in
practice, as the rest of the rule shows. Thus Olivi ransacks his storehouse
of previous conclusions to argue that a passage seemingly tailor-made for
his enemies could not possibly mean what it seems to mean.

An important issue peers out for a moment, then abruptly disappears.
Olivi again contests the notion that one is bound by vow only to those

portions of the rule which contain words like *precipio* or *teneantur*. In effect, he leafs through the rule highlighting what Nicholas would call "equivalent words," but he does substantially more. In a brief discussion of the phrase "promising to observe this life and rule" he argues that, in vowing the rule, Franciscans bind themselves by vow to all its parts.[21] Is this view reconcilable with Nicholas's insistence that Franciscans are bound by precept only to what is demanded through precept, prohibition or equivalent words? Here again we encounter the difficulty which Olivi ignored when citing Pecham and Nicholas III, and here again we must defer consideration until later.

The Highest Poverty

Beyond these appeals to authority, question nine and the *Treatise* both insist that inclusion of *usus pauper* in the vow is logically implied by the Franciscan claim that the order observes the highest poverty. In question nine, over half of Olivi's total argument is devoted to working laboriously through his case in question eight for the superiority of poverty over wealth, attempting to show that it is valid only if that poverty includes *usus pauper*. Only thus, he argues, can the virtues mentioned in question eight be fully realized and the vices fully avoided.

In the *Treatise* Olivi makes the same point in mercifully shorter form, then goes on to observe that any poverty which allowed opulent use would be inferior, not only to that of the ancient anchorites but also to that of monks who practice common ownership, since even they place some restriction upon use. Moreover, if the Franciscan vow did not demand *usus pauper*, it would follow that one could leave the Franciscan order and join a higher one, which is contrary to the rule. In fact, since it is logical to anticipate an ultimate order to which all previous orders were ordained (just as the various personalities of the Old Testament were ordained to Christ's person according to the flesh), it would follow that a higher and more perfect order than the Franciscans must certainly appear in the future.[22] Olivi adds an intriguing historical aside: "Through the aforesaid error, certain foolish people, impelled by demonic instigation, left this state and transferred to a stupid eremetical life, believing they could institute and observe a more perfect rule. Far be such an apostate error from me, however!"[23]

Olivi's general point is clear enough. A Franciscan cannot transfer to some other, higher *religio* because there can be none. For that very reason, if there is to be an ultimate order in the final stage of history it must follow the Franciscan rule. Nevertheless, a gnawing question remains:

Who were those foolish people who deserted the order and embarked upon an eremetical life? Is he referring to earlier developments in Italy as he understands them?

Dangers of the Opposing View

In the final section of his *Treatise*, Olivi outlines in cursory fashion seven "especially vile errors" which follow from his opponents' view. In brief, he suggests that their stand, if triumphant, would destroy evangelical perfection, turn the Franciscan life into an empty charade, and make the order a laughingstock throughout Christendom, giving its enemies the chance they long have awaited. He also sounds an apocalyptic note, suggesting that his opponents are preparing the way for "the infernal sect of Antichrist."

There is little reason to examine these points in detail, since they largely summarize what he says elsewhere; yet one element in the discussion, the "public defamation of our state" foreseen by Olivi if his opponents' views should triumph, is worth noting because it is related to an argument offered with some effect in question nine. There, besides quoting popes and scholars, Olivi appeals to an entirely different level of opinion, that of common laymen. Twice he invites the reader to ask how valid the majority of men would consider a profession of poverty to be if it allowed luxurious use of goods.[24]

Opposing Arguments

Having examined Olivi's arguments, we must now consider those offered by his opponents. There is nowhere to turn at this stage except to Olivi himself. Fortunately, question nine, question fifteen, and the *Treatise* all present and refute opposing arguments in good scholastic fashion.[25] Thus a great deal of information about Olivi's antagonists is available, even if it does not come from them directly.

Olivi is a better source for his enemies' views than one might at first imagine. Although it seems unlikely that his opponents would have applauded Olivi's presentation, there is reason to believe that both his own personality and the nature of the quarrel encouraged accuracy on his part. As for his personality, Olivi was a man who took ideas seriously and saw the complexity of the issues being argued in his day. While it would be naive to credit him with a degree of objectivity unattained by modern scholars, it is equally unlikely that he would construct and demolish an opponent of pure, unadulterated straw.

As to the nature of the debate, in its early stages the *usus pauper* controversy was primarily a battle of ideas, with little *ad hominem* argument involved. Questions nine and fifteen give the impression that Olivi and his adversaries began by saying a great deal about one another's arguments and little about one another's behavior. This situation contrasts strongly with the one that would prevail close to three decades later at the Council of Vienne, when an opponent's moral turpitude became as interesting as his logic.

Of course, however one may feel about the authenticity of the opposing arguments as Olivi presents them, they would be worth examining simply for Olivi's responses to them; yet our tendency to trust their authenticity is actually strengthened by his responses. After question nine, in which the arguments do seem a bit too easily refuted, one does not normally get the impression that Olivi is making life easy for himself, and some of his replies might even be characterized as evasive.

It is no mean feat to organize these arguments into a coherent presentation. Here again the *Treatise* is our best document. It offers the clearest presentation of central arguments already seen in earlier works, and it adds a few not previously encountered. Nevertheless, because it omits some arguments found in earlier writings, the best course is to follow no single work, but rather to present a synthesis of the arguments found in all of them.

The shifting nature of these arguments, and particularly the omission in the *Treatise* of some offered in earlier works, raises a question: had his opponents stopped using them, or was Olivi simply being selective? There is some evidence for the latter view.[26] Thus Olivi is a reliable witness to his opponents' arguments but is less trustworthy as an indication of how their attack altered in the course of debate.

Spiritual Dangers

The most basic objection to *usus pauper* as an essential part of the vow reverberates through the controversy from question nine to the *Treatise* and beyond it to the Council of Vienne. It is that such a situation would involve spiritual dangers. These dangers are developed in two different ways. Sometimes opponents emphasize the absoluteness of such a vow. It would bind Franciscans to use only what was necessary for immediate survival. Thus a friar would sin mortally if he ate good bread or chicken, drank white wine, or otherwise used something he could survive without.[27] References to chicken and white wine are more to the point than one might at first imagine. When out of their convents, friars found it impossible to control the menu. They had to eat what was placed before them if they were to eat at all. Francis himself had anticipated this situation in the rule, as we shall see. The apparent absoluteness of the vow was seen as dangerous even within convents, however. If a group accepted only what was necessary for the moment it would constantly be on the brink of famine. This situation would engender great anxiety, impeding spiritual progress. In question nine a series of objections reduce this notion to absurdity by arguing that limitation of use to what is necessary would condemn Franciscans to seeking new shelter and clothing as needed at that particular moment. The result would be constant wandering, destruction of discipline, curtailment of prayer, and perhaps indecent exposure.[28]

On other occasions emphasis falls not on the absoluteness of such a vow but on its indeterminacy.[29] There would be no way of judging the precise point at which it was violated, and thus the friar would live in constant anxiety. As the *Treatise* neatly puts it, a vow cannot properly be made in situations where reason cannot determine what is required. Both of these objections gather strength from the conviction—assumed throughout and explicitly argued in the *Treatise*—that any deviation from a vow involves mortal sin.[30] This view is presented as the unanimous opinion of Franciscan masters.

These are not minor objections. They lie at the heart of opposition to the notion of *usus pauper* as an essential part of the vow. Thus Olivi takes some care in refuting them. He counters the first by denying that *usus pauper* is identifiable as a state in which death is imminent unless relief comes immediately. The "extreme necessity" involved in *usus pauper* is substantially less dramatic. It is "a need manifestly existing for the present or the immediate future, of such a nature that one cannot remain in one's proper state without its fulfillment."[31]

Granting such a definition, there is nothing wrong with accepting supplies for an entire year when they cannot be obtained in any other way. One must distinguish between necessity in the present (*de presenti*) and for the present (*pro presenti*). Sometimes it is necessary to provide in the present for future needs, as when one sows in the spring anticipating a fall harvest. *Usus pauper* limits Franciscans to necessity in the present, which includes whatever must be done right now for the satisfaction of present or future needs. Thus it does not condemn them to concentrate on the present day, hour, or minute. This point is crucial, and Olivi returns to it on several occasions in dealing not only with present exigencies but with biblical precedents as well.[32]

The more Olivi elaborates on this notion, the more moderate his position seems. Present necessity, he says, should be judged discretely, neither too strictly nor too broadly. It is taken too strictly if nothing is included except what is needed for the present moment, too broadly if it includes everything required for the rest of our lives.[33] Between these extremes, the idea of excess varies with specific cases. Some things, like bread and wine, are needed in great quantity and can be conserved easily. They can also be given easily and are currently donated in large quantities, because they are normally possessed and used by all. Other things, like oil and legumes, are needed rarely and in small quantities but are possessed by few people and only in small quantities. Still other things, like vegetables, are needed frequently and in quantity, yet cannot be obtained without continually growing them.

Given these variables, the limits of necessity will vary with different items. In the normal course of events, stockpiling of wine in cellars and of wheat in barns seems more questionable to the observer than does storage of oil, unless the oil is very expensive or one has a great deal of it. Since legumes and oil are not commonly used in large and expensive amounts and cannot be obtained easily through gifts, there is nothing wrong with storing them for a few months, particularly since the staples, bread and wine, will still be lacking. Since vegetables are used frequently and cannot be obtained by gift in sufficient quantity for a large community, there is nothing amiss in planting a garden, at least when the specter of property does not rear its head.

Nor are these the only variables to be considered. The size of the group is a factor. What seems like *usus dives* in a group of two or three may pass for *usus pauper* in a large community.[34] Health is important, too. The sick may deserve treatment that would be unfitting for the healthy.[35] Then there is location. Necessity takes on different contours when one is traveling than when one is at home.[36] Durability is also significant. Food is used up at a ferocious rate, but garments and houses endure.

Again, while everything mentioned so far serves the body, some things like churches, ecclesiastical ornaments, and books have spiritual utility. In a moment of self-disclosure Olivi notes that books are of spiritual benefit and are needed in quantity if we are to investigate the many things to be known. Thus excess is harder to judge in this area than in others unless it is a question of multiple copies or ornamentation serving vanity rather than spiritual advancement.[37]

In view of the myriad possibilities of earthly existence, no rule is absolutely immutable in the final analysis. Every situation has its own particular requirements. Thus the Franciscan rule stipulates that particular injunctions are to be observed unless manifest necessity or utility dictates otherwise.[38] Even the prohibition against money is not exempt from this condition, for Christ and the disciples saw fit to carry a purse when traveling through Samaria, where they could expect to receive supplies only by buying them.[39]

If there is that much latitude at home, one should expect no less when the friar is dining at the tables of the great. Faced with chicken and white wine, he can proceed with confidence, knowing that a good meal will not damn anyone. He will not sin mortally simply by using something he could do without unless he takes so much of it or takes it so frequently that his behavior deviates from *usus pauper* enough to be called *usus dives*.[40]

Even "being able to do without something" is open to two interpretations. It can mean either that a person could survive without the item in question or that he could fulfill without it all the functions befitting his status and office. The second interpretation can in turn have two meanings: either the item is neither fitting nor useful to the person, or it is useful but its function can be fulfilled by using something else. If we accept the first interpretation, there are many things without which we can survive yet which do not violate *usus pauper*. If we accept the second interpretation and examine those things which are in no way useful to our state, use of such things is a minor or major sin depending on the nature and degree of use. If we are speaking of what is useful but for which something else can be substituted, use of it is no sin unless the other item is simultaneously employed.[41]

Certainly Olivi is no absolutist; yet as he goes about proving as much he seems to become increasingly vulnerable to the charge of indeterminacy. If scores of variables turn "present necessity" into such a complex notion, how can we determine the point at which *usus pauper* becomes *usus dives*? Olivi's answer is essentially that we cannot do so but need not worry about it. If *usus pauper* fell under the vow precisely, so that one sinned mortally whenever a determined limit was transgressed, it would be dangerous indeed. Instead, it falls under the vow indeterminately, so that a small violation involves venial sin. We are guilty of mortal sin only when the violation is so great that our conduct should be called *usus dives*, the opposite of *usus pauper*.

Usus pauper is not the only thing indeterminately contained in the vow. It is impossible to determine precisely the point at which relations with women become suspect; or the degree to which such relations must be avoided; or how much or how long one is required to resist carnal thoughts; or how often the words of a prelate can be disobeyed when they are anything less than a direct command; or at what point failure to obey such words implies contempt and becomes a mortal sin. In all such cases, nothing better than a probable judgment can be offered.[42] The precepts of the Franciscan rule are no different in this respect than those of the divine law. How does one judge the degree in which pride, envy, or vainglory must be present in order to become mortal sins? Only "a general and very confused opinion" can be formed on such matters. The best we can do is determine the limits of mortal sin with some degree of probability, then avoid any conduct which carries us close to those limits. That is exactly what should be done regarding *usus pauper*.[43]

In short, certain things like lack of property and sexual abstention fall under the vow precisely and thus any violation is a mortal sin. Other things like sobriety in food and speech fall under the vow indeterminately and thus a minor violation is a venial sin. Such is the case, Olivi explains, for two reasons. First, in some cases one simply cannot locate any clear-cut, unchangeable boundary beyond which one must not stray. Second, human nature is particularly prone to certain vices because of its own fallen nature and because the world is generous in providing temptation.

Evangelical vows must contain nothing dangerous yet must bind votaries to the summit of perfection. If all evangelical counsels fell under the vow precisely, the vow would fail in the first respect. If some counsels were omitted entirely, it would fail in the second. The only tenable solution is for some counsels to be included precisely, others indeterminately. The vow will then lead people to perfection forcefully in some areas and gently in others, according to the strength and grace given to each person.

Thus *usus pauper* can be defined as "that use which, all things considered, befits the evangelical poor and mendicant. And there can be diverse grades of it: befitting, more befitting, most befitting." One can observe *usus pauper* more or less strictly, more or less perfectly. The vow encourages friars to observe it perfectly, but failure to do so will not involve mortal sin unless, all circumstances considered, one's behavior should be called *usus dives* rather than *usus pauper*. A minor lapse implies nothing so drastic. *Usus pauper* can and normally does exist with an admixture of venial sin.[44]

Obviously Olivi disagrees with his opponents' assumption that any deviation from a precept involves mortal sin. He acknowledges that many modern theologians reserve the name *precept* for that which cannot be transgressed without mortal sin. Thus violating *usus pauper*, socializing with women, entertaining carnal thoughts, and ignoring the words of a prelate would involve traducing precepts of the rule only at that level beyond which violation would be a mortal sin. The same would be true for vices like pride, envy, and the like forbidden by precept through the divine law.

Olivi's opponents may adopt this view if they wish, but they must recognize that the theologians who hold it see venial sins as distortions inclining us to transgression of precepts. These theologians acknowledge many venial sins in connection with the divine precepts. Thus they should do the same regarding regular vows, which are divine precepts to those who have taken them. This position may not be fully commensurate with Olivi's, but neither is it commensurate with the notion that Franciscans can live luxuriously without sin.

In any case, whatever many modern theologians may think, the *sancti* think otherwise. For them, both venial and mortal sins are contrary to the precept. Olivi alludes to Augustine, then shifts to his own order, citing Alexander of Hales's *Summa*, William de la Mare's *Correctorium*, and two of his own works.[45] Thus it is hardly suprising that he sees this view as leading directly to his own position on *usus pauper*.[46]

The Vow

Olivi's opponents also argue from the wording of the vow and from the intention of those taking it. As question fifteen says, no one is obliged to anything through a vow unless he vows it explicitly, or intends so to oblige himself, or, upon hearing the vow, would understand himself to be so obliged through the common meaning of the words used. He who vows the Franciscan rule does not explicitly say, "I promise not to eat good bread, live in a beautiful home," and so on; nor does he intend to so oblige himself; nor do those who hear the rule commonly take it to demand any such thing.[47]

Olivi denies every part of this statement. By the same logic, he says, one could argue that a Franciscan does not vow to renounce common property, since that is not explicitly vowed either. Nor is there any point in vowing not to eat good bread. One does not pursue *usus pauper* by vowing not to do a series of specific things. *Usus pauper* is "that use which, all circumstances considered, is more consonant with the poverty and condition of Christ than with the condition of the rich," and within it there can be degrees of greater and lesser purity.[48]

Equally false are the accompanying assertions that one vowing the rule does not intend to oblige himself to *usus pauper* and that those hearing the vow do not understand it to include *usus pauper* according to the normal meaning of the words. In reality, there is scarcely a Christian anywhere who does not believe that the Franciscans are bound to limited use by their rule. Here again, Olivi appeals to the commonsense understanding of his order held by laymen.[49]

Usus Pauper *as an Essential Part of Poverty*

Question fifteen contains an objection the importance of which can easily be overlooked, because it is explicitly formulated only in that work: limited use is not an essential part of the highest poverty, nor is abundant use an essential part of wealth, for a rich man can use goods sparingly and a poor man can use them lavishly.[50] In his reply, suprisingly, Olivi concedes that such is the case. Only lack of property can be considered "poverty itself, or its radical part." Nevertheless, he balks at the idea that limited use and extravagent use are equally accidental to poverty. Such is true, he says, in the case of poverty unenforced by any vow, such as that of a bailiff who may consume his lord's goods without owning them. If one is speaking of evangelical poverty, however, "this is not only false but assumes what it ought to prove."[51]

Olivi drops the matter at this point, leaving the reader with a feeling that something more should have been said. If use is not an essential part of evangelical poverty, yet rich and poor use are not equally accidental to it, how might one describe the relationship between limited use and evangelical poverty? In effect, Olivi awards himself a serious handicap by granting one of his opponents' most vital presuppositions. The problem would return to haunt his supporters three decades later at the Council of Vienne.[52]

One might profitably link Olivi's attempt to field this objection with a series of passages in which he tries to link *usus pauper* with lack of property. In question nine he argues that, since virtues are directed to concrete virtuous acts and anyone bound by vow to a virtue is therefore bound to the corresponding acts, anyone vowing abdication of property must also be bound to restricted use.[53] Somewhat later in the same question he contends that restricted use is related to abdication of property rights as form to matter. Matter without form is confused, unstable, changeable, empty, vain, and unfruitful. Just so, those who vow evangelical poverty yet aspire to opulent use are unstable, flowing from desire to desire, exhausting themselves in vanity and vainglory, empty of virtuous acts, and lacking in the fruit of contemplation. On the other hand, as form requires matter in order to exist, so *usus pauper* presupposes abdication of property rights. Just as we come to know matter through form and deduce from the presence of form that matter is also present, so it is with *usus pauper* and the abdication of property rights.[54] Although neither of these passages explicitly identifies poverty with lack of property rights alone, both show a tendency to neutralize any such identification by arguing a strong connection between lack of ownership and *usus pauper*.

The Problem of Size

Olivi's opponents also attempt to argue that the size of the order or even of a single convent makes it impossible to vow *usus pauper*. The needs of different people vary, and what helps one hurts another. If all vowed a single standard of conduct, a great number of people would be impeded from enjoying the advantages of Franciscan life.[55]

Olivi replies to this objection in a number of ways. In question fifteen he refers his opponents to *Exiit qui seminat*, which was written to correct the notion that the Franciscan rule is dangerous and unobservable. He also observes that, if their argument were correct, it would apply to any monastic vow requiring silence, dietary restrictions, and the like. No one expects such things to be determined precisely and uniformly for all, but only "as right reason dictates, considering the special circumstances of person, task, time and place."[56]

His reply in the *Tractatus* is notably harsher. This view, Olivi says, contains a whole nest of heresies. It implies that strict maceration of the flesh is not generally expedient for those in religious orders, even though all saints and masters say the opposite. This is nothing less than a recrudescence of the heresy introduced by Vigilantius. Nor is it the first time modern writers have espoused this heresy, for Pecham and Bonaventure both battled against it.[57] As for their assertion that what is necessary for one is superfluous for another, "I wonder," Olivi asks himself, "if they really intend to say that there can be no common life unless food, drink and all other supplies are equal in quality and quantity for all, right down to the last iota." If so, their position is patently ridiculous.[58]

The Possibility of a Higher Vow

By the time Olivi wrote question fifteen, his opponents already had adjusted to his argument in question nine that, if *usus pauper* were not included in the Franciscan vow, it would be possible to imagine another vow that would include it and thus be higher than evangelical poverty. They now reply that there is nothing disturbing about the possibility of an individual doing just that. For example, someone could vow evangelical poverty and simultaneously vow not to eat meat. Such a vow cannot be recommended to a group, however.[59]

This idea inspires a lengthy and heated rebuttal. Olivi charges that it is heretical and contradicted by all the *sancti* and *doctores*. There can be no greater poverty, no higher perfection, than is found in the life of Christ and his disciples or, more recently, in the life and rule of Saint Francis. Having said so much, however, Olivi must explain what is wrong with his opponents' argument. It fails, he says, in at least three ways. First and least germane to the present problem, there is no reason why one person should be any more able to observe such a vow than a multitude would be. Here we are back to his opponents' consistent assertion that vows of *usus pauper* befit an individual but not a large group.

Second, evangelical vows should have a universal perfection extending to all times. A vow to abstain from meat cannot be perfect in this sense, because individual circumstances might make it dangerous. Nevertheless, insofar as such vows contain something of value, they are included in evangelical vows as the particular is contained in the universal, for evangelical perfection inclines one to do whatever is pleasing to God and to love whatever is entailed in perfection, even though it does not commit one to achieve all types of personal perfection, just as the universal is not totally explicated in particulars.

One might imagine Olivi's adversaries chortling at this reply. If abstention from meat could be dangerous on occasion, then so could the rejection of money, horseback riding, or more than two tunics, all of which are prohibited by the rule. In question nine Olivi has argued that such prohibitions involve no danger because they need not be observed if manifest necessity or utility dictates otherwise. Could Olivi's opponents not add a "necessity or utility" clause to their hypothetical vow and have a valid argument? The answer implicit in Olivi's response is that there is a deeper issue at stake. Evangelical poverty cannot be reduced to a finite number of things one vows to avoid. He who adopts evangelical perfection commits himself to the pursuit of a general goal. Lack of money, houses, and tunics can be viewed as nothing more than particular manifestations of that goal. A person cannot achieve all, but he does what he can.

Olivi's third objection to his opponents' hypothetical case is that abstaining from meat on these terms would directly pertain not to *usus pauper* and the virtue of poverty but to the virtue of temperance, although it is related to *usus pauper* insofar as it involves need and want. This seems a curious distinction on his part, since, when he wants to depict violations of evangelical poverty, he normally evokes the specter of *haute cuisine*. It also proved a dangerous distinction because it could easily be modified to support the opposite position.[60]

Appeal to Authority

One might expect both sides in the controversy to line up friendly witnesses. Olivi's opponents do so, but their appeal to the Bible and church fathers is surprisingly limited when compared with the barrage of citations laid down by Olivi himself. They mention Paul's collection for the church at Jerusalem, his acknowledgment that the Philippians subsidized him in Thessalonica, and his announcement that he can experience abundance and want, fullness and hunger in Christ. They also mention those passages which show Christ dining well (as at the house of Levi) or providing for the future (as when he and the disciples saved the remaining bread for later). The purse carried by Christ and his disciples is also duly noted, as are his words, "Eat and drink whatever is set before you."[61]

The latter words are particularly significant, since they are echoed in the rule. In the *Treatise* Olivi's opponents turn them in an odd direction. It is consistent with evangelical perfection for Franciscans to eat fancy meals in the homes of the rich and powerful, just as Christ did. Thus there is nothing wrong with eating them at home because, to avoid setting a bad example, Franciscans should behave more soberly outside their houses than within. Moreover, they inhabit their houses as pilgrims, just as they inhabit other people's, and the food they eat at home is no more theirs than if they ate it elsewhere.[62]

In dealing with such citations, Olivi can often walk comfortably in the footsteps of his predecessors, since the same citations had constituted a problem for those who defended the order in the secular-mendicant controversy. In any case, his response follows logically from what he has said about the flexibility built into the rule. His reaction to the words "Eat and drink whatever is set before you" does deserve some attention, if only because these words were to become a constant refrain among those who combatted *usus pauper* at Vienne. Olivi argues that Christ acted "out of condescension, like a kindly doctor." Francis, in like manner, was soothing brothers with tender consciences, who might otherwise have assumed that as guests they could accept only the same modest fare eaten at home. One can hardly deduce from his words, Olivi says, that "if a thousand varieties of wine and meat were set before them, they could gobble down all of them. Even the Epicureans wouldn't have said that!" It is one thing for the evangelical poor to take what is necessary for them from the many things offered by others, and quite another to seek delicious and superfluous items. Again, it is one thing to be served lavishly in someone else's house, another to serve oneself lavishly at home.[63]

Olivi's opponents also make limited use of Augustine's words, "Not use of things but desire for them is to be blamed, and a wise man can use the most precious food without sin."[64] They are raising an issue already discussed in Hugh of Digne's *Dispute* and destined to play a major role in the controversy, that of inner attitude versus external act.[65] Olivi remarks that if attitude alone were important, then luxurious possessions would not derogate from perfection, nor would fasting and other ascetic practices contribute to it, all of which is patently heretical. He handles Augustine with care, acknowledging that desire for things rather than use of them is to be blamed. Nevertheless, he says, abstaining from property rights and from abundant use contributes more to the extirpation of such desire than riches do, is in itself more arduous, and leads more to perfection of the virtues. As for the second part of Augustine's statement, that the wise man can eat expensive food without sin, Olivi remarks that it is not quite to the point, since eating precious food is not the same as *usus dives*. The former is sometimes necessary, but *usus dives* in the sense rejected by evangelical perfection is, like marriage, never necessary to those seeking perfection in the Christian era.[66] A Franciscan, dependent as he is upon others, may occasionally have to eat *coq au vin* or starve, since he can hardly expect the rich to keep a supply of gruel just for him; yet he does not have to eat too much *coq au vin* or eat it regularly when other dining arrangements are available.

Although this particular argument appears only in question fifteen, the *Treatise* contains a close relative of it. There Olivi quotes his adversaries as saying that habits fall under the precept but virtuous acts do not. "Wonderful," he says. "We can be holy lying in bed!" Then he runs through the Ten Commandments, showing that they deal more expressly with acts than with habits.[67]

As one might anticipate, Olivi's opponents make some appeal both to papal authority and to Franciscan tradition. Question fifteen contains a rather straightforward argument which attempts to parry Olivi's citations in question nine: the holy fathers of the Franciscan order spoke zealously against opulent use because it was their practice to avoid not only mortal but even venial sin, in fact everything that impedes perfection. Opulent use impedes perfection but is not a mortal sin. This tactic indirectly raises the central question of whether violation of a vow inevitably entails mortal sin; yet it does not meet that question head-on, and neither does Olivi until the *Treatise*. In question fifteen he simply remarks that his opponents contradict their own position by admitting that opulent use destroys perfection.

The Franciscan fathers are considered again in the *Treatise*, but in a new and surprising way. Olivi's adversaries announce that Bonaventure and others who wrote on this subject could not have believed *usus pauper* was included in the vow, because they themselves lived laxly.[68] We can almost see Olivi reeling back in horror.

> It was hitherto customary to cite pious men as examples of perfection; yet today, alas, they are cited as examples of laxity by these people, thus at one stroke wounding the men by their accusations, mutilating themselves by the example they draw from it, and infusing poisoned doctrine into others. I say, therefore, what I know of the aforesaid father. He was of the best and most pious inner disposition, and in his words he always endorsed whatever is consistent with perfect purity, as is clear from what has been said above; yet he had a frail body and was perhaps a bit self-indulgent in this respect, as I often heard him humbly confess. For he was not greater than the apostle, who said, "We all offend in many things." Nevertheless, he so grieved at the widespread laxity of this age that in Paris, in full chapter with me present, he said there was no time since he became minister general when he would not have consented to be ground to dust if it would help the order to reach the purity of Saint Francis and his companions, which Francis indeed intended his order to attain. Thus the holy man was largely if not entirely innocent of these charges, for he was not among the number of those defending relaxations and assailing the purity of the rule, nor among the number of those who seem to enjoy wallowing in the aforesaid impurities. On the contrary, if he shared any of them he did so with sorrow and lamentation. Such defects, I believe, are not to be considered mortal sins unless, all circumstances considered, they are very great.[69]

This cameo portrait of Bonaventure is particularly intriguing in view of what some Italian spirituals would later say about him.[70] Angelo Clareno's portrayal of Bonaventure as an exponent of laxity and as John of Parma's would-be destroyer might be considered reverse hagiography. In contrast, Olivi sees neither a saint nor a devil but a man, human like the rest of us but on the right side in the great debate. Olivi neither asks nor expects any more of him.

Olivi's opponents evoke papal authority in a similar way. It is commonly recognized that Franciscans today eat and drink well, often dress well, and live in big, beautiful houses; yet the pope is known to have approved and confirmed their state. Such behavior must be compatible with the vow, or else the pope would have ratified mortal sin.[71] Olivi's reply is prefaced with a brief personal credo: "It is to be held, not only that the Franciscan state is good, but that it will never fail from now until the final judgment. What is more, I hold without a trace of doubt that it will be totally purged of the afflictions brought on by some of its own members."[72]

On that note of hope he turns to the question of what Nicholas III thought he was approving. He intended to approve the Franciscan rule and those who strive to observe it purely, not the many corrupt practices presently found in the order. Olivi cites, among other things, Bonagratia of San Giovanni in Persiceto's statement that Nicholas, speaking to a group of ministers, told them the order would be "shaken to the hairs of our head" unless friars observed the rule more carefully.[73]

Reference to such enormities naturally raises the question of whether a number of Franciscans are living in mortal sin. Olivi's answer is carefully qualified. The gravity of the offense, he says, depends on three considerations. First, there is the individual's attitude. Does he abhor or welcome the corruption? Second, there is a certain ratio between the individual's act and his specific situation as determined by personal and environmental factors. Some excesses are difficult for a particular person to avoid because of mental or physical weakness; or because he lives in a community where such excesses are hallowed by an old, established custom; or because his community lacks experienced spiritual directors. Under such conditions, what might otherwise be easy becomes difficult. Again, the individual's state of spiritual development must be considered. The same behavior might rank as minor imperfection in a neophyte, serious deviation in a veteran, and unthinkable self-indulgence in one of the early anchorites. The size of the community also plays a role. What might constitute *usus dives* among a few people could rank as *usus pauper* in a large group. Third, one must consider the importance of scandal or good example to others. Fourth, there is perhaps "some hidden condescension and tolerance on God's part up to a time predetermined by Him." The last two are simply mentioned without elaboration, but the fourth is clearly a reference to Olivi's apocalyptic view of history.

"By examining all these factors carefully and combining or comparing them in various ways," Olivi says, "one can attain some insight into how excusable present behavior is in some cases, how inexcusable in others." How much insight one can expect is, of course, another question. Olivi must be aware that here, as elsewhere, his carefully nuanced presentation has shown the impossibility of weighing guilt as accurately as apples.

The Importance of Usus Pauper

What has been said so far does not include every argument placed by Olivi in the mouths of his adversaries, but it comes close to doing so. Clearly his opponents did not consider *usus pauper* to be an essential part of the vow. What *did* they think of it, then? In the *Treatise* Olivi offers an intriguing comment. Because their case is weak, he says, they twist words and mislead the simple through deceitful demeanor rather than by strong and subtle arguments.

> For all their arguments conclude that in no sense does *usus pauper* fall under the vow or precept of the rule. Lest, however, what they seem to be saying about use of possessions should ring horribly in the ears of the brethren, they add that, even if use of possessions is not directly against the vow or precept of the rule, it is nevertheless against its intention (*contra mentem eius*). They say this, however, to twist their words and cover themselves with a cloak of deception, for they go on to remark that, according to Brother John Pecham in his book, we are held to this—and to some other things in which the word "precept" or something similar is absent—only by approved custom in situations where, by reason of the scandal involved, different conduct could lead to mortal sin. Thus they finally add, fraudulently as it were, "I nevertheless believe it to be against the intention of the rule," etc. Moreover, lest they seem to say that we can live as luxuriously and splendidly as kings, they insist that such regal consumption, though not directly against the precept of the rule, is nonetheless against its intention. All other use beyond regal use is allowed to us, however ostentatious and opulent it might be. Moreover, lest they be taxed with contempt for *usus pauper* or with support for laxity, they sometimes say that, even though *usus pauper* does not fall within the vow, it is nevertheless so perfect, useful and, as it were, necessary for the avoidance of vice that the profession of poverty has little or no value without it. In this way, with astonishing duplicity, they simultaneously bless and curse the aforesaid behavior.[74]

Olivi objects that it is fraudulent to characterize excessive use as contrary to the intention of the rule but not contrary to the vow. In reality, he says, his adversaries' arguments point to a different conclusion, namely that excessive use could not be contradictory to the rule in any sense. Whether included in the vow or only in the intention of the rule, *usus pauper* would still be indeterminate and thus dangerous by their standards. Olivi's response is less satisfying than it might appear, partly because it ignores what one would take to be a major preoccupation of his critics, the desire to show that *usus pauper* is enjoined, but not in such a way that its violation would entail mortal sin. According to their understanding, violation of a vow inevitably entails mortal sin whereas violation of an intention of the rule, whatever that may mean (a question justifiably raised by Olivi),[75] does not. Therefore the two are not dangerous in the same way.

Olivi's discussion is also befogged by the fact that his opponents seem to twist in two directions calling for different responses. He presents them as praising *usus pauper* and terming it necessary (though not a part of the vow); yet he also portrays them as saying that only regal use is against the intention of the rule. Given their belief that violation of a vow entails mortal sin, one can appreciate why they might have taken the former position, and we will see later that current circumstances may have encouraged them to move in that direction. In contrast, the second position seems arbitrary and inexplicable. If we assume that Olivi is neither putting words in his opponents' mouths nor distorting theirs beyond recognition, it is tempting to infer that his adversaries were themselves divided into different camps. They agreed that *usus pauper* was not part of the vow but differed on the extent to which it was required anyway.

Notes

1. *Tractatus*, 10rb–va.
2. Ibid., 10va–11vb; Q. 9, 84rb–vb.
3. *Tractatus*, 10va–vb. See Pecham, *Tractatus pauperis*, c. 10. Chapters 1–6 are published in *Tractatus pauperis* (Paris, 1925); cc. 7–9 in *SF* 29 (1932): 47–62, 164–93; cc. 10 and 16 in *Tractatus tres de paupertate* (Aberdeen, 1910), 21–87; cc. 11–14 in *CF* 14 (1944): 84–120; and c. 15 in *Fratris Riccardi de Mediavilla quaestio disputata* (Quaracchi, 1925), 79–88. I will cite only by chapter numbers.
4. See *Tractatus*, 25va (quoted in note 74 below) and 29va, citing *Tractatus pauperis*, c. 9.
5. But see Chapter 2, note 29.
6. *Apologia pauperum*, in *Opera*, 8:276.
7. Ibid., 322f.
8. The constitutions of Narbonne, in dictating the form of the vow, describe it as the *professio*. See Bihl, "Statuta generalia," 40.
9. *Epistola* I, in *Opera*, 8:469.
10. It was a subtle one. The community offered just such an exegesis at the time of the Council of Vienne, although it was not directed toward this passage in particular. Richard of Conington and Pierre Auriole both argue, though in different ways, that the Franciscan does not vow *usus pauper*

and yet *usus pauper* is somehow required by the vow. Richard's work is published by Albanus Heysse, "Fr. Richardi de Conington, O.F.M., tractatus de paupertate fratrum minorum," *AFH* 23 (1930): 57–105, 340–60. Aureole's work is published by Ephrem Longpré, "Le quolibet de Nicolas de Lyre, O.F.M.," *AFH* 23 (1930): 42–56, where Pierre's quodlibet is published under Nicholas's name. For the proper attribution see Franz Pelster, "Nikolaus von Lyra und seine Quaestio de usu paupere," *AFH* 46 (1953): 213. Other polemical writings reflecting the conventual position make a similar point. See, for example, Anicetus Chiappini, "Communitas responsio 'Religiosi viri' ad rotulum fr. Ubertini de Casale," in *AFH* 7 (1914): 671.

11. *Epistola* II, 470f.
12. Printed in Wadding, *Annales*, 5:75.
13. *Tractatus*, 15ra–rb.
14. Q. 9, 84rb. See *BF*, 1:69.
15. Q. 15, 96vb–97ra.
16. *Declaratio communitatis* in Albanus Heysse, "Ubertini de Casali opusculum 'Super tribus sceleribus,' " *AFH* 10 (1917): 118.
17. Q. 15, 96vb–97ra.
18. See *Regula*, c. 1.
19. Q. 9, 83ra–va; *Tractatus*, 20va–22vb.
20. Q. 9, 83va–84ra; *Tractatus*, 22vb–24rb.
21. *Tractatus*, 23rb: "Cum igitur absolute mandet regulam promitti, oportet quod in hanc promissione intelligantur omnia illa capitula ex quibus sic regula specialiter conflatur, quod merito potest censeri una pars regule detruncata esse in ablatione unius eorum."
22. See the discussion of Olivi's apocalyptic thought in Chapter 6.
23. *Tractatus*, 24vb: "Ex predicto autem errore quidam fatui instinctu dyabolico incitati statum istum deserendo transvolaverunt ad vitam stultorum heremiticam, credentes se posse perfectiorem regulam instituere et servare."
24. Q. 9, 80vb, 84vb. Jean Batany, "L'Image des Franciscains dans les 'revues d'états' du XIIIe au XVIe siècle," in *Mouvements franciscains et société francaise, XIIe–XXe siècles* (Paris, 1984), 62, argues that laymen did not see Franciscan poverty as qualitatively different from traditional monastic austerity. On these terms, poverty and luxury would be mutually exclusive.
25. Opposing arguments and Olivi's responses are found in q. 9, 76rb–79rb and 85va–88va; q. 15, 95va–96va and 98ra–100vb; *Mtt.*, 81ra–va; *Tractatus*, 24vb–31rb.
26. For example, the idea that limited use is not an essential part of the highest poverty does not appear within Olivi's presentation of opposing arguments in the *Tractatus*; nor does the argument from Christ's (and Francis's) words, "Eat whatever is placed before you;" nor does Augustine's suggestion that desire rather than use of things is to be blamed; nor does the argument that he who vows something to attain an end does not necessarily vow the end itself; yet later in the *Tractatus* Olivi credits his opponents with advancing the third and fourth of these arguments in slightly different

form, and the first three were destined to become part of the weaponry deployed by the community three decades later at the Council of Vienne.

27. Q. 9, 76rb–va; *Tractatus*, 24vb.

28. Q. 9, 76va–vb, where another argument presents the positive result of the opposite extreme: having sufficient goods for one's entire life or at least a long period would release one from temporal distractions and free one for the contemplative life. Q. 9, 76va, also notes that doling out wheat and wine by the day would be hard on donors, who might prefer to make yearly contributions.

29. Q. 15, 95vb; *Tractatus*, 24vb.

30. *Tractatus*, 24vb.

31. Q. 9, 85va: "Extrema autem necessitas prout sub voto pauperis usus cadit dicit indigentiam iam manifeste existentem aut manifeste de proximo imminentem, et talem quod debitus status corporis seu persone deo servientis nisi sibi succurratur stare non potest."

32. For example, Q. 9, 86ra–rb, 87ra, 88ra. Olivi is speaking of the friar's needs, not the donor's. The demands of evangelical poverty, he says, should always weigh more heavily than a bit of inconvenience to the giver.

33. Q. 9, 87ra: "Presens necessitas discrete est intelligenda, quia non nimis stricte nec nimis large. Nimis enim stricte sumeretur si nihil aliud de presenti reputetur esse necessarium nisi illud quo necessario indigeo pro usu presentis momenti, nimis autem large si totum illud quo ad totam vitam nostram posset esse necessarium pro presenti necessitate accipiatur."

34. Q. 9, 88rb.

35. Q. 9, 86rb.

36. Q. 9, 87vb.

37. Q. 9, 88ra–va.

38. Q. 9, 85ra. Olivi is expanding the rule here, moving it closer to the language of thirteenth-century interpretations. *Regula*, cc. 2–3, speaks only of necessity.

39. See Q. 9, 89ra, which generalizes this case to apply to any situation in which one is moving through hostile territory; 86rb, which justifies Paul's collection on similar grounds; and 87vb, which notes the different demands made by life on the road. The problem of Christ's purse is a recurring theme in polemical works by Bonaventure and Pecham.

40. *Tractatus*, 26rb.

41. Ibid., 26rb. Again, note Olivi's willingness to credit not only necessity but utility as well.

42. Ibid., 25vb: "Si simpliciter et universaliter volunt astruere quod nihil cadat sub voto vel precepto de quo non est totaliter determinatum usque ad quem gradum teneamur illud servare et usque ad quem non, primo habent apertas instantias in aliis regule votis. Quero enim si semper ad plenum est eis determinatum quando consortium vel colloquium mulierum est suspectum et usque ad quem gradum tenentur illud vitare, aut usque ad quantum temporis vel augmenti illecebris cogitationum et affectionum carnalium tenentur necessario resistere, aut usque ad quantam frequentiam possunt transgredi simplex verbum prelati absque mortali, aut usque ad quantum

negligentia obediendi simplici verbo eius includit in se contemptum mortalem et usque ad quantum non. Et credo quod cogentur dicere se non posse hoc ad plenum scire nisi solum per modum iudicicii probabilis."

43. Ibid., 25vb. "Habent apertas instantias in preceptis divine legis. Quero enim an sciant usque ad quem punctum vel terminum sit eis mortalis affectus superbie vel invidie vel vanaglorie vel accidie vel edacitatis vel ire et usque ad quem non. Et quidem cogitentur dicere quod non sciunt hoc nisi solum sub determinatione generali et nobis valde confusa."

44. Q. 9, 85vb: "Unde non omnis deviacio a paupere usu in professoribus suis mortale inducit, sed quando est talis aut tanta quod pensatis hinc circumstanciis pocius debet censeri dives usus quam pauper. . . . Ex hoc autem quod pauper usus sub voto indeterminate cadit contingit quod diversi gradus perfectionum esse possunt in eodem statu paupertatis altissime secundum quod pauper usus perfeccius vel imperfeccius striccius vel lacius observatur." See also *Tractatus*, 26vb: "Ex hiis autem patet quid hic vocatur pauper usus, scilicet ille usus qui omnibus hinc inde pensatis decet evangelicum pauperem et mendicum. Et in hoc possunt esse diversi gradus, scilicet decens, decentior, decentissimus. Et primus scilicet decens potest esse decens cum venialibus indecentiis aut sine omni indecentia etiam veniali, quamvis in vita ista vix hoc inveniri possit nisi forte in eo qui est decentissimus in summo." See *Mtt.*, 81rb, which speaks of sins as *venialia*, *mortalia*, and *mortaliora*.

In q. 9, 85va, Olivi distinguishes natural anxiety ruled by reason and virtue from anxiety exceeding such bounds. If those who practice restricted use must face anxiety, it will be of the former type, and they will gain merit by mastering it.

45. Alexander Halensis, *Summa theologica* (Venice, 1575), lib. 3, q. 37, 150r; William de la Mare, in *Le Correctorium Corruptorii "Quare"* (Le Saulchoir, 1927), 302–8, 405–7; Olivi, *Quaestiones in secundum librum sententiarum*, q. 118 (pp. 380f.); Olivi, "Fr. P. J. Olivi Quaestio de voto regulam aliquam profitentis," *Antonianum* 16 (1941): 147f.

46. *Tractatus*, 26va–vb.

47. Q. 15, obj. 3, 95vb: "Nullus per votum ad aliquid obligatur nisi obligans exprimat illud vel ad hoc se obligare intendat, vel audiens obligari ipsum iudicet vel intelligant per talia verba secundum communem usum et sensum verborum. Sed cum quis vovet paupertatem evangelicam et non exprimit quod ipse se obliget ad talem usum pauperem necque enim dicit promicto deo quod non commedam bonum panem, vel quod non habitabo pulchram domum et consimilia, et si diceret stulte diceret, non etiam ad hoc se obligare intendit, nec audientes verba voti sui accipiunt communiter illa secundum talem intellectum." In *Tractatus*, 25ra, these points are divided among objections 7, 8, and 9. There it is said that Franciscans are bound by vow only to what they explicitly vow, and no one says, "I vow *usus pauper*." Again, they are bound by precept of the rule only to what is explicitly prescribed or forbidden there (*preceptorie vel inhibitorie sunt expressa*), and nowhere does the rule use words like *precipio* or *teneantur* in connection with matters of restricted use, except in the case of money.

48. Q. 15, 98vb: "Usus enim pauper censendum est omnis ille usus qui omnibus circumstantiis pensatis potius consonat paupertati Christi et statui eius quam statui divitiarum, in quo plures possunt esse gradus puritatis maioris et minoris."

49. Q. 15, 98vb–99ra. In the *Tractatus* his reply to the first assertion follows q. 15. His reply to the assertion about intention is refreshingly *ad hominem*: "Si isti ut dicunt hoc non intenderunt certus sum quod nunquam veri fratres minores fuerunt. Si autem hoc intenderunt et modo hoc negant, veri apostate censendi sunt." Their denial is contradicted by the common opinion not only of the order but of the whole world (*Tractatus*, 28va).

50. Q. 15, 95va: "Moderantia vel tenuitas usus non cadit sub voto professionis eorum. Dicunt enim quod duplex est usus. Unus est uti re cum dominio vel absque dominio. Usus autem rei absque dominio est essentialis paupertati altissime, sicut uti rebus ut propriis est essentiale diviti. Alius usus est uti rebus habundanter vel tenuiter, seu uti pluribus vel paucis, et iste secundum eos est accidentalis paupertati altissime, sicut usus habundans est accidentalis divitibus. Unde multi divites parce utuntur rebus suis propter cupiditatem vel aliam causam. Pauper vero manens pauper sepe utitur copiose, ut patet in baiulo alicuius magni domini qui tamen nichil habet proprium."

51. Q. 15, 98rb.

52. For example, Heysse, "Fr. Richardi de Conington," 70–72; Longpré, "Le Quolibet," 52–54.

53. Q. 9, 83vb: "Cum abrenunciacio iuris principaliter inventa esse videatur propter pauperem usum, et sine eo vix bene teneri possit, cum etiam omnium virtutum intencio finaliter dirigatur ad usum virtuosum et actum, ita quod qui voto vel precepto ad virtutem aliquam astringitur eo ipso sit astrictus ad eius usum et actum, nullo modo est credibile aliquam regulam rationabiliter et divinitus institutam abdicacionem iuris vovere sine professione pauperis usus."

54. Q. 9, 84vb: "Sicut forma se habet ad materiam sic usus pauper se habet ad abdicacionem omnis iuris. Unde sicut materia sine forma est informis et confusa, instabilis et fluxibilis, et vacua seu vana et infructuosa, sic abdicacio omnis iuris sine paupere usu se habet. Cuius rei manifestum signum est quod omnis homo deridet et contempnit professores eius ex quo ad opulencias ardenter et inhianter suspirant tanquam certissime sencientes professionem talem esse deformem et confusam. Altera pars eiusdem signi est quod professores eius opulentari querentes nichil habent stabilitatis, sed ita fluunt per questus et desideria et ita evanescunt per occiositates et inanes glorias et verborum vanitates et sic inveniuntur vacui altis virtutum exerciciis, et sine fructu et gustu contemplationis celestis, sicut et terra arida sine aqua sicut autem forma ad sui existentiam preexigit materiam tanquam sue existencie fundamentum sic professio pauperis usus preexigit abdicacionem omnis iuris tanquam sue grandissime existencie et ambitus capacissimam materiam et altissimum fundamentum et ideo quia per formam devenimus in cognicionem materie, et posita forma necessario intelligitur materiam positam esse, tam Christus in evangeliis

quam sancti in dictis suis principalius intencionem verbi ferunt ad expressionem pauperis usus."

55. Q. 15, 95va–vb; *Tractatus*, 25rb.

56. Q. 15, 98rb–98va, 99ra.

57. Olivi cites Pecham, *Tractatus pauperis*, c. 12, and Bonaventure, *Apologia*, c. 6, thus identifying his antagonists with the opposing side in the secular-mendicant controversy. Neither Bonaventure nor Pecham explicitly refers to Vigilantius in the chapters mentioned by Olivi, but Pecham does so in c. 11.

58. *Tractatus*, 28vb: "Miror si intendunt quod nisi omnes in quantitate et qualitate cibi et potus et aliorum victualium et utibilium sint penitus usque ad unum iota equales non possit in eis vita esse concors et communis. Quis tantum ridiculum patienter audiat quod infirmi et sani, senes et iuvenes, scolastici et laboratores, clerici et sanguinei, magni et parvi, in omnibus hiis equari debeant."

59. Q. 15, 100ra–rb; In *Tractatus*, 24vb, this view is attributed to Bonaventure.

60. In his question on poverty (see note 10), Pierre Aureole argues that restricted use pertains to the virtue of temperance rather than poverty.

61. Q. 9, 76vb–77va; *Mtt.*, 81ra–rb; *Regula*, ch. 3.

62. *Tractatus*, 25rb–va.

63. *Mtt.*, 81vb. *Tractatus*, 29ra–rb, makes roughly the same point. For community use of "Eat what is placed before you" see *Declaratio communitatis* in Heysse, "Ubertini," 118, 121.

64. Q. 15, 96ra.

65. For use of Augustine at Vienne see *Infrascripta dant*, in *Archiv*, 3:155.

66. There is a precedent in Hugh's *Disputatio*, which uses the phrase *usus dives* as well.

67. *Tractatus*, 31va–vb.

68. Ibid., 25ra.

69. Ibid., 28ra–rb: "Hactenus solebant omnes adducere viros sollempnes in exemplum perfectionis. Sed heu domine deus hodie ab istis inducuntur in exemplum laxationis uno ictu illos vituperando confodientes et ex deducto exemplo se ipsos excecantes et aliis doctrinam venenatam infundentes. Dico igitur quod de predicto patre sentio. Fuit enim interius optimi et piissimi affectus, et in doctrine verbo semper predicans ea que sunt perfecte puritatis, sicut ex supradictis ab eo satis liquere potest. Fragilis tamen fuit secundum corpus et forte in hoc aliquid humanum sapiens quod et ipse humiliter sicut ego ipse ab eo sepius audivi confitebatur. Nec enim maior fuit apostolo dicente in multis offendimus omnes. Nichilominus tamen in tantum dolebat de communibus laxationibus huius temporis quod parisius in pleno capitulo me astante dixit quod ex quo fuit generalis nunquam fuit quin vellet esse pulverizatus ut ordo ad puritatem beati Francisci et sotiorum eius et ad illud quod ipse de ordine suo intendebat perveniret. Ex hiis igitur vir sanctus excusari potuit a tanto et si non a toto. Non enim fuit de numero defendentium laxationes et impugnantium regule puritatem, aut de numero iniacentium predictis impuritatibus qui eas sequi videntur quasi toto corde."

70. See Chapter 1. Did the attempt by later, laxer brethren to claim Bonaventure contribute to Angelo's view of him?

71. *Tractatus,* 25ra. Ibid., 25rb, cites *Exiit* and other papal declarations in support of the assertions that Franciscans are bound by precept of the rule only to what the rule explicitly prescribes or forbids, and are bound by vow only to that to which they intended to bind themselves when vowing.

72. Ibid., 27ra: "Non solum est tenendum statum minorum esse bonum, sed quod nunquam deficiet usque ad finale iudicium, et quod plus est absque omni scrupulo dubietatis teneo quod adhuc totaliter purgabitur a miseriis quas per aliquos de suis contraxit."

73. Ibid., 27va. Bonagratia's letter is published in Wadding, *Annales,* 5:75.

74. Ibid., 25va: "Fere enim in omnibus rationibus quibus suum errorem astruunt concludunt pauperem usum nullo modo cadere sub regule voto vel precepto. Ne autem videantur quo ad usum possessionum in auribus fratrum rem horrendam dicere, subdunt quod usus possessionum et si non sit directe contra regule votum vel preceptum est tamen contra mentem eius. Hec ipsum tamen valde intorte et cum pallio multe duplicitatis dicunt. Premittunt enim quod secundum fratrem Iohannem de Picciano in libro suo nos non tenemur ad istud nec ad aliqua in quibus non ponitur verbum precipiendi vel aliquid simile nisi solum ex consuetudine approbata que ratione scandali posset generare peccatum mortale et sic tandem quasi in dolo subdunt ego tamen credo quod sit contra mentem regule etc. Insuper ne videantur dicere quod secundum hoc possemus vivere ita laute et splendide sicut reges dicunt quod usus regum et si non sit directe contra votum nostre professionis vel contra precepta regule est tamen contra mentem eius. Sed omnis usus alius citra usum regalem quantumque pomposus et opulentus est nobis licitus. Insuper ne de contemptu pauperis usus aut de doctrina laxationis possint nominari, dicunt aliquando quod quamvis pauper usus non cadat in voto est tamen quid valde perfectum et valde utile et quasi necessarium ad vitia evitanda, intantum quod professio paupertatis modicum aut nihil habet utilitatis sine ipso et per hunc modum cum miris dolis simul predicto usui benedicunt et maledicunt." See Pecham, *Tractatus pauperis,* c. 9.

75. *Tractatus,* 30ra: "Item quero ab istis, quando dicunt quod est contra mentem regule, quid intendunt significare per contra mentem. Numquid per hoc volunt solum dicere quod est contra finalem intentionem eius?"

CHAPTER 4

The Censure of 1283

Unfortunately for Olivi, what began as an academic dispute was rapidly turning into something more. His views on poverty had led to a quarrel with another lector and his followers. Each contestant had tried to strengthen his case by questioning other aspects of his opponent's teaching, and Olivi's adversaries apparently sent a list of nineteen suspect opinions to the minister general, Bonagratia of San Giovanni in Persiceto, who forwarded it to Olivi's provincial minister. The latter demanded clarification from Olivi and, when he complied, sent his response to Bonagratia. The precise chronology of this battle continues to elude us, but by Easter 1283 Olivi's writings had been confiscated and he was awaiting judgment by the minister general.

Censure and Response

Bonagratia, faced with a portfolio of suspect Olivian opinions, called for an investigation. The *Chronicle of the Twenty-four Generals* states that he dealt with the matter by collecting all the Olivian views which "seemed to ring poorly" and submitting them to a commission of Parisian scholars consisting of three bachelors and four masters of theology. This suggests that he gave them excerpts, but, as we have seen, other evidence seems to indicate that Bonagratia gave the commission entire works from which they themselves excerpted offending passages. The four masters were Droco (provincial minister of France), John of Wales, Simon of Lens, and Arlotto of Prato. The three bachelors were Richard of Middleton, John of Murrovalle, and Giles of Bensa (or Baise).[1]

The *Chronicle of the Twenty-four Generals* explains what happened next.

> After mature deliberation, these men agreed to reprove some of the things as dangerous and poorly stated (*male sonantia*). They

sent this reproof to all the brothers in a letter under their seals
called the *Letter of the Seven Seals*. With this letter the aforementioned minister general went to Avignon in order to suppress
there those who ascribed to the reproved articles. And there,
since he was gravely ill, he instructed his companion Brother Gerard of Prato that, according to the decision made at Paris in the
council of the aforesaid masters and bachelors, he should collect
and interdict the books of the aforementioned Peter John and no
one should dare to say or hold anything contrary to the contents
of the *Letter of the Seven Seals*.

Olivi, in a letter to the Paris commission written in 1285, says that
passages from his writings were excerpted by the commission and collected in a *rotulus* with various judgments written in the margin. "Some
were judged false, some heretical, some doubtful in the context of the
faith, some dangerous to our order, some ignorant, some presumptuously
stated, and some crucified as it were or marked with the sign of the
cross." To this *rotulus* they added another document, the *Letter of the
Seven Seals*, which presented a series of positive assertions contradicting
Olivi's errors. Both documents were sent to every house in Olivi's province, where they were to be read before all the brothers. Olivi's writings
were to be confiscated from anyone possessing them.[2]

The *rotulus* has disappeared, but Olivi's 1285 *apologia* and three
manuscripts apparently used by the commission provide insight into its
form and content. Joseph Koch concludes from this evidence that it contained at least fifty articles consisting of excerpts from Olivi's writings,
each with a specific judgment such as "heretical," "dangerous," "presumptuous" or "false."[3] The second document, the *Letter of the Seven
Seals*, is extant.[4] It consists of twenty-two articles, each a brief positive
statement of the orthodox view concerning some subject on which Olivi
presumably went awry.

In the fall of 1283, Olivi was summoned to Avignon. There he assented
to the *Letter of the Seven Seals* before a special council.[5] His response
has survived, and it shows that he ascribed to the *Letter* only with reservations.[6] In his 1285 *apologia* to the commission Olivi explains his
dilemma. The *Letter* was composed of positive statements written in
opposition to Olivi's views as the commission understood them. Refusal
to accept the document would imply rejection of the articles of faith contained in the positive statements; yet endorsement of it would suggest
that Olivi accepted the commission's interpretation of (and judgment
upon) his own writings. Olivi concluded that a more nuanced approach
was in order. He elected to "confess some articles simply and absolutely

and others under distinction" but to offer no defense whatsoever concerning purely philosophical matters.[7]

Thus Olivi managed to retain his dignity, but he saved little else. His works were confiscated and the *Letter of the Seven Seals* disseminated throughout his province. His teaching career lay in ruins. Olivi felt he had been treated shabbily and wanted to tell the commission as much. He applied to the provincial minister for permission to go and confront them in Paris, but permission was denied. He would have liked to continue the debate by letter but found it hard to speak forcefully in his own defense when he was denied access not only to his own writings but to the commission's *rotulus* as well.[8]

Then, sometime between January and May 1285, Olivi gained access to the documents necessary for a respectable defense.[9] He was now able to send the commission members an *apologia* in which he elaborated his own views, noted the ambiguity of their censures, and asked them to explain themselves. There is no record of their having done so.

Olivi's *apologia* is an important source for our knowledge of the 1283 condemnation because it replicates parts of the *rotulus* in which the commission cited passages from Olivi's works and passed judgment upon them. Thus the *apologia*, in quoting the *rotulus*, indicates which works the commission examined and what it thought of them.

Usus Pauper and the Vow

Both the *Letter of the Seven Seals* and the *rotulus* show concern about Olivi's thoughts on *usus pauper*. The former announces that "*usus pauper*, insofar as it includes extreme necessity (meaning manifestly existing or imminent need of such a sort that the proper state of one's body or person cannot be maintained without its satisfaction) is in no way included in the vow of evangelical poverty, and to say the contrary is erroneous."[10]

In his 1283 reply to the *Letter of the Seven Seals* Olivi says, "I accept this view if *extreme necessity* is taken to mean extreme deprivation (*penuria*), as the masters seem to take it. I do not believe I have said the opposite, and if I did so then I recant. Nevertheless, taking *extreme* for the mean of virtue, not as an indivisible point (*pro medio virtutis non in puncto indivisibili*), but with the required latitude and in a way befitting status and offices, I have said that it is included in the vow of evangelical poverty."[11]

Olivi's distinction is consistent with his earlier pronouncements on the subject, and what he means to say is clarified by these pronouncements.

It is less clear what the commission means to say. Is it simply criticizing a specific statement, or is it denying that *usus pauper* as it includes extreme necessity (in the Olivian sense) is part of the vow? If the latter, would it consider *usus pauper* to be part of the vow in some other sense? One can appreciate why Olivi approached the *Letter of the Seven Seals* cautiously.

In the *apologia*, Olivi says that the commission quoted the following passages from question nine in the *rotulus*:

> (1) It is so solidly and clearly true that *usus pauper* is substantially included in the Franciscan vow that this point follows unquestionably from all things said in the preceding question in order to show that poverty is one of the principal councils of evangelical perfection. In fact, *usus pauper* follows more directly than renunciation of common possessions or jurisdiction. (2) It is not only false but heretical to say that some poverty is more perfect than evangelical poverty; yet a poverty which included the vow of *usus pauper* would be more perfect than one which did not. Therefore, etc. (3) Since *usus pauper* falls under the vow indeterminately, not every deviation from it involves mortal sin, but only such a deviation as, all things considered, should be regarded as rich rather than poor use. (4) Extreme necessity, taken strictly so that death is immediately imminent unless help is given, does not necessarily fall under the profession of *usus pauper*. Extreme necessity as it falls under the vow means manifestly existing or imminent need of such a sort that the proper state of one's body or person cannot be maintained without its satisfaction, although even necessity of this sort falls under the vow only indeterminately.[12]

The fourth excerpt is obviously the one criticized in the *Letter of the Seven Seals*; but here it seems likely that the commission does interpret it in the Olivian sense, since the four statements, taken together, roughly summarize Olivi's position. The members of the commission did understand Olivi. What, then, did they think of him? In the margin, Olivi observes, the commission has written "commonly false and dangerous to our state." The word *commonly* would seem to indicate that the commission agreed on this verdict.

Joseph Koch, who considers the 1283 censure an important step in the development of techniques for dealing with theological error, has called the *rotulus* "a first-rate scientific job."[13] It is hard to agree with this judgment if one happens to believe that a decent public censure should at least tell people what is wrong with the view in question. This one is not even clear as to what is being censured.

Olivi himself is confused. In the 1285 *apologia* he asks whether the marginal comment refers to everything stated in the four excerpts or only to part of it. He gathers from the *Letter of the Seven Seals* that the commission found the fourth statement most offensive, but there is really no way of knowing. He also asks whether the commission wishes to say that *usus pauper* taken in this particular sense is not a part of the vow, or intends to deny that the vow involves *usus pauper* in any sense. If the former, and the commission's target is the idea of extreme necessity, then its members should realize that extreme necessity can be defined in two ways. Here he repeats at greater length the same explanation offered in his response to the *Letter of the Seven Seals*, underscoring the moderate nature of his own definition with a judicious selection of quotations from questions nine and fifteen. If his censors object to the basic notion of something falling under the vow indeterminately because they feel that a vow should include only precisely determinable obligations, then he can only refer them to his own argument for the opposite opinion in questions nine and fifteen and in the *Treatise on Usus Pauper*.

If, however, the commission is taking the latter, more extreme course and denying that the vow includes *usus pauper* in any sense, then while they are at it they might as well censure Bonaventure, Pecham, Hugh of Digne and Nicholas III. Having dealt at length with three of these authorities in his previous works, Olivi now simply waves in their direction. Hugh is a new face, however, and Olivi quotes him at length. In two passages from his work *On the Ends of Poverty*,[14] Hugh, "a most holy and famous man in his own day," asserts that Franciscans are bound by their vows to observe what he calls "the *insignia* of extreme poverty." He also states that these *insignia* are destroyed by superfluity. Since Hugh means by "the *insignia* of extreme poverty" pretty much what Olivi means by *usus pauper*, he makes an excellent witness for the defense.

Why is Hugh not mentioned until 1285, even though the passages quoted from him come closer to supporting Olivi's position than anything offered previously? Given the modern tendency to see Olivi as heir to a southern French spiritual tradition descending from Hugh and including concern for both poverty and apocalyptic speculation, the omission seems odd. Could Olivi have come across Hugh's *On the Ends of Poverty* only in the mid-1280s? That seems quite unbelievable. There are enough similarities to encourage a suspicion that he knew at least some of Hugh's works very early. Perhaps the answer lies in his description of Hugh as "famous in his own day." Olivi originally rested his case on Bonaventure and Pecham because they were recognized as eminent spokesmen for Franciscan poverty. Nicholas was cited because, once *Exiit qui seminat* appeared, it would have been unthinkable to ignore him. Hugh was overlooked because Olivi felt that his name carried insufficient weight to make him a potent authority.

Bishops

The commission also objected to certain Olivian opinions on the more practical aspects of *usus pauper*. Here again, its source was question nine. In the first place, the commission members disapproved of his contention that when Franciscans become bishops "they are in some sense even more strongly obliged than before to observe *usus pauper*."[15] The *Letter of the Seven Seals* says, "It is false and erroneous to say that those of the evangelical state who assume episcopal office are more fully obliged to *usus pauper* than before, and that there can be no dispensation from this obligation."[16] In his 1283 reply, Olivi agrees that Franciscan bishops are not held to *usus pauper* more than before in areas where such would impede them in the performance of their duties. Nor does he claim that they are obliged in all cases, but only under certain conditions. Nor should the words *more than before* be taken *simpliciter* but only *secundum quid*, according to congruity of status. He willingly acknowledges that they can be excused from the obligation in some way during their tenure as bishops. Here again, Olivi justifiably points to his avoidance of overgeneralization in discussing such matters. He also observes that, although he has written on the subject, he has not stated his opinion in the schools and is not happy that his views were spread about.[17]

In the 1285 *apologia*, Olivi says that the *rotulus* contained four statements from question nine regarding bishops.[18] One is, oddly enough, a quotation from John Pecham;[19] yet the commission labels it "commonly false." Thus, in a sense, the commission actually did follow Olivi's suggestion and censure Pecham while they were at it. Another statement cited is the assertion implicitly rejected by the *Letter of the Seven Seals*: "It is to be held without doubt that [bishops] are in some way obliged even more than before to observe *usus pauper*." The masters add two further sentences by Olivi which insist that there can be no dispensation from this obligation.

Here again Olivi confesses ignorance as to what the commission finds objectionable. Is he being censured because he believes Franciscan bishops are obliged to observe *usus pauper*; because he considers them more obliged than before; or because he thinks there is no possibility of dispensation? If the first, then evangelical poverty is not the highest state after all, we are wrong about Christ and the apostles, and the Franciscan order is built on a gigantic misunderstanding. If the second, then he must remind his readers that the phrase "more than before" should be taken not *simpliciter* but *secundum quid*, meaning "more in some way." If the third, then it should be understood that this does not rule out whatever behavior may be useful or necessary for the rule of souls, for the vow is never prejudicial to perfection, necessity, and spiritual utility. In other words, no dispensation is necessary because the vow itself provides the flexibility needed in such situations.

Obviously Olivi's stance regarding bishops is closely related to his notion that the vow of *usus pauper* is binding yet flexible. Viewing the matter from this perspective, he can grant a Franciscan bishop freedom to enjoy worldly comforts when the occasion demands without dispensing him from his vow. Nevertheless, there is something else lurking in Olivi's argument as he develops it in question nine, something well worth pondering.

In the question, Olivi cites and refutes three arguments in favor of dispensation.[20] One insists that it is necessary for a more effective ministry. Most people respect wealth. The simple believer, who does not appreciate inner virtue, looks upon *usus pauper* as contemptible, and his contempt will compromise episcopal authority. "As the vulgar proverb says, 'familiarity breeds contempt.' " Moreover, dispensation will aid one's ministry by allowing adequate resources to perform episcopal duties. For example, the bishop can get around his diocese and minister more effectively if he travels on horseback, but he cannot do so unless he is dispensed from the Franciscan vow not to ride horses.

Olivi's answer is a flat denial that dispensation will lead to a more effective ministry. Reverence, he says, comes in two varieties. One is based on sanctity, the other on temporal magnificence. The former is holier than the latter and inflames the faithful with love for both virtue and the bishop. The latter is more likely to induce fear, not only of evildoing, but of the bishop as well. As for familiarity breeding contempt, too much of it may well do so, but at the moment there is little danger that the faithful will become excessively familiar with the phenomenon of bishops who are dedicated observers of evangelical poverty. As for providing the bishop with resources to do his job, that depends on what job he is expected to do. Dispensation may help him to accomplish temporal goals. He may find it easier to gain wealth and worldly power for the church. Nevertheless, his spiritual goals will become correspondingly harder to achieve. Even in the temporal realm the blessing will be a mixed one, since episcopal poverty would allow more money to be spent on the poor, as it should be.

Another argument suggests that *usus pauper* cannot be required of bishops because the church has not required it in the past and does not require it now. In fact, it encourages the opposite behavior. Why would it do so unless the opposite behavior were more useful and rational? Certainly one should not believe that the church is in error. Olivi replies that it is good to follow the example of previous churchmen but even better to follow that of Christ and the disciples. Moreover, breaking with precedent does not imply that the church is in error unless the matter is one on which the church has made an official determination. Olivi recalls the case of Cyprian, who defended an erroneous opinion regarding heretics yet was not himself heretical for defending it, because the point at issue would only later be settled by a general council. The matter of Franciscan bishops is still very much an open question.

The final argument is that dispensation is possible because the episcopal status is higher than that of the simple monk or friar. It is an accepted axiom that a lesser vow can be commuted to a better one and a less perfect state can be commuted to a more perfect one. Olivi's response is confused by a complex welter of distinctions, but his basic point is clear enough. The episcopal state is indeed higher than that of the simple monk or friar because it calls for all the perfections of their state and more besides. There is a type of perfection which necessarily presupposes another to which it is added and upon which it is founded. The episcopal state is just this type. It is ordained to perfecting others, whereas the state of *religio* (that is, the state of the monk or friar) is ordained to perfecting oneself; yet the episcopal state can perfect others precisely because it is rooted in that prior personal perfection offered by the state of *religio*. Thus the episcopal state "demands, presupposes and binds one *de congruo* to the perfection of *religio* and also to all perfection of this life." In short, though the episcopal state is higher than that of a friar, it does not dispense one from the latter but is instead superimposed upon it. It is not as if one state were commuted to another, higher state incompatible with it, as when a married man takes a vow of chastity.

Obviously the discussion has taken an odd turn. Olivi is arguing that the Franciscan bishop's duty to observe *usus pauper* rests upon more than his vow. The vow simply binds him more indissolubly to a moral obligation already inherent in the episcopal status. He should practice *usus pauper* because all bishops should do so.[21] This view is something more than a passing whim on Olivi's part. He makes the same point in the *responsio* section of the question, where he argues that there can be no dispensation for Franciscan bishops because there can be no dispensation from evangelical vows in any situation[22] and, even if there could be, this certainly would not be an appropriate situation since the episcopal state "demands evangelical perfection in the highest way ... , so much so that the state is never achieved in full decency and perfection unless evangelical perfection is observed along with it." As a sign of this fact Christ imposed evangelical perfection, especially *usus pauper*, on his followers when he sent them out to preach and later when he appointed them to the apostolate.

Olivi invites us to imagine what the world would be like if all bishops lived as the apostles did. The wealth of the church would be spent on the poor. Faithful and responsible stewards would supervise the use of such temporal possessions according to canon law while the bishops devoted themselves to prayer, preaching, spiritual guidance and good example. Would the faithful and even the infidel not be drawn more easily to God if such were the case? Yes, indeed!

He now turns our unwilling minds to reality. Not only secular bishops but even those who are bound to some rule travel about by horse with a crowd of overdressed retainers. They dine elegantly and occupy themselves with the administration of temporal possessions. As a result, *religiosi* who have become bishops "provide as scandalous an example to their subordinates as other prelates do."[23]

There is more to this discussion than meets the eye. The hidden ingredient can be glimpsed briefly in Olivi's evocation of Christ and the apostles, but particularly in his oblique reference (during the meditation on Cyprian) to various *status ecclesiae*. Olivi's attitude is fully comprehensible only when viewed in the light of his theology of history. That, however, is another matter, which must be considered later. For the moment it is important only observe that, however fraught with significance Olivi's notion of bishops might seem to us, there is no evidence as to what the Parisian commission saw in it. Like Olivi, the modern historian must ultimately confess his ignorance as to why the commission members considered his comments worth censuring. Presumably they would have thought twice before denying that a Franciscan bishop remained bound to his vow of poverty, since Olivi was correct in claiming agreement with Bonaventure on that issue.[24] Two possibilities remain: either they objected to the idea that Franciscan bishops were more bound than before, or they felt that *usus pauper* was not part of the vow.

Burial

Olivi was also criticized for his comments on Franciscan involvement in the burial of laymen. One article in the *Letter of the Seven Seals* asserts that "burying the dead is a work of mercy, spiritual and in no way out of harmony with evangelical perfection." Another says that "having the right to bury is not contrary to the highest poverty."[25] In ascribing to these propositions, Olivi says that the first is true as long as the burial "is not under unworthy or imperfect circumstances, such as for reasons of cupidity or with impediment to some worthier actions." The second is true if one is speaking of a spiritual right concerning the body but not if one refers to a right concerning burial fees or the place of burial.[26]

In his 1285 *apologia* Olivi reports that the commission's target was a passage from question eight in which he argues that having a right to bury a body or to retrieve it if someone else takes it is not directly repugnant to the highest poverty, except perhaps insofar as the right to retrieve something which is not directly spiritual seems contrary to such poverty, and insofar as the act of burial, being the lowest and least perfect of spiritual acts, does not accord well with the perfection found in poverty. He says in the same passage that there is great imperfection in the office of burial unless it is a case of necessity, for the act is of little utility or spirituality, involves a rather unspiritual matter, and impedes the performance of more perfect activities. Baptizing is more spiritual than burying, yet Paul told the Corinthians that he was sent to preach and not to baptize. Christ, wishing to remove this impediment to more spiritual acts, told the man, "Let the dead bury the dead, you go and announce the kingdom of God." In the margin beside this passage the commission wrote, "commonly very false and dangerous."[27]

Olivi protests that he has allowed burial its status as a spiritual act, albeit an imperfect and less important one, and has granted that it is not directly opposed to the highest poverty. He has said, however, that jurisdiction over the place of burial and over burial fees *is* so opposed, since such jurisdiction can be held only by those who have private or common property.[28] He has said, moreover, that great attention to the office of burial is not good for Franciscans if it keeps them from higher occupations. Friars who are not committed to such duties by pastoral or episcopal office would do well to meddle in them as little as possible, because the dangers of cupidity and simony abound. So does the danger of evil example. The clergy are scandalized as well as offended when Franciscans haggle with them over burial rights, and the laity fail to appreciate the grandeur of evangelical poverty when they see that brothers bury the rich more willingly than the poor. "What," Olivi asks, "is false or dangerous in all this? Is it dangerous to try as hard as possible to avoid such impurities or dangers?"[29]

Of course not, but it might be very costly. The question of burial had become an important element in the secular-mendicant controversy because of the considerable profit involved.[30] The Franciscans insisted, of course, that their motives were pure, but conscientious leaders recognized that some of the brethren were endangering their souls and their image through an unedifying scramble for bodies. Olivi has no difficulty in documenting Bonaventure's concern on this matter.[31]

Thus, if we credit the commission with a desire to save something besides revenues, we are left asking, along with Olivi, just what it had in mind. Certainly it could not have disagreed with much in Olivi's statement without being prepared to criticize Bonaventure as well, although Olivi is exaggerating when he protests that he is actually more lax than Bonaventure. It is hard to believe that the commission simply felt the two positive assertions included in the *Letter of the Seven Seals* had become submerged in Olivi's argument and needed to be stated clearly. If so, its judgment of "very false and dangerous" would be inexplicable.

Procurators

A final issue, unmentioned in the *Letter of the Seven Seals*, emerges in the 1285 *apologia*. Olivi says that the *rotulus* included a passage from question nine in which he discusses whether observers of evangelical poverty can have procurators who collect what is willed or given to the order and carry on legal processes against debtors.[32] Olivi argues there that some things are licit according to the perfection of one's state, while others are licit only as concessions to the imperfect in order to keep them from doing something even worse. Again, one can have a procurator in either of two ways. One either gives him authority and jurisdiction or simply nominates someone who is given authority and jurisdiction by others. Franciscans cannot give a procurator authority and jurisdiction because they have none to give. Thus they can only nominate, but Olivi confesses that at the moment he does not clearly understand how even this much can be in accordance with the Franciscan state. Much less can they ask procurators to institute legal action and bring people to judgment, except perhaps as a concession to the weak. The commission has labeled this statement "commonly false."

Olivi comments that he had thought he was speaking rather laxly. He wonders what the commission found objectionable. Certainly his censors cannot imagine that the order has jurisdiction, for that would contradict the papal bulls *Quo elongati* and *Exiit qui seminat*. Nor does it seem likely that they would think of litigation as commensurate with the perfection of the Franciscan state.

It is worth emphasizing that Olivi does not reject the institution of procurators. He simply wants to clarify who controls them, what they should be asked to do, and whether their existence should be celebrated or merely tolerated. Nor does he reject them elsewhere. In other parts of question nine he grants that, though Franciscans cannot handle money, they can receive items purchased with it through *dispensatores* controlled by the givers.[33] In question sixteen he accepts the legitimacy of procurators but suggests that the money held by them should be used only for present or imminent necessities and that the brothers should police their own attitudes toward money, making sure that they regard it as belonging to the donor rather than themselves and that they do not think the procurator is obliged to spend it, even for their necessities. Here again he cites *Quo elongati* and *Exiit qui seminat*.[34]

The issue at stake was an important one for thirteenth-century Franciscans, who came to rely heavily on contributions as they ceased to engage in manual labor outside their houses.[35] The rule itself recognized the need for recourse to a "spiritual friend" who could use money to buy clothes and to care for ailing brothers.[36] In *Quo elongati* (1230), Gregory IX allowed the services of a *nuntius* who would be the representative of the giver and thus not subject to Franciscan control.[37] The role of such intermediaries and the extent of Franciscan control over them were increased by Innocent IV in *Ordinem vestrum* (1245) and *Quanto studiosus* (1247). The former allows that the rule prohibits Franciscans from receiving money. Nevertheless, "if they wish to buy something necessary or useful to them or pay for something already purchased," they can present a *nuntius* to perform that task. The *nuntius* can represent either the seller or those who give alms, or can even be the almsgiver himself. The important thing is that he does not belong to the Franciscans. The order can also nominate someone to take custody of contributions and make occasional payment *pro aliis fratrum necessitatibus aut commodis* as the brothers deem expedient. Here again, however, it is clear that the *nuntius* represents those who give the money, not the Franciscans themselves.[38] *Quanto studiosus* gives provincial ministers the right to install (*constituere*) "God-fearing men," who, through papal authority, can spend money *pro necessitatibus vel commodis fratrum* according to the decision of the ministers. It also gives them the authority to remove these agents and replace them with others if it seems necessary.[39]

The privileges granted by Innocent were not entirely welcome to the Franciscans. By the generalates of John of Parma (1247–57) and Bonaventure (1257–74), those who worried about the effects of papal privileges were numerous enough to have some impact. At the general chapter of Genoa in 1251, the provincial ministers of England and Ireland argued that the order should avoid procuratorial practices allowed by *Ordinem vestrum*.[40] Their goal was to hold the line at the interpretation offered in *Quo elongati*, and they seem to have carried the day. Moreover, succeeding general chapters at Metz (1254) and Narbonne (1260) agreed to abstain from using the privileges granted by Innocent IV,[41] even though *Ordinem vestrum* was reissued by Alexander IV in 1257.[42]

However suspicious some Franciscans may have been concerning papal privileges, they were due to see more of them. In *Exiit qui seminat* (1279), Nicholas III observes that Franciscans cannot receive money themselves, but it can be spent for their needs by the donor or someone nominated by him.[43] He emphasizes that this person is nominated by the donor and not by the Franciscans, yet immediately adds that they may nominate him themselves if the donor cannot or will not do so. If the procurator[44] cannot perform his duties because of illness, absence, or some other impediment, the Franciscans can nominate another. In fact, they can nominate several if the situation seems to demand it. Throughout the discussion, Nicholas shows a lively awareness that varying conditions call for flexibility. He demands that the money be spent on necessities but appreciates the protean nature of that category, observing that it cannot be limited to provision for the immediate future. He insists, however, that the money be seen as belonging entirely to the donor until the moment it is spent. The brothers have no right to tell the procurator how it should be used or bring him to justice if he spends it poorly. They can only inform him of their needs and desires, exhorting him to fulfill his commission responsibly for the sake of his soul. Nicholas realizes that this interpretation seems to deprive the Franciscans of any legal claim to legacies or even to funds given but not yet expended at the donor's death.[45] He treads very lightly around this problem, but does finally state his intention to assure "by means licit and congruent with the rule" that the Franciscans will not be defrauded by rapacious heirs.

Another important step was taken in 1283, when Martin IV published *Exultantes in domino*. The bull is a straightforward assertion, unencumbered by the restrictions and warnings Nicholas stuffed into *Exiit qui seminat*, of what Franciscans can do in this area. Martin gives them permission to nominate at their discretion "special persons" who will have full power to receive money in the name of the church and spend it for the *utilitates* of the order as required by the minister general (or others with his approval). The person in question can take legal action against those who fraudulently deprive the order of legacies. The order can remove the person and nominate another when it seems opportune to do so. Martin's one oblique reference to limitations on expenditure is his comment that the "special person" will use the money "as the rule or declaration of the rule allows." [46]

Exultantes in domino was officially accepted by the order at the general chapter of Milan in 1285, where it was ordained that "the privilege of Pope Martin concerning the naming of procurators . . . can be used." It was stipulated, however, that Franciscans "should be wary of multiplying litigation and should do nothing against the integrity of the order." [47]

Thus Olivi spoke to a situation in flux when he wrote the words that offended the commission. He was writing only months before *Exiit qui seminat* and not long after the order had attempted to distance itself from the privileges granted by Innocent IV. He was thus discussing a question to which the order could give no definitive answer. Nor was his view wildly at variance with the one to be offered shortly thereafter by Nicholas III. Olivi resembles Nicholas in the cautionary tone he assumes. Both emphasize Franciscan lack of control over the procurator and both stress that the money must be used for necessities, although both work with a flexible notion of necessity. Olivi went beyond the words of *Exiit qui seminat* in questioning whether nomination of procurators by the order was consistent with Franciscan perfection; yet even Nicholas sanctioned this process as a second line of defense to be utilized if the donor failed to settle matters himself.

Thus when Olivi, writing the *apologia* in 1285, says his view is in line with *Quo elongati* and *Exiit qui seminat*, he is more or less right; yet he is choosing his bulls rather carefully. By that time Martin IV had spoken in words similar to those of Innocent IV. Shortly after, the order officially accepted Martin's privilege. Whether one thinks Olivi differed from Martin depends on whether one interprets Martin and Innocent as granting more than Nicholas did. They certainly left a few more doors open, doors which Olivi and Nicholas seemed anxious to shut. One can at least say that by 1285, although Olivi may not have been hopelessly out of step with his order, he and it were hardly moving in the same direction on the matter of procurators.

That does not answer Olivi's question as to what the commission found repugnant in his statement. Here again the commission chooses to remain silent; yet it is perhaps significant that, in listing the possibilities, Olivi leaps nimbly over what might seem a likely explanation. Perhaps the commission members were offended, not by his denial that Franciscans could give authority or his assertion that there was something seedy about litigation, but by his unwillingness to see the institution of procurators as anything more than a lamentable concession to imperfection.

Notes

1. The names are given in *Chronica XXIV generalium*, 374, and Olivi, *Responsio* II, 130.
2. *Responsio* II, 132. Presumably he surrendered his own copies for examination before he wrote to R, and then, after the censure, all copies were confiscated.
3. "Verurteilung," 505f.
4. Geroldus Fussenegger, "'Littera septem sigillarum' contra doctrinam Petri Ioannis Olivi edita," *AFH*, 47 (1954): 45–53.
5. Raymundus de Fronciacho, *Sol ortus*, 14; *Chronica XXIV generalium*, 376. Raymundus and Bonagratia de Bergamo, *Infrascripta dant*, 144, quote Raymond Geoffroi as saying that Olivi ascribed before Gerard of Prato rather than Bonagratia. The recantation in *Chronica XXIV generalium* refers to Bonagratia as *tunc generalis*, suggesting he was already dead.
6. *Responsio* I, 126–30.
7. *Responsio* II, 134. The confession in *Chronica XXIV generalium* seems to offer an unconditional submission, but in it Olivi says of the commission: "Credo ipsos habuisse sanum intellectum, et secundum sanum intellectum quem credo ipsos habuisse in verbis illis, illa verba accepto." Thus he accepts his own idea of what the commission must have meant in order to be correct.
8. *Responsio* II, 132–35.
9. The resultant work, *Responsio* II, is dated 1285 and is addressed to the seven scholars, including Arlotto of Prato, whom it addresses as a master of theology. In May 1285 Arlotto was elected minister general. If Olivi was using the southern French system of dating, the document was submitted between Easter and Pentecost.
10. "Littera septem sigillarum," 52: "Item usus pauper rerum prout in se claudit extremam necessitatem, que dicit indigentiam manifeste existentem vel de proximo imminentem et talem quod debitus status corporis sui vel persone Deo servientis, nisi sibi succurratur, stare non potest, nullo modo includitur in voto evangelice paupertatis; et contrarium dicere est erroneum."
11. *Responsio* I, 129: "Hanc sententiam accepto, sumendo li extremam necessitatem pro extrema penuria, sicut magistri hic accipere videntur; et sub hoc sensu non credo me dixisse contrarium, et si dixi revoco. Sumendo autem li extremam pro medio virtutis non in puncto indivisibili, sed in latitudine debita, et convenienti statui et officiis, sic dixi quod includitur in voto evangelicae paupertatis."
12. *Responsio* II, 381–86.
13. Koch, "Verurteilung," 506f.; Koch, "Philosophische und theologische

Irrtumslisten von 1270–1329," in *Mélanges Mandonnet* (Paris, 1930), 309–29.

14. *Responsio* II, 383: "Praeter autem praedictas adhuc exstat ad hoc auctoritas fratris Hugonis, viri in diebus suis famosissimi atque sanctissimi."

15. Q. 9, f. 91vb.

16. "Littera septem sigillarum," 52.

17. *Responsio* I, 12. See his remark in *Responsio* II, 132, that the commission made excerpts from questions secretly written by him for his own intellectual exercise and made public by his confreres without his consent. Would he produce anything as massive as qq. 8 and 9 just to clarify his own thinking? Perhaps he showed his questions to a few people before he was ready to "publish" them, and somehow they were circulated more widely than he had intended. One assumes q. 15 was produced for public consumption, since it counters objections apparently raised by others against his argument in q. 9.

18. *Responsio* II, 386–90.

19. It is from *Tractatus pauperis*, ch. 14.

20. These arguments are found at 78va–79ra, but in a different order than the one followed here. Olivi's reply to them is at 92rb–93vb and the *responsio* section concerning bishops is at 91vb–92rb.

21. Aquinas, who also relies on Pseudo-Dionysius, says something similar in *Summa theologiae*, IIa IIae, q. 185, a. 8, and *De perfectione spiritualis vitae*, c. 20, in *Opera* (Rome, 1882–), 41:B-92; yet he gives the argument a different twist because he does not rate poverty as highly as Olivi does. He argues that a bishop is "in a certain way" obliged to the same things as a religious, but that means chastity, obedience to the duty of serving his flock, and willingness to sacrifice his possessions for the sake of that flock *should that become necessary*. Olivi commits the bishop to *usus pauper*, but Thomas does not even see the religious as committed to it. Bonaventure, *Apologia pauperum*, in *Opera*, 8:244–52, avoids this problem. He compares *religio* and *prelatio* without submitting both to a set of common attributes.

22. He refers ahead to his question on dispensation from vows, q. 14 in Vat. lat. 4986.

23. Did Olivi have anyone special in mind? There were no Franciscan bishops in the ecclesiastical provinces of Narbonne, Arles, or Aix at the time, although there had been a Franciscan bishop of Orange from 1270 to 1276. See Bernard Guillemain and Catherine Martin, "Les origines sociales, intellectuelles et ecclésiastiques des évêques de la province de Narbonne entre 1219 et 1317," *Les évêques, les clercs, et le roi* (Toulouse, 1972), 102f; Edouard Baratier, "Nominations et origines des évêques des provinces d'Aix et Arles," in ibid., 128. For early Franciscan bishops in Rodez (1247–74) and perhaps Marseilles see Williell Thomson, *Friars in the Cathedral* (Toronto, 1975), 212–17 and 228–30.

24. Bonaventure, *Commentarius in I, II, III, IV librum sententiarum* (hereafter *Sent.*), IV, d. 38, q. 3, ad 5, in *Opera*, 4:824. Richard of Middleton, a member of the Paris commission, would later deny that a bishop is dispensed from his vows (*Super quattuor libros sententiarum* [Brescia, 1591],

IV, d. 38, a. 5, q. 1, and a. 9, q. 1). The passage from Pecham, *Tractatus pauperis*, c. 14, which Olivi cites twice in q. 9 is actually quoted slightly out of context.

25. *Littera septem sigillarum*, 52.
26. *Responsio* I, 129.
27. *Responsio* II, 378f.
28. In q. 8, 52ra–rb he adds that jurisdiction over the body to be buried is not thus opposed since it is spiritual, like the right to administer the sacraments. Nevertheless, it is least among all such *spiritualia et sacramentalia*.
29. *Responsio* II, 378–80.
30. In Narbonne, where Olivi's own body would rest until 1319, the Franciscans were at odds with the chapter of St. Just over burials in 1280, when the *usus pauper* controversy was heating up. See Richard Emery, *Heresy and Inquisition at Narbonne* (New York, 1941), 123. Emery suggests that the Franciscans did relatively well from wills there, but evidence is slight. For Franciscan legislation on burials see the 1260 constitutions of Narbonne, in Bihl, "Statuta generalia," 48, which say that no one should be buried in Franciscan vestments if he can be refused without notable scandal; the 1274 Lyons chapter, in Bonaventure, *Opera*, 8:467, which enjoins Franciscans to avoid scandalizing the clergy on this account; Jerome of Ascoli's 1274 letter in Abate, "Memoriali," *MF* 33 (1933): 22, which tells Franciscans "on the order of the pope" to induce no one to be buried elsewhere than in his family burial place; the 1279 chapter of Assisi, in Bihl, "Statuta generalia," 53, which orders that brothers should induce no one to be buried elsewhere than in his or her family sepulcher, should receive no one for burial without compensating the local church according to the local custom, and should not enter into litigation over bodies; the late thirteenth-century provincial statutes of Aquitaine, in Little, "Statuta provincialia provinciarum Aquitaniae et Franciae," 472, ordering the brothers not to seek burial fees through lawsuits or violence; and the 1303 provincial statute from upper Germany, in Fussenegger, "Statuta," 253, which says no one is to be buried in a Franciscan church unless deemed by *discreti* to be of such sanctity or dignity as to merit it.
31. In *Responsio* II, 380, he quotes the two letters by Bonaventure cited in Chapter 1, notes 1 and 2 above.
32. *Responsio* II, 390–94.
33. Q. 9, 67rb, 69vb–71rb.
34. In David Burr and David Flood, "Peter Olivi: On Poverty and Revenue," *FS* 40 (1980): 48f. See also Flood, *Olivi's Rule Commentary*, 142f., where Olivi cites the same two bulls.
35. But see the warning on this subject by Anna Imelde Galletti, "Insediamento e primo sviluppo dei frati minori a Perugia," in *Francescanesimo e societa cittadina* (Perugia, 1979), 22.
36. *Regula*, c. 4.
37. *BF*, 1:69.
38. Ibid., 400f.
39. Ibid., 487f.
40. Thomas of Eccleston, *De adventu*, c. 8.

41. Ferdinand Delorme, "Diffinitiones capituli generalis Narbonnensis," *AFH* 3 (1910): 503. See also Hugo de Digna, *Rule Commentary*, 59–64; Brooke, *Early Franciscan Government*, 264f. This was not the only area in which the order ignored papal decisions.
42. *BF*, 1:196.
43. *Corpus iuris canonici*, 1115–1118.
44. Nicholas does not use the term at this point but later says that Franciscans wishing to convert books or other expensive durables into other necessities can do so through a procurator appointed by the pope or cardinal protector.
45. The status of money left to the Franciscans in wills was a problem. Apparently Dominican critics argued that such legacies disproved the Franciscan claim to absolute poverty. See Pecham, *Contra Kilwardby*, published in *Tractatus tres de paupertate* (Aberdeen, 1910), 138; and *Canticum pauperis*, published in *Biblioteca franciscana ascetica medii aevi* (Quaracchi, 1908), 4:170.
46. *BF*, 3:501f.
47. Callebaut, "Acta capituli generalis Mediolani," *AFH* 22 (1929):283.

CHAPTER 5

Rehabilitation and Reversal, 1283–1309

Olivi's Rehabilitation

We have only a shadowy notion of how the *usus pauper* controversy fared between 1283 and Olivi's death in 1298. According to Angelo Clareno, Olivi managed to settle the score with his minister general almost immediately. He came to Avignon without permission from his provincial minister and requested an interview with Bonagratia, who asked why a simple brother, and a censured one at that, had dared to flout protocol in this manner. Olivi said he was impelled by urgent necessity, the matter being so important that it would be advisable for the brothers at large to hear what he was about to say. Bonagratia complied, intending to hear Olivi before a group and then make an example of him by imposing a stiff penance for his flagrant disregard of proper channels.

The result was spectacularly different. Olivi, moved mightily by the Holy Spirit, spoke so eloquently that Bonagratia could not bring himself to mention the penance. Instead, stricken to the heart, he sickened and died, as did two of the people who had moved him to proceed against Olivi in the first place.[1]

The story is obviously more emotionally satisfying than informative. Olivi did journey to Avignon in the fall of 1283, but it was by order of the minister general, and he came to submit rather than to prophesy. Bonagratia did die around that time, but probably not from remorse. Olivi stood helplessly by as the *Letter of the Seven Seals* was distributed throughout his province, his works were confiscated, and his reputation sank.

Then, in early 1285 Olivi managed to get his hands on the requisite documents and composed his *apologia* to the commission of seven. His comments in that work need not be reexamined here. More important for our purposes is the fact that other events in 1285 suggest a continuing interest in his case. Arnold of Roquefeuil, his provincial minister, joined with thirty-five other colleagues in a petition calling Olivi the head of a superstitious sect and a sower of discord.[2] The problem was discussed in May 1285 at the general chapter held in Milan, and the ministers officially renewed the ban on Olivi's writings until the minister general should order otherwise.[3]

The new minister general chosen at Milan was Arlotto of Prato, a former member of the seven-man commission. Perhaps Olivi's *apologia*, penned sometime in the previous five months, had arrived at his doorstep and impressed him, or perhaps Arlotto simply had decided on his own to hear Olivi out. In any case, the *Chronicle of the Twenty-four Generals* states that Arlotto "summoned Olivi to Paris so that he could answer personally."[4]

Whatever the true story may be, Angelo Clareno again provides the most entertaining one. According to Angelo, Olivi went to Paris and appeared before Arlotto in the presence of two other commission members, Richard of Middleton and John of Murrovalle. Arlotto asked him to explain his view of the divine nature and, when he finished, smilingly invited the others to respond. Neither was able to do so. Olivi proceeded to expound other issues with the same result, "for they could not resist the wisdom and spirit which spoke in him."[5]

The *Chronicle of the Twenty-four Generals* offers a shorter and more credible account. It notes that Arlotto died after a year in office, "and thus the matter remained undiscussed."[6] Olivi's rehabilitation was delayed until a new minister general was chosen at the next chapter meeting. Nevertheless, it is likely that Arlotto took some significant action, since Ubertino da Casale names him along with Matthew of Aquasparta and Raymond Geoffroi as one of the ministers who rescinded the censures against Olivi.[7]

The next general chapter meeting was held in 1287 at Montpellier, Olivi's own territory.[8] He attended and clarified his view of *usus pauper*. His explanation seems to have met with approval, since the new minister general, Matthew of Aquasparta, appointed him lector in the order *studium* at the convent of Santa Croce in Florence. From this point until his death in 1298, Olivi stayed in relatively good odor with the authorities, good enough at least to safeguard his teaching position.[9]

That proved to be no easy task, because the poverty dispute escalated. In 1289, those who sought a more rigorous observance were blessed with a new minister general, Raymond Geoffroi, whose sympathy for their cause undoubtedly encouraged them to take a strong stand. Raymond, who may have been the friend to whom Olivi wrote defending himself in the early 1280s, was himself from southern France and had served as lector at Marseilles.[10] His most dramatic gesture on behalf of the rigorists was to free the Anconan zealots from prison and dispatch them as missionaries to Armenia. More important for us, he approved Olivi's transfer from Florence to the Franciscan *studium* at Montpellier.

Raymond's election certainly suggests that those who sought a stricter observance were anything but defeated. It might even be interpreted as evidence that they were temporarily in control, particularly since the *Chronicle of the Twenty-four Generals* says that Pope Nicholas IV, the Franciscan pope in whose presence the election was carried out, had wished to see someone else elected.[11] It would be dangerous to conclude too much from this event, however. Raymond was related to the counts of Provence and was friendly with the house of Anjou, to which he rendered some service at least from 1286 through 1288. Thus his elevation may reflect French influence. It is probably significant that, on the day after his election, the coronation of the Angevin King Charles II of Naples (whom Raymond had aided while Charles was in Aragonese captivity) took place *in loco fratrum*.[12] It is also worth noting that, when Angelo Clareno and his colleagues returned from Armenia and were told they were unwelcome in Ancona, Raymond authorized them to seek a remedy from Celestine V.[13] His action suggests that he acknowledged his own inability to restrain their provincial superiors.

Further Battles

Olivi remained in southern France (though not at Montpellier) for the rest of his life. Thus it is hardly surprising that he soon found himself embroiled in the same old battles. We can follow those battles only at a distance. In 1290 they were acrimonious enough to catch the attention of Pope Nicholas IV (the former Jerome of Ascoli), who wrote Raymond Geoffroi telling him, as the *Chronicle of the Twenty-four Generals* says, to look into "certain brothers who seemed to introduce schism into the province of Provence, condemning the state of the other brethren and considering themselves to be more spiritual than the others."[14] Some of these friars were also reputed to hold incorrect views. The chronicle reports that the investigation was carried out by the inquisitor of the province, the result was submitted to the general chapter at Paris in 1292, and some southern French brothers were punished for sowing schism.[15]

Olivi himself was spared, but only after appearing before the general chapter and again explaining his notion of *usus pauper*. So, at least, the

Chronicle of the Twenty-four Generals tells us, and other evidence supports that claim. Some early fourteenth-century spokesmen for the community attempt to include Olivi in the condemnation of 1292, but their way of stating the matter suggests that they are stretching the evidence for their own purposes.[16]

The poverty dispute probably continued to smolder in southern France during the last six years of Olivi's life, for it erupted immediately after his death; yet we hear almost nothing about it. Nor is there any evidence that Olivi himself was troubled. His provincial minister during at least part of this time was Bertrand de Sigotier, who as inquisitor had conducted the investigation leading to the condemnation of 1292. Bertrand had been guardian of the Franciscan house at Marseilles when Raymond Geoffroi was a lector there in the late 1270s, and it was probably Raymond who involved him in the investigation. One might also assume that his appearance as provincial minister owed something to Raymond's influence. Thus it is unlikely that Olivi was threatened much by his leadership.

Some evidence of polemical activity on Olivi's part does survive from this period. In May 1295 he sent a letter to the three sons of King Charles of Naples.[17] The three were being held as hostages in Catalonia and had requested that Olivi visit or write them. Olivi, now at Narbonne, says he chose the latter alternative partly because of their father's fear that he might "beguinize" (*inbeguiniri*) them. His comment reveals that Olivi's faction and pious laymen were already joined in the alliance that would produce a thriving Olivi cult and then revolution in the early fourteenth century. It also reveals that the alliance was already making some people nervous. Further evidence of tension might be wrested from Olivi's observation that "if I do not come to you I may have to hurry off to another place," which could be interpreted as an indication that he was still under attack and might eventually have to flee Narbonne. On the other hand, it may mean nothing of the sort.

Three Confessions

Olivi's works during the period 1287–98 do not cast as much light on the *usus pauper* controversy as those written during the critical period 1279–85, but they are significant nonetheless. No less than three confessions have been attributed to this period. One was supposedly delivered on Olivi's deathbed but is probably the earliest of the lot, since in it he announces his loyalty to the church, "the governor of which is now Pope Martin."[18] Martin IV was pope from February 1281 to March 1285.

Perhaps the confession was delivered at the 1282 general chapter. That would explain why Ubertino da Casale, who cites two confessions by Olivi, assigns the other one quoted by him to a specific general chapter (1287) but does not do the same for this one. He might have considered it diplomatically wise to associate the other confession with a chapter at which Olivi defended himself successfully, but less so to identify this one with a chapter so unimpressed by it that Olivi was censured the following year.[19] Why it eventually should have been ascribed to the dying Olivi remains unexplained and perhaps inexplicable.[20]

The confession could almost be described as a summary of Olivi's conclusions reached in question nine. It describes *usus pauper* as a substantive part of the vow and defines it as "that use which, all things considered, should be thought of as poor rather than rich." Many of the relaxations attacked in question nine, such as wearing shoes, riding horses, annual *pietantiae*, and abuses of burial rights or procurators appear here as well.

Another confession does belong in the 1287–98 period. Ubertino says it was delivered to the general chapter at Montpellier in 1287 and then repeated at the Paris general chapter in 1292.[21] In it, Olivi clarifies what he means by *usus pauper* and how it is included in the vow. Again he emphasizes that its observance will vary in accordance with individual circumstances and that the vow of *usus pauper* is broken only when the violation is great enough to traduce the state of evangelical poverty, lesser transgressions being nothing more than venial sins. He asserts that his view is in line with those of Nicholas III, Bonaventure, Pecham and Hugh of Digne, adding that he never has said anything contrary and, if he has, he rejects it.

The *Chronicle of the Twenty-four Generals* corroborates Ubertino's assertion that Olivi repeated his Montpellier confession at Paris but claims that he made a significant addition. At Paris he affirmed that Franciscans were bound to *usus pauper* only in the sense defined by Nicholas III, that he had never said otherwise, and that, if he had, he withdrew it. He also promised not to support anyone holding a contrary opinion.

There is no reason to doubt the statement in the *Chronicle* that at Paris Olivi added an expression of allegiance to *Exiit* and explicitly dissociated himself from those who were about to be disciplined. This addition may explain why Raymond of Fronsac, who interprets *Exiit* as supporting his own anti-Olivian views, pictures Olivi as having recanted his former position. Olivi, who had been quoting *Exiit* all along, would have seen the matter differently. It may also explain why the confession has survived in two different lengths, one of which (found in Ubertino and a single manuscript of the *Treatise on Usus Pauper*) ends with a disclaimer substantially and at some points literally the same as that found in the *Chronicle*. It is less clear why this longer version should differ at all from the *Chronicle* report, since the latter seems to think it is quoting directly. Perhaps Olivi reworked the latter part of the confession one more time after 1292. Or perhaps the problem simply lies in the *Chronicle*'s sources. It is impossible to say.[22]

Unfortunately, we have another confession ascribed to the 1287 general chapter.[23] In this one, Olivi responds to eight specific questions. He asserts that Franciscans are bound by their vow to observe *usus pauper* but not to practice such extreme self-deprivation that they endanger their health. This, he says, is the position of Nicholas III, whom he quotes at length. As to whether Franciscans can receive privileges from the pope, he denies that they can licitly have those that derogate from the purity of the rule, such as privileges involving them directly or indirectly in litigation or temporal rights. As for procurators, he affirms that recurring to them in order to engage in litigation regarding wills, gifts, burials, or the like constitutes impurity. Burial, he says, is a legitimate activity for Franciscans if performed for charitable reasons without claiming any rights or seeking profit, without scandalizing clergy or laymen, and without impeding engagement in higher pursuits. The confession is clearly an effort to explain his position on many of the subjects at issue in the early 1280s. It is easy to imagine such a statement being required of him at the 1287 chapter meeting, but Ubertino seems to forbid it.[24]

These confessions corroborate what can be gathered from other sources: the views for which Olivi was censured in 1283 continued to plague him through 1292 and probably until his death, yet he was never forced to recant them.

The *Rule Commentary*

Another relevant document, Olivi's commentary on the Franciscan rule, was written in the period between the two general chapters, probably in late 1288.[25] During his discussion of chapter six, he cites a passage from the *Exposition of the Four Masters* in which they suggest that Franciscan poverty involves both lack of possessions and *paupertatem tanquam usum*.[26] Olivi comments that these words agree with what he has asserted elsewhere concerning *usus pauper* and supported by reference to popes and great Franciscan masters. "Thus it is amazing that certain people should accuse me of inventing something new when, almost by compulsion, I advanced and defended the idea of *usus pauper* against those who strongly denied and opposed it, particularly in view of the fact that such denial involves an explicit, powerful denial of the Christian faith, our rule, and the whole evangelical state."[27] Olivi then catalogs seven places in the rule that seem to support his view of *usus pauper*.

Obviously Olivi sees no change in his view regarding poverty. Nor does the *Rule Commentary* diverge in any significant way from his earlier views. Again Olivi advocates a flexible approach to the rule which will allow practice to alter with the demands of necessity.[28] Again he simply takes for granted major alterations in form and function which separate the primitive order from that of his own day.[29] His relatively sanguine attitude toward Franciscan history is manifested in his emphasis on the rightness of papal interpretations and his acceptance of papal privileges.[30]

On the other hand, the implicit tensions between Olivi's thought and developments in his time are still visible in the *Rule Commentary*. He affirms the pope's right to interpret the rule but alludes to his own earlier question on the subject without mentioning that his position there limits papal power in this respect.[31] He cites Gregory IX and Nicholas III in his discussion of *amici spirituales* but omits mention of the recent pronouncement by Martin IV.[32] Most significant for our purposes, in discussing how to interpret the opening statement of the rule that "the rule and life of the friars minor is . . . to observe the holy gospel," he refers back to his own question seventeen and does not even mention papal solutions to the problem, which lead in a different direction.[33]

The Letter to Conrad of Offida

The final document worth considering at length is Olivi's letter to Conrad of Offida, written September 14, 1295.[34] Nine months earlier, on December 13, 1294, in the fourth month of what promised to be a disastrous pontificate, Celestine V had resigned. Celestine's story is too well known to need retelling here.[35] We need only remind ourselves that the legitimacy of his resignation was questioned in several quarters. Some of these doubts were at least partly inspired by political alignment, since Celestine's successor, Boniface VIII, soon found himself at odds with the king of France and with the Colonna family.

Some doubters were motivated by their own shattered dreams. The election of a relatively obscure hermit as pope had been, to say the least, surprising. It is understandable that reformers might have felt encouraged to hope they were seeing the birth of a new era. A group of Italian Franciscan zealots, finding themselves inhibited by their own order from observing the rule as strictly as they thought necessary, appealed to

Celestine. He established them as the Poor Hermits of Pope Celestine, with Fra Liberato as their leader and Cardinal Napoleon Orsini as their protector. As one modern historian succinctly observes, the pope listened to their complaints "and in his kindly simplicity reached a decision that was to ruin them."[36] On December 27, fourteen days after Celestine's resignation, Boniface VIII rescinded most of his legislation and the Poor Hermits were thrown back upon the mercy of their enraged Franciscan superiors.

Liberato, Angelo Clareno, and others avoided confrontation by departing for Greece. While it is impossible to trace the fate of those poor hermits who remained in Italy, we do know what happened to certain Italian zealots who seem to have supported the Poor Hermits and whose association with that group remains unclear. Jacopone da Todi and at least two other Franciscans eventually threw in their lot with the Colonna family, while Conrad of Offida was one of those who eventually made their peace with the new minister general, John of Murrovalle, and thus with the new pope.

Olivi's letter to Conrad tells what one group of Italian zealots were doing in late 1295. He begins by announcing that he has received some terrible news from certain letters sent to him (and perhaps in other ways as well, although that may be reading too much into Olivi's turn of phrase). He has been told that certain people, motivated by zeal for the highest poverty, have fallen into various errors and left the order. Having had long experience of Conrad's sanctity and discretion, he has decided to write and beg his friend that, "should any of these people come to your attention, you recall them from their errors."

The errant brothers are claiming, first, that Celestine V is still the pope because he cannot resign. Moreover, they insist that anyone accepting Boniface VIII as pope is part of the synagogue of Satan and outside the one true church. Olivi, having just completed a *quaestio* on the subject of papal resignation,[37] is ready for them. He refutes their arguments curtly and rather cuttingly so that "these temerarious, presumptuous people can see how disgracefully and brutally they err."

They combine their repudiation of Boniface VIII with an attack on previous papal declarations concerning the rule, insisting that *Quo elongati* and *Exiit qui seminat* have violated the rule, the testament of St. Francis, and the gospel by permitting the use of money through procurators and by granting ministers, custodes, and other leaders the right to provide each friar with more than two tunics in case of necessity. Far from simply criticizing, they are calling for rebellion. "They seem to think that these popes and all who obey them are heretics," and they urge their colleagues to separate from the carnal leaders of church and order. They take their call to separate from Revelation 18:4, "Come out of her, my people!"

Olivi is appalled. He reminds his opponents that others before them said the same thing about Innocent III and the fourth Lateran council because the latter condemned Joachim of Fiore's doctrine of the trinity. By that reasoning, Francis, Dominic, and their orders would be heretical, since Innocent approved them after condemning Joachim's view. Francis would be worse than Lucifer, since in the rule he exhorts his order to obey Innocent's successor Honorius, and Honorius's successors in turn.

Olivi deals at length with Francis's testament. "These people—insane, blind and ignorant of the holy scriptures as they are—must realize that the papal declaration does not condemn the holy father's letter, called by some his 'testament.'" In fact, Gregory IX commends it in *Quo elongati*, saying he believes Francis wrote it with good intention. The pope goes on to say, quite accurately, that if in writing this letter, Francis intended to impose on his order and his successors new precepts beyond those found in the rule, he was trying to do something beyond his power. In fact, however, Francis wanted to do nothing of the kind. He simply wanted the rule to be observed without fraud or comment. Some "simple and ignorant people" may protest at this point that the testament orders literal obedience to everything in the gospel and rule. Nicholas III has settled this problem. Heaven help us if Francis meant that we should literally tear out an eye or slice off a hand when it offends us or literally turn the right cheek to whoever strikes us on the left one.

As for procurators, papal declarations are right in asserting that, when money is entrusted to them for the brothers' necessities, the friars themselves do not receive it. To think otherwise is to argue not only against papal declarations but against the rule as well, not to mention Paul's collection for the saints at Jerusalem. The Franciscans themselves have no right to say how the money will be spent. If some friars currently use *bursarii* or *depositarii* in such a way as to suggest the opposite, they are guilty of abusing what is in itself a valid procedure.

The rule and right reason both militate against the rebels' stand on clothing. The rule says that ministers and custodes shall provide such clothing as befits local conditions. As for the need to escape from carnal society, Olivi rhetorically asks whether Giles, Leo, and other companions of Saint Francis left the order because of such problems.

Olivi accuses the rebels of exposing the rule to external and internal attack. Critics outside the order can take their interpretation of the rule as proof of the old accusation that it is impossible to observe and therefore injurious, while laxer brethren within the order can cite their revolt as evidence that the rigorist wing (or, as Olivi calls his faction, "the spiritual professors of the rule") advocates extreme solutions and is tainted with heresy.

Some historians see in the letter to Conrad of Offida a melancholy instance of Olivi warding off attacks by distancing himself from views that were really quite similar to his own.[38] Franz Ehrle regards it as evidence that Olivi "was no longer lord of the spirits he had conjured up."[39] Such appraisals seem unjust. In the first place, Olivi's letter can hardly be seen as a defensive move on his part. If self-protection was his aim, Olivi would have been better off writing to the minister general. He addressed his thoughts to Conrad of Offida because he was genuinely concerned. A reputation was indeed at stake, but not his own. He saw the renegade Italians as a threat to the Franciscan rule.

As for the assertion that Olivi attacks his own previous views in the letter, quite the contrary is true. He may seem to do so at first glance because his thoughts on procurators and clothing in the *Questions on Evangelical Perfection* are written to refute a position diametrically opposed to that countered in the letter to Conrad. Whereas the letter attacks an opinion so rigorous that it seems to cast doubt on the rule itself, the ninth of the *Questions on Evangelical Perfection* joins battle with those who would distort the rule in such a way as to compromise *usus pauper*. At times in the latter work it is easier to see what Olivi rejects than what he accepts, but he always accepts the basic institution of procurators and the right of ministers to exercise discretion regarding tunics.

There is, of course, another problem concerning consistency. One is struck by the extent to which Olivi and his targets share a common apocalyptic perspective. He differs from them in being an apocalyptic thinker who takes his theology, history, and canon law seriously, but in the final analysis his quarrel with them is not over whether the dragon will emerge in history but where and when. Thus one must ask whether, in rejecting the Italian zealots' call to abandon ship, Olivi traduces his own apocalyptic program. A later chapter will show that he does not.

Ehrle's portrayal of Olivi as sorcerer's apprentice is even less justifiable. Olivi did not "conjure up" the Italian zealots. They existed long before the *usus pauper* controversy began. They were in some ways similar to Olivi and his friends in southern France, but in other ways they were very different, informed by diverse experiences and pursuing diverse programs. Olivi's letter marks one of the points at which these differences surface for the modern scholar's inspection.

Such considerations may explain Olivi's attitude, but they do not necessarily condone it. Lydia von Auw, author of an excellent modern work on Angelo Clareno, seems genuinely indignant when she recounts the episode. Noting that Olivi "did not understand or did not wish to understand" the tragedy of the Italian situation, she observes that his letter "is not very generous." He did not take account of the way passions had been exacerbated in Italy, nor did he appreciate the severity of the persecutions undergone by Liberato, Angelo Clareno, and their associates.[40]

Moral considerations aside, there is much to be said for this analysis. Olivi was deprived of his writings and his position for a while, but his body remained inviolate until twenty years after his death. Reality took on a different hue for those who had spent years in an Anconan prison and lived in constant danger of spending several more there. Those Italian zealots who had been absolved from obedience by Celestine now faced the prospect of falling back into the clutches of Franciscan leaders whose hostility had been increased by the zealots' successful dealings with the hermit pope.

Olivi certainly felt some existential involvement in the affair, but at a much different level. His program for reform involved at least a theoretical acceptance of papal declarations. In practice that meant accepting them on most issues and explaining them away or simply ignoring them when they said something he could not accept. His program also involved reforming a single, united Franciscan order. The Italian troublemakers were challenging him on both counts and in the process were endangering his chance of success. Olivi saw—quite correctly as it turned out—that the more radical Italian zealots were offering enemies of reform precisely the weapon they needed to enlist papal support.

Who were these zealots, and why did Olivi write to Conrad about them? He must have thought that Conrad, whom he had probably known since the late 1270s,[41] was in a position to address the rebels. It is less obvious whether he thought Conrad himself needed convincing. Conrad had been an instigator of the delegation to Celestine V which had resulted in the Poor Hermits of Pope Celestine.[42] He had a strong vested interest in questioning the legitimacy of Boniface's election and may have done so. Who knows what information had percolated up to Narbonne? If Olivi's correspondents were well connected, he may have known a great deal more than his letter suggests, and his imprecation to set the erring brothers right "if you run into any" may suggest that Olivi had a remarkably delicate touch when correcting his friends.

Nevertheless, there is no evidence that Conrad took an active role in the campaign against Boniface as Jacopone da Todi did, and some reason to believe that he did not, since he did not share Jacopone's fate. Nor does such involvement square with what little can be derived from Angelo Clareno and the *Fioretti*. Angelo says that when John of Murrovalle became minister general, some people complained to him about Conrad. They accused him of having said that neither the declarations nor the rule were being observed; that those who wished to do so found their efforts impeded by the laxer brethren; and that another order (presumably the Poor Hermits of Pope Celestine) was the real order of brothers minor. They also accused him of having counseled those wishing to obey the rule that they should leave the Franciscan order.[43]

These charges are easy to believe because Angelo acknowledges that they were well documented and they agree with what Angelo says elsewhere about Conrad. Thus it is all the more intriguing that his interview with the minister general turned out as it did. According to Angelo, John read all the charges aloud and then, with great emotion, cried, "I can barely restrain myself from tearing all my clothing into shreds, just as you have torn my heart!" Conrad, seeing his genuine grief, prayed for him and, "with a few humble, simple, words," won him over so thoroughly that John frequently called on Conrad for spiritual comfort until the latter's death in 1306.

Obviously this story belongs in what should be a familiar category by now, "Vindication of the Spirituals Before Those in High Places." Having heard Angelo tell a few apocryphal stories of that genre involving Olivi, we might pause before accepting one about Conrad. Nevertheless, one senses a general core of fact here. Conrad probably was accused and probably did manage to avert John's punishment, perhaps even to gain his favor.

Since John was elected minister general in the spring of 1296 and Olivi wrote his letter in September 1295, the invidious brothers had not yet lodged their charges against Conrad by the time he wrote. Nevertheless, there is still something to be gained from comparing the charges—and what little else is known of Conrad—with what Olivi says in his letter. Some of it fits. Obviously Conrad, like a series of other Italian brothers including Angelo and Ubertino da Casale, thought current problems could be settled by splitting the order, a notion Olivi considered well beyond the pale.

Other things might fit. One rather assumes that Conrad shared the veneration of Francis's testament which was so widespread among Italian zealots; yet even if he did, it is hard to judge how he might have differed from Olivi on the matter. Ubertino da Casale appealed to the testament at the Council of Vienne, constantly emphasizing that Francis's intention as seen in that document must be the touchstone in determining how the rule should be interpreted. Nevertheless, Ubertino stated this view in terms which he claimed were perfectly consistent with *Quo elongati.* They were, in fact, oddly similar to Olivi's words in his letter to Conrad. Ubertino agreed that Franciscans were not bound to observe the testament, since by human law Francis had renounced authority earlier; yet it was true nonetheless that in the testament "he wished to explain to us, in the manner of a precept, what he meant to say in the rule, a meaning given to him by the Holy Spirit and asserted by him with certainty to be the will of the Lord." Thus Ubertino deferred to the pope in denying the testament one sort of authority, yet simultaneously granted it another, higher sort.[44] One wonders how Olivi would have reacted if asked to comment on Ubertino's formulation. French and Italian spiritual leaders did view the testament differently, but that difference proved hard to formulate.

In some very central ways, however, what we hear of Conrad does not seem to fit Olivi's strictures at all. Angelo says Conrad's enemies accused him of saying that "neither the declarations nor the rule were being observed." Although one could say this much and still consider the declarations to be an unfortunate dilution of the rule—Ubertino would say both at Vienne[45]—it still seems unlikely that Conrad's assailants could have accused him of saying only this when he was in fact proclaiming that the popes had deposed themselves by issuing declarations and that all who remained obedient to them were heretics separate from the true church.

Nor, for the same reason, does it seem likely that Olivi is obliquely referring to Conrad when he castigates those who deny the legitimacy of Celestine's resignation and thus of Boniface's election. Granting that Conrad may have thought or even said as much, it is hard to believe that his views were so public as to have been known to Olivi in France by late 1295. If they had been, certainly his enemies would have told the minister general about it, and it would have taken more than a few humble, simple words on Conrad's part to clear him. Thus, if we can give any credence to Angelo's story, Olivi probably did not think he was describing Conrad.

Could he have been criticizing Angelo Clareno himself, or—more precisely—Angelo, Liberato, and the other founding fathers of the Poor Hermits of Pope Celestine? They fled to Greece sometime after Boniface became pope and, within days after his consecration, canceled the Celestinian decree on which their legitimacy rested. It is hard to tell what this group was doing or saying in September 1295. Perhaps they were already gone from Italy. A more or less contemporary source says they did not go until 1300, but Angelo's narrative gives the impression that they must have departed at least three years earlier, perhaps more.[46] They were in legal limbo by the end of 1294, and it is unlikely that the order delayed long before attempting to retrieve them. Indeed, according to Angelo it was already trying to do so during Celestine's pontificate, and his resignation convinced Liberato, leader of the Poor Hermits, that they should "retreat to remote and secluded places in order to achieve greater peace and safety."[47] Thus it is at least possible that Olivi could have heard of their departure by September 1295.

The real problem is whether Angelo and friends could have said everything Olivi reports in his letter. Angelo's reminiscences offer little evidence, but what they do say does not encourage such a view. Certainly he accepted separation from the order. He also emphasized the obligation to observe Francis's testament along with his rule.[48] Did he also deny the legitimacy of Boniface's election? Angelo complains that his enemies turned Boniface against him and his colleagues by saying as much,[49] but Angelo himself constantly denies this charge. Some modern scholars take Olivi's letter as evidence that it was Angelo who was prevaricating, but that argument seems to assume precisely what most needs proof, namely that it is Angelo whom Olivi is describing.

The papal bull condemning Angelo's group, *Saepe sacram ecclesiam*, was addressed to the patriarch of Constantinople and the bishops of Athens and Patras. Angelo reports that the two bishops refused to take action and the patriarch did nothing until he had returned from Venice. In the meantime, the intended targets knew they were the subjects of an unpleasant papal communication and patiently awaited its delivery so that they could obey it. Unfortunately, they found that the temporal rulers wanted them out of their territories immediately. The rest of the story is long and tortuous, but the upshot is that, according to Angelo, his group did not openly defy the papal condemnation because they never received it.[50]

Raymond of Fronsac, writing around 1318, possessed both *Saepe sacram ecclesiam* and the patriarch of Constantinople's resultant letter executing the pope's commands.[51] We have neither. We do not even know when the bull was written, although a letter of January 11, 1300, mentions it and Peter, the patriarch of Constantinople who executed the pope's commands, died in 1301.[52]

On the other hand, both the *Historia* and Angelo's earlier letter to John XXII suggest a substantial delay between the group's arrival in Greece and Boniface's action against them. He pictures them as settling in and building a reputation for holiness. Two years after their arrival that reputation so inflamed the Franciscans with jealousy that the latter tried to undermine their reputation, appealing first to the secular and ecclesiastical rulers of Greece and then to Boniface VIII.[53] Although it is hard to believe that the Franciscans were motivated solely by jealousy—after all, they had been after the Anconan zealots for some time—there is reason to accept the notion of a delay. It is likely that they did not go to the pope until John of Murrovalle became minister general in the spring of 1296. Angelo observes that John's predecessor, Raymond Geoffroi, had encouraged the spirituals to petition Celestine V, but in John their opponents "had a willing promotor of all they requested."[54] Angelo's suggestion of a two-year interval would then be close to the truth.

All this is intriguing in light of George Digard's identification of *Saepe sacram ecclesiam* with an extant document dated August 1, 1296, and written *ad perpetuam rei memoriam*.[55] If he is correct, then Boniface certainly thought the worst of Angelo's group, for this document speaks of heretics, some of them apostates from approved orders, who say they have the power to loose and bind, denying that power to the institutional church. It also accuses these heretics of preaching without authority, saying they can confer the Holy Spirit by laying on hands, saying that manual labor is forbidden, and thinking it more effective to pray naked.

Ehrle, on the other hand, thinks *Saepe sacram ecclesiam* resembled the bull *Firma cautela*, sent September 26, 1296, to bishops, archbishops, and other ecclesiastics. In it Boniface recalls that his predecessor, Honorius IV, realizing that a flood of undisciplined new groups could harm the church, ordered those seeking the religious life to join an established order. He has heard, however, that this advice is being ignored by a group which includes some apostates from approved orders. These people wander about as *girovagi*, having no stable residence, and wear clothes suggesting that they belong to an order. Others claim to be faithful members of the established church and to practice the eremitical life but are actually spreading heresy. In effect, Boniface wants his subordinates to look closely at hermits. Those whose conduct seems innocent may continue, but they should be forbidden to hear confessions or preach without proper authority. Those who seem suspect should be told to stop wearing a religious habit and entirely desist from preaching or hearing confessions. Boniface complements this letter with another to inquisitors telling them to prod any prelates who do not carry out his instructions and report them to Rome if they do not mend their ways.[56]

Firma cautela is similar to another letter which Boniface directed to the inquisitor Matthew of Chieti on May 7, 1297.[57] It tells the inquisitor to proceed against a group in the Abruzzi and Marches, and describes the offenders in almost the same terms used by *Firma cautela*. Both speak of "some apostates from diverse orders, along with some who have professed no approved orders, calling themselves 'Bizochi' or some other name." Both letters say the offenders are violating the prohibition of such groups by previous popes and spreading diverse heresies, although neither identifies the heresies.

Two other documents deserve at least brief mention. On July 7, 1297, Boniface wrote to the Franciscans at Besançon, who had petitioned to him complaining that apostate Franciscans were flocking to the *locus Sancti Pauli* there, a place of sanctuary since ancient times. Boniface solved their problem by exempting the runaway friars from the law of sanctuary.[58] We also have a letter from Charles II, king of Naples, to Isabelle Villehardouin.[59] Written on January 11, 1300, it alludes to *Saepe sacram ecclesiam*, saying that it is directed against certain people who wear "the habit of religion or of *bizochi* but belong to no approved order." Some mendaciously claim to observe the Franciscan rule yet do not live in obedience to the Franciscan leaders.

Finally, there is Angelo's important letter to John XXII, written in 1317 after the pope had belatedly applied *Saepe sacram ecclesiam* and imprisoned him.[60] In it, Angelo seems to embark on a point-by-point refutation of charges made in *Saepe sacram ecclesiam*. He assures the pope that he and his associates are not apostates, heretics, or excommunicates "unless it is a heresy worthy of excommunication to believe and confess . . . what Saint Francis believed and confessed concerning the observance of his rule." As for "the other things contained in the letters of Pope Boniface, that of Peter, patriarch of Constantinople, and the brothers' petition against me and my group," they are all false. Oddly enough, the first of these "other things" Angelo denies is that they observe the rule of the brothers minor. They are, he says, poor hermits living according to the concession granted by Pope Celestine. Bewildering as this denial may seem—particularly since Angelo has just elected to stand with Saint Francis on the rule—it probably makes sense. Angelo is really denying the charge that his group attempts to gain legitimacy by feigning some vague connection with the Franciscan rule and order, a charge we have seen reflected in papal letters.

Angelo then rejects the charge that they have constructed residences, insisting instead that they live like pilgrims and paupers in other people's buildings. He also denies that they would ever dream of preaching or hearing confessions unless ordered to do so by ecclesiastical authority. Then he vigorously rejects a series of charges which he runs together into a single accusation: "that papal authority has vanished; that Pope Boniface is not really pope; that authority has long since fled from the church and resides in us until such time as the church is reformed; that only we and those who have the Spirit like us are true priests, while those who receive ecclesiastical ordination are not; and that the eastern church is better than the western." Angelo protests that he would refuse to believe such things "even if I heard them announced by angels or apostles, complete with miracles, nor was I ever so flighty or stupid that I would even consent to listen." In fact, he says, he always has asserted the opposite.

These documents show that the pope was worried about unauthorized groups that dressed and behaved like approved orders. Some contained both laymen and renegades from established orders, mainly the Franciscan order. Some still claimed an attachment to the Franciscan rule. Some were acting not only like regulars but like priests as well, and some felt that they were the only priests left, power having departed from the pope and his hierarchy. Some, cut loose from ecclesiastical control, had drifted deeper into heresy. A few had progressed beyond mere heresy to the genuinely bizarre.

Olivi and Boniface viewed the world from different perspectives and were dependent on secondhand information derived from different sources. Although both received much of their information from Franciscans, it is hard to imagine that the brothers whom Angelo describes as poisoning Boniface's mind were the same ones who corresponded with Olivi. Nevertheless, pope and friar both seem to be incensed at the same phenomenon. By combining Olivi's letter, the various papal bulls, and reflections of *Saepe sacram ecclesiam* in the letters of Angelo and Charles II, we can produce something resembling the composite portrait derived by police artists from the descriptions of several witnesses. Does that composite portrait bear any resemblance to Angelo Clareno?

Some features do remind one of Angelo, but others do not. His group was currently unauthorized, yet it acted like an order. It combined adherence to the Franciscan rule with independence from the Franciscan hierarchy. These were charges Angelo found himself dodging rather than refuting. The rest he rejected forthrightly, and there is no evidence that he was lying. There is, indeed, some evidence to support his denials. It is in his letters, which unfortunately date only from the Council of Vienne on. They show a remarkable tendency to accept papal authority in theory while ignoring it in practice. When a group of Tuscan spirituals defied the Franciscan leadership in 1312 and elected its own chain of command from minister general down, Angelo was aghast and delivered a long epistolary lecture on the centrality of obedience.[61] When John XXII and Franciscan leaders fell out in the 1320s, Angelo advised his correspondents to stay out of the battle. Over and over he emphasized his acquiescence in the hierarchical system and his allegiance to its leader, the pope. Even as he said these things, however, he continued to ignore a whole series of papal decisions ordering him and all Franciscans to submit to their superiors. He hid behind a long-abrogated privilege from a four-month pope, a provisional absolution from excommunication once granted by John of Murrovalle's vicar in the east, and the patronage of great men such as James Colonna and the abbot of Subiaco. His Italian followers derived a degree of protection from bishops, abbots, and sheer inaccessibility.

The general impression one receives from Angelo's letters is that he believed strongly in obedience to duly constituted authority. He found this conviction not only prudent but theologically compelling, since he identified obedience with humility, charity, and doctrinal orthodoxy. He also thought himself bound to observe the rule and testament. Unfortunately, these two goals proved mutually exclusive. Angelo chose to solve the problem by ignoring it or at least avoiding reference to it. Lydia von Auw accuses him of illogicality, and she is probably correct;[62] yet one suspects that Angelo's particular brand of illogicality reflects not opportunism or stupidity but life itself. That is another matter, however.

As for other salient features in the composite portrait, there is no evidence that Angelo's veneration for the testament led him to believe that Gregory IX, Nicholas III, and those who obeyed them were heretics. Nor is there reason to think that he felt authority had departed from the ecclesiastical hierarchy or saw exodus from carnal church and order as a religious duty. He must have found the events of December 1294 very disappointing. It would be understandable if he had entertained doubts concerning Boniface's legitimacy and even expressed those doubts; yet it is hard to imagine him actively campaigning against Boniface. The point is not simply that we lack positive evidence for such beliefs but that they seem quite incompatible with Angelo's mentality as revealed his voluminous correspondence. To accept his belief in such things would be equivalent to postulating that he underwent a major transformation between the 1290s and the Council of Vienne.

Of course, Angelo was not the entire group, nor was he even the leader until Liberato's death around 1307. Little is known of Liberato, but what Angelo says about him, coupled with the fact of their close association, suggests that his views on such matters could not have been strikingly different from Angelo's. Moreover, their flock seems to have been small and bound more by conviction than by juridical ties. Thus, though it is not impossible that some members of their immediate circle held the views condemned by Boniface and Olivi, it does seem unlikely.

Did Boniface and Olivi at least think they were describing Angelo and his group? Here the key document seems to be Angelo's letter to John XXII. It shows that *Saepe sacram ecclesiam* did contain many of these charges. Thus it seems that the group was at least included in the attack. Nevertheless, Boniface's letters show that the problem was not confined to Angelo's flock in Greece. Other renegade Franciscans were running in other directions. Thus many of the charges, though not true of Angelo and his companions in Greece, might fit others. They might even fit persons originally included in the Celestinian disposition who took different paths after December 1294, although such people are hard to identify. Jacopone da Todi is worth mentioning, since he, like Conrad of Offida, was one of those by whose council the Italian zealots petitioned Celestine V. Unlike Conrad, he actively opposed Boniface VIII. Jacopone described Boniface as "a new Lucifer," accused him of "either heresy or despair," and signed the Longhezza manifesto.[63] Of course, the manifesto questioned only the legitimacy of Boniface's election, not that of the papacy itself, let alone the entire institutional church. Nevertheless, in some lauds Jacopone denounces the church of his time (including his own order) in terms straight out of the Apocalypse, lamenting that "the members of Antichrist call themselves the church."[64] It is difficult to say what Jacopone thought or even what he did during the 1290s, but he does come closer than Conrad and Angelo to fitting the composite.

Others probably fit it even more closely. The spirituals at their most organized were a loose coalition of like-minded individuals. When our focus narrows to Italy or even to a single community in Ancona, the coherence increases but never displays that tight structure considered *de rigueur* by leaders of the order.[65] It is easy to see how different views and even outright heresies could germinate in such an environment, particularly after Boniface destroyed the legal basis of the Poor Hermits and they became fugitives from Franciscan and papal discipline. From that point on they were free to splinter into sects and encouraged to believe the worst about established authority.

Reversal

Olivi's letter to Conrad of Offida seems to have been his last appearance in the lists, though not the end of his literary career.[66] He died at Narbonne on March 14, 1298, and was laid to rest in the choir of the Franciscan church there.[67] Though execrated by some, he was revered by others, and his tomb soon became a pilgrimage site. Angelo Clareno says that on the anniversary of his death the crowds rivaled those at the Portiuncula.[68] Another source announces that the pilgrims included not only laymen but cardinals, bishops, and other church leaders.[69] Olivi's writings circulated not only in the original Latin but in translation as well.[70]

At that very moment, however, those who opposed his views were ready to launch a counteroffensive. The groundwork had been laid somewhat earler. Boniface VIII had become pope in December 1294 following Celestine V's "great refusal." In October 1295 Boniface had removed Raymond Geoffroi from the office of minister general. In May 1296 John of Murrovalle had succeeded Raymond. By the fall of 1297 Arnold of Roquefeuil was again provincial minister in southern France, probably replacing Bertrand of Sigotier.[71] Thus there was a whole new cast of characters by Olivi's death in March 1298. Perhaps he died just in time.

John's election might suggest that sentiment was swinging away from the rigorist position; yet the truth may be more complex. The election took place at Anagni under the pope's watchful eye.[72] The legitimacy of Celestine's resignation was already being challenged by Italian Franciscans and Boniface would naturally welcome a minister general who was willing to control his order. There is no reason to assume that the pope wanted John in office just to harass the spirituals, however. John was an old acquaintance who had proved useful to Boniface long before he became supreme pontiff and who would serve him well thereafter.[73] Boniface made him a cardinal in 1302. It is natural that he should have wanted to replace Raymond Geoffroi with a man he could rely on, particularly since the French connection, which made Raymond attractive to the electors in 1289, would have made him decidedly less so to Boniface in 1295. Moreover, one should not hastily grant that John's election caused rejoicing among the laxer brethren.

Olivi's admirers from Languedoc to the Marches of Ancona soon felt the weight of the new regime, and Olivi himself was not spared. At the general chapter meeting of 1299, his teachings were condemned and those who used his books were excommunicated.[74] This legislation was followed by a series of letters from the minister general ordering that "the sect of Brother Peter John" be broken up, his apparently recalcitrant disciples punished or dispersed, and his writings collected and burned.[75] Visitors were dispatched to the province of Provence to carry out the purge. One of them, the provincial minister of Aragon, was commissioned to draw up a form of abjuration to be forced on all the brothers in the entire province. Those who ascribed to it were forgiven for past offenses. Those who did not were severely punished.[76] Boniface VIII lent even more manpower to the hunt by sending the minister of the province of Genoa to southern France. He conducted an investigation leading to such extensive results that "a great book was made of the punishments and errors involved."[77]

These punishments seem to have been well worth avoiding. Both Ubertino da Casale and Angelo Clareno refer to the case of one Pons Bautugat, who was incarcerated for saying that, although he had no writings by Olivi, even if he had any he would refuse to hand them over to the order, although he would surrender them to the pope for correction. According to Angelo, Pons remained so tightly fettered in prison that he sat ill in his own urine and excrement until he died. When they removed him, they discovered that his body was largely eaten away by worms.[78] Mention of Pons by both Ubertino and Angelo suggests that his case was something of a cause célèbre and thus hardly the norm, but it does not take many cases like his to establish that the persecution was a savage one.

Arnold ceased to be provincial minister sometime between late 1300 and early 1304, Boniface to be pope in 1303, and John to be minister general in 1304; yet none of these changes brought relief to the beleaguered spirituals. The persecution had attained a momentum that would carry it almost through the first decade of the fourteenth century. It abated only in 1309, when the spirituals' lay supporters managed to convince Pope Clement V that intervention was necessary. He summoned spokesmen for both sides, thus initiating a new phase in the controversy.[79]

What did this attack on the spirituals have to do with *usus pauper*? According to Ubertino, a provincial chapter meeting in southern France under Arnold of Roquefeuil's successor, Elzéar of Clermont, wrote to John asking why the campaign against Olivi's followers was taking place. John replied, "All those who dare to assert that *usus pauper* is a substantial part of our vow of poverty should be judged superstitious holders of a pernicious doctrine."[80]

It is impossible to say whether this was the only Olivian view criticized in John's letter, since Ubertino is attempting to establish the centrality of *usus pauper* in the repeated attacks against Olivi and it suits his purpose to cite only this issue. Other issues were involved in the persecution, however, as is clear from Raymond of Fronsac's reference to the form of abjuration forced on all brothers throughout the province. It seems that John of Murrovalle commissioned the provincial minister of Aragon to draw up a document stating what was be held on three topics: *usus pauper*, the wound in Christ's side, and veneration of those who had not been officially canonized.[81] The second item refers to an Olivian view that would receive close attention from that moment on, his suggestion that, despite the apparent announcement of scripture to the contrary, Christ's death came after he was wounded by the spear.[82] The third is obviously directed at the growing Olivi cult.[83]

Thus *usus pauper* was not the only issue by this time, but it was obviously an important one. Perhaps it was the central one. Ubertino certainly thought so, and his view receives at least some confirmation from Arnold of Villanova. In a 1304 letter to Pope Benedict XII, Arnold protested that those Franciscans who attacked notable laxity, asserting that the life of Christ and his apostles should be observed and that *usus pauper* pertained to the substance of the rule, were being oppressed by their superiors and subjected to barbarous punishment.[84]

If *usus pauper* was an important issue, can we conclude that John of Murrovalle was an apostle of relaxation? Here we encounter what may seem at first a strange paradox. John's predecessor, Raymond, displayed his spiritual sympathies, not only by rescuing Angelo Clareno and his friends while minister general but by defending the spirituals later at Vienne. John, in the meantime, was moving steadily up the institutional ladder: bachelor and then master of theology at Paris (through papal intervention),[85] lector at the papal curia, minister general, and finally cardinal-bishop, a position he held for the last decade of his life. Along the way his activities marked him as an opponent of the very tendencies Raymond protected. He sat on the commission that censured the living Olivi, then orchestrated an attack on the dead Olivi's teachings and supporters.

Knowing this much, one might feel justified in assuming that John must have dedicated his generalate to the reversal of Raymond's reforms; yet the evidence points in a different direction. Legislation from Raymond's generalate does not suggest any move toward greater rigor, but a substantial body of evidence from the opening decade of the fourteenth century, when John was first minister general and then cardinal protector, shows a tightening of discipline. In fairness to Raymond we must remember that during the first three years of his generalate, which included the critical Paris chapter of 1292, he worked under the shadow of a Franciscan pope, Nicholas IV. This situation may have inhibited him from any significant action. A glance at Nicholas's correspondence suggests that his idea of helping the order was to heap indulgences on its churches, liberate it from episcopal jurisdiction, and support it in its quarrels with outsiders. In his legislation regarding the Franciscans he is distinguished from Boniface VIII by the degree of his favoritism toward the order, not by any superior sensitivity to its original aims.[86]

It is John and not Raymond, however, with whom we are most concerned at the moment. In his 1302 letter he noted that, "as if the Lord's hand had been shortened so that he could not provide for his poor," some houses were warding off uncertainty by receiving income from fields, houses, vineyards, and annual pensions. He forbade these practices and ordered convents to divest themselves of their present holdings "if it can be done."[87]

Even spiritual leaders at the Council of Vienne offered at least reluctant witness to John's reform measures. Ubertino da Casale granted that John had tried to do something about Franciscans returning to their home-towns and creating an enclave. Raymond Geoffroi acknowledged that there had been some improvement in the handling of legacies.[88]

Gonsalvo of Spain, John's successor as minister general, seems to have shared his desire for reform. In 1304, at the Assisi general chapter, he commanded the brothers to get rid of all wine-producing vineyards.[89] The same chapter announced that ministers could absolve from the sentence of excommunication incurred by transgressing the constitutions concerning perpetual incomes. This statement might seem evidence of relaxation, but it could just as easily be seen as part of a campaign to end the particular abuse in question.

In 1307 the general chapter of Toulouse revoked all special arrangements giving individual brothers a claim to books after the holder's death. It also tried to stop Franciscans from returning home and dominating their own native territories.[90] In 1310 Gonsalvo wrote to provincial ministers ordering them to end all arrangements whereby any convent or individual brother received an annual income in return for fulfilling some obligation, and to be quick about it if they wanted to avoid visitors.[91] Other sources show that visitors were already being employed effectively at least two years before that date.[92]

If all this activity had taken place in 1310, one might be tempted to see it as an attempt to steal the march on the spirituals, who by that time had launched a rather successful publicity campaign in the papal court. As things stand, however, it seems just as likely that throughout the decade John of Murrovalle and Gonsalvo of Spain were genuinely concerned about ridding the order of precisely those abuses seen earlier in the Bolognese wills. If so, then was their attack on *usus pauper* actually an assault not on its practice but on Olivi's discussion of its theoretical basis? Did poor Pons Bautugat rot away in prison for *that*? One gathers—in fact one hopes—that there was a bit more involved. What, then, did people find objectionable about Olivi's view?

Notes

1. *Historia septem tribulationum*, 291f. According to a Fraticelli chronicle in MS Florence Bibl. Naz. (Magliab.) XXXIV 76, 97v, they all died on the spot.
2. Raymundus de Fronciacho, *Sol ortus*, 14.
3. Callebaut, "Acta capituli generalis Mediolani," 289.
4. *Chronica XXIV generalium*, 382.
5. *Historia septem tribulationum*, 295ff.
6. *Chronica XXIV generalium*, 382.
7. Ubertino da Casale, *Sanctitati apostolicae*, in *Archiv*, 2:387.
8. He had written the letter to R from there, although the 1285 *apologia* was written at Nîmes.
9. Ubertino da Casale, *Sanctitati apostolicae*, 389, says he continued to teach without further censure until his death.
10. Péano, "Raymond Geoffroi," 190–203, furnishes biographical details.
11. *Chronica XXIV generalium*, 419.
12. Péano, "Raymond Geoffroi," 194f. Raymond's connection with the Angevins continued after his removal from office. An intimate of St. Louis of Toulouse, Raymond was designated as one of his executors and was holding Louis's hand when the latter died.
13. Angelo says as much in *Historia septem tribulationum*, 308 and in his *epistola excusatoria* to John XXII in *Epistole*, 243.
14. *Chronica XXIV generalium*, 420–22. There is no adequate history of how the term *spiritual* developed within the order, but see Stanislao da Campagnola, "Dai 'viri spirituales' di Gioacchino da Fiore ai 'fratres spirituales' di Francesco d'Assisi," *Picenum seraphicum* 11 (1974): 24–52. The central problem is how to balance the influence of Joachite apocalyptic, in which an *ecclesia spiritualis* governed by *viri spirituales* triumphs in the age of the Holy Spirit, with the influence of traditional Franciscan usage dating back to Francis's own time as seen, for example, in *Regula*, c. 10, which instructs those brothers who find they cannot observe the rule *spiritualiter*. See also *Scripta Leonis*, 94, 96, 110, 142.
15. The *Chronica* simply says who carried out the investigation. His status is given in other documents. See Raymundus de Fronciacho and Bonaventura de Bergamo, *Infrascripta dant*, 157; BF, 4:139. According to Raymundus de Fronciacho, *Sol ortus*, 15, twenty-nine friars were disciplined. On the inquisitor, Bertrand de Sigotier, and his connection with Raymond Geoffroi, see Pierre Péano's articles, "Ministres provinciaux de Provence et spirituels," 50; "Raymond Geoffroi," 194–99; "Ministres provinciaux de la primitive province de Provence," 31–33.
16. For support of the version found in the *Chronica* see L. Amorós, "Series condemnationum," 504; Ubertino da Casale, *Sanctitati apostolicae*, 389. Raymundus de Fronciacho, *Sol ortus*, 14f., says that one of the pope's letters attacked Olivi personally, but that claim is refuted by Ubertino, *Sanctitati apostolicae*, 389. Raymond, in fact, says the pope did so "in general terms." Raymond also says that Olivi was forced to recant his view of *usus pauper*, but this claim probably rests on a questionable interpre-

tation of the Paris confession. Raymundus de Fronciacho and Bonagratia de Bergamo, *Infrascripta dant*, 157, say that Nicholas IV punished Olivi on this occasion, but their assertion is unsubstantiated by any other source and is openly disputed by Ubertino, *Declaratio*, in *Archiv*, 3:192.

17. *Epistola ad regis Sicilie filios*, in *Archiv*, 3:534–40.

18. There are two extant manuscripts: MS Florence, Bibl. Laur. S. Croce Plut. 31 sin. cod. 3, 175ra–rb, published by Albanus Heysse, "Descriptio codicis bibliothecae Laurentianae Florentinae, S. Crucis plut. 31 sin. cod. 3," *AFH* 11 (1918): 267–69; and MS Pistoia, Fort. D298, 253v–255v. In both it is prefaced by an abridged version of the account of Olivi's death reported by Bernardus Guidonis, *Practica inquisitionis heretice pravitatis* (Paris, 1886), 287, as frequently read in Beguin circles. Wadding, *Annales*, 5:378–81, gives essentially the same confession (with extensive differences in wording) but does not link it with an account of Olivi's death. Ubertino da Casale, *Sanctitati apostolicae*, 411, quotes part of it. The Florence MS and Ubertino say "Martin," Wadding says "Boniface," and the Pistoia MS leaves a blank space (suggesting the copyist encountered a blank in his exemplar or saw something that made no sense to him).

19. Some scholars, seduced by Ubertino, assume that it was part of his 1285 *apologia* to the Parisian commission. Ubertino actually says that Olivi's allegiance to the papacy is seen "in a certain confession which he made . . . ; and it is in the declarations, from which they claim to have drawn many errors." By "the declarations" he does mean the 1285 *apologia*, since *Responsio* II, 131f. contains a passage similar to the one Ubertino quotes from the confession. Ubertino is saying that Olivi stated his allegiance in both documents.

20. Perhaps, as Heysse suggests, the confusion was caused by Ubertino, who quotes the excerpt immediately after announcing that Olivi, at his death, submitted all his works to the pope for correction. *Chronica XXIV generalium*, 498, supports the claim that Olivi submitted his works to the pope for correction at the time of his death.

21. *Sanctitati apostolicae*, 400–402. The same confession is found, either wholly or in part, in five of the seven extant manuscripts of the *Tractatus*, but in such a way as to suggest that it is a later addition. Omitted in the most trustworthy manuscript, it appears at the end of c. 6 in three others and at the end of c. 7 in two; yet only one manuscript contains the entire text given by Ubertino. The *Chronica XXIV generalium*, 421f., gives what amounts to a paraphrase of the last few lines of the longer text found in Ubertino and the single manuscript of the *Tractatus*. Raymundus de Fronciacho, *Sol ortus*, 15, seems to refer to the 1292 confession when he says that Olivi recanted his view of *usus pauper*.

22. The difference between the Ubertino and *Chronicle* citations is no greater than that between the Wadding and early manuscript versions of the first confession. In each case, substantially the same points are made in different language.

23. It is so labeled in MS Pistoia, Fort. D298, 251v. Another manuscript, Florence, Bibl. Laur. S. Crucis Plut. 31 sin. cod. 3, 174vb, simply says it was

given "in general chapter." The text of the latter manuscript is published in Heysse, "Descriptio codicis," 264–67.

24. The problem cannot be solved by concluding that Ubertino and the *Chronicle of the Twenty-four Generals* give us varying reports of the 1292 confession and that the other confession was given in 1287. According to Ubertino and the *Chronicle*, substantially the same confession was delivered in 1287 and 1292; yet the confession given by Ubertino and the *Chronicle* differs sharply from this one in content as well as wording.

25. Flood, *Olivi's Rule Commentary*, 69.

26. *Expositio quatuor magistrorum*, 94–98.

27. Flood, *Olivi's Rule Commentary*, 163.

28. Ibid., 132.

29. See, for example, his comments on study (ibid., 188) or on Francis's statement that the brothers should be *tanquam peregrini* (pp. 164f.).

30. Ibid., 124, 130f., 142f., 148.

31. Ibid., 131. He is citing *Qq. de perf. evang.*, q. 14.

32. Ibid., 143.

33. Ibid., 119f.

34. *Epistola ad Conradum de Offida*, in Livarius Oliger, "Petri Iohannis Olivi de renuntiatione papae Coelestini V quaestio et epistola," *AFH* 11 (1918): 309–73 (letter on pp. 366–73).

35. For an excellent recent discussion see Peter Herde, *Cölestin V* (Stuttgart, 1981).

36. George Peck, *The Fool of God* (University, Ala., 1980), 116.

37. See note 34 for edition.

38. See, for example, Oliger's comment in his introduction to the letter, "Petri Iohannis Olivi de renuntiatione papae Coelestini V," 335: "Quis non mirabitur Olivi sic loquentem et Spirituales durioribus verbis increpantem? Nonne ipse similia et peiora etaim suis scriptis disseminavit?"

39. Ehrle, "Petrus Johannis Olivi," 438.

40. *Angelo Clareno*, 48f. Auw also suggests that in writing the letter "Olivi meant to free himself from all responsibility in the Italian spirituals' affair and avoid new difficulties."

41. See Chapter 2, note 7 above.

42. Angelo Clareno, *Historia septem tribulationum*, 308.

43. Ibid., 312.

44. *Sanctitas vestra*, in *Archiv*, 3:53, 71, 74, 76.

45. *Sanctitas vestra*, 67, 69; *Rotulus*, in *Archiv*, 3:105.

46. Auw, *Angelo Clareno*, 46, is correct on this point, although Paul of Venice's reference to Sicily as point of embarkation should at least be considered, even if his date should not. See Decima Douie, *The Nature and the Effect of the Heresy of the Fraticelli* (Manchester, 1932), 56.

47. *Epistole*, 245 and *Historia septem tribulationum*, 309f. say the Franciscans sent an armed posse to capture them as soon as they heard that Celestine had absolved them from obedience. Angelo's status as our major source for the group will necessitate referring to it as "Angelo's group" in the following discussion, although he was not leader of it until ca. 1307.

48. In his letters he routinely speaks of "rule and testament," seldom mentioning one without the other.

49. *Epistole*, 246; *Historia septem tribulationum*, 316.

50. *Epistole*, 246–48; *Historia septem tribulationum*, 316f.

51. *Sol ortus*, 12f.

52. The letter is published in Ehrle, "Die Spiritualen," *Archiv*, 2:335f. Angelo, *Historia septem tribulationum*, 315, says, "Habebant tunc fratres dominum Johannem de Murro sancte romane ecclesie cardinalem, qui eorum minister generalis extiterat, spontaneum promotorem omnium, que petebant;" yet John did not become a cardinal until December 1302. Perhaps Angelo simply means that the brothers had a willing helper in John, who had been minister general before becoming a cardinal.

53. *Historia septem tribulationum*, 316; *Epistole*, 246. Boniface's immediate response—"Leave them alone, they're doing better than you are"— implies no prior knowledge of their exploits in Greece, since the preceding sentence in both narratives says the complainants began by informing Boniface of the group's existence. The whole anecdote, one of several used by Angelo to suggest a continuing trend in papal-spiritual relations, must be regarded with caution.

54. *Epistole*, 243, and *Historia septem tribulationum*, 308, for the remark about Raymond; *Historia septem tribulationum*, 315 (quoted in note 52) for the one about John.

55. George Digard, *Philip le bel et le Saint-Siège de 1285 à 1304* (Paris, 1936), 1:240f. The bull is in *BF*, 4:409f.

56. Both letters are in *Archiv*, 2:155–58.

57. *BF*, 4:435f.

58. *BF*, 4:440, written two days before another in which Boniface instructed inquisitors to proceed against the Colonna and their families. The Longhezza manifesto had been published and the Colonna excommunicated two months earlier. See Boase, *Boniface VIII*, ch. 6, and Herde, *Cölestin V*, 161–70.

59. See note 52. On Isabelle see Auw, *Angelo Clareno*, 57f.

60. Published in *Archiv*, 1:521–33 and *Epistole*, 236–53.

61. *Epistole*, 121–31, which suggests that the group was claiming Olivi as an authority. In *Epistole*, 280, written when some of them were wandering as fugitives, Angelo is critical and yet advises his followers to shelter them.

62. Angelo Clareno, *Epistole*, 124, note 3. Auw is actually criticizing Angelo's stand on the Tuscan rebels, which she sees as inspired by opportunism.

63. *Laude*, lauda 83. The Longhezza manifesto is published by Heinrich Denifle, "Die Denkschriften der Colonna gegen Bonifaz VIII," *Archiv*, 5:509–15. For a recent biography of Jacopone see Peck, *Fool of God*.

64. See especially *laude* 6, 8, 29, 36. Jacopone describes himself as a *bizocone*, but he is apparently alluding to a phase that ended with his entrance into the Franciscan order two decades earlier. On the significance of the word see Auw, *Angelo Clareno*, 47.

65. See Gentile da Foligno's letter describing Anconan organization in the 1320s, published in Angelo Clareno, *Epistole*, 359, and Auw's comment in *Epistole*, 354.

66. *Rev.*, 84ra, seems to place that part of the work in the year 1297, and Olivi may have worked on other projects up to the time of his death.
67. Bernardus Guidonis, *Practica inquisitionis*, 287.
68. *Epistole*, 175.
69. Ehrle, "Petrus Johannis Olivi," 443, citing MS Vat. Borgh. 85, 102r–v.
70. Manselli, *Spirituali e beghini in Provenza* (Rome, 1959), 36ff.
71. Péano, "Ministres provinciaux de Provence et spirituels," 51.
72. Wadding, *Annales*, 5:348.
73. Boase, *Boniface VIII*, 21f. and 203, discusses the use made of John by Boniface in 1290 when he was still Benedetto Caetani, papal legate, and in 1297 when as pope he was trying to stop English-French hostilities.
74. L. Amorós, "Series condemnationum," 504.
75. Raymundus de Fronciacho, *Sol ortus*, 15f. For fuller treatment of these events see Lambert, *Franciscan Poverty*, ch. 7.
76. *Sol ortus*, 16, which mentions Vitalis de Furno, then a lector at Toulouse, as a participant in the purge.
77. Amorós, "Series condemnationum," 505.
78. Ubertino da Casale, *Sanctitati apostolicae*, 386; Angelo Clareno, *Historia septem tribulationum*, 300.
79. On these events see Lambert, *Franciscan Poverty*, 180–83. John of Murrovalle was succeeded by Gonsalvo of Spain. On Gonsalvus's name and career see Leo Amorós's introduction to Gonsalvus Hispanus, *Quaestiones disputatae et de quodlibet* (Quaracchi, 1935), xiv–xxxvii. John himself became protector of the Franciscans in 1307 and thus continued to exert considerable leverage.
80. *Sanctitati apostolicae*, 385f.
81. *Sol ortus*, 17.
82. See Burr, *Persecution*, 76.
83. On the Olivi cult at Narbonne see also Angelo Clareno, *Epistole*, 175, and *Historia septem tribulationum*, 142; and the 1316 self-defense of Narbonne spirituals in *Archiv*, 3:443, and in Delorme, "Constitutiones provinciae," 415–34. Abate, "Memoriali," *MF* 33 (1933): 30, presents an announcement by the 1307 Toulouse general chapter that, if any uncanonized dead are depicted with crowns or diadems, those crowns or diadems should be removed; yet the following comment that the same should be done with pictures of the trinity suggests a somewhat larger issue, however it may be related to Olivi's posthumous fortunes.
84. In Heinrich Finke, *Aus den Tagen Bonifaz VIII* (Münster i. W., 1902), 3:clxxxvi.
85. See Ernest Langlois, *Les registres de Nicholas IV* (Paris, 1886), 952, 975f., 980. For a summary of John's career see Ephrem Longpré, "L'ouvre scolastique du cardinal Jean de Murro, O.F.M.," in *Mélanges Augustin Pelzer* (Louvain, 1947), 468–70.
86. Nor in the rest of his papal activities did he display any characteristically Franciscan qualities. Otto Schiff, *Papst Nikolaus IV* (Berlin, 1897), sees him as formed by his bourgeois upbringing rather than his Franciscan affiliation. James Ryan, "Nicholas IV and the Evolution of the Eastern Missionary Effort," *Archivum historiae pontificiae* 19 (1981): 79–95, notes

the increasing papal missionary interest during his pontificate, and one might identify this much with his Franciscan roots; yet Ryan also suggests that when political and missionary interests clashed, Nicholas considered the political ones more important. As minister general, Nicholas (then Jerome of Ascoli) had ordered Olivi to burn some writings on the Virgin Mary and probably challenged other works as well. See Angelo, *Historia septem tribulationum*, 288; Olivi, *Responsio* I, 127; Olivi, *Epistola ad R*, 51(63)v and 52(64)r; *Infrascripta dant*, in *Archiv*, 3:13; Ferdinand Delorme, "Notice et extraits d'un manuscrit franciscain," *MF* 15 (1945):86; Amorós, "Series condemnationum," 502. Angelo Clareno, *Historia septem tribulationum*, 288, says that years later, when Olivi's enemies sought Nicholas's support, he praised Olivi, announcing that the writings on the Virgin had been orthodox and their burning merely an exercise in humility. This seems unlikely.

87. Wadding, *Annales*, 3:7f.
88. Ubertino, *Rotulus*, 112; Raymond, *Ad primum*, in *Archiv*, 3:143. Angelo Clareno, *Historia septem tribulationum*, 312–16 reports John's admiration for Conrad of Offida and notes that he appointed Jacobo da Monte, another *vir mirabilis puritatis et sanctitatis*, as his vicar in the east. Arnold of Villanova thought John a great hypocrite, however. See Auw, *Angelo Clareno*, 68, for citations. The 1300 Umbrian statutes would provide additional evidence if Cenci, "Ordinazioni," 8f. were correct in suggesting that John influenced them by his presence at the provincial chapter; yet the evidence is ambiguous.
89. Abate, "Memoriali," *MF* 35 (1935): 238.
90. Abate, "Memoriali," *MF* 33 (1933): 30–32. The latter problem would be discussed in greater detail in the acts of the 1313 Barcelona general chapter and in the 1316 Assisi general statutes. See ibid., 32f. for the 1313 chapter and Armandus Carlini, "Constitutiones generales ordinis fratrum minorum anno 1316 Assisii conditae," *AFH* 4 (1911): 282, for the 1316 statutes.
91. The same letter is in *Chronica fratris Nicolai Glassberger*, in *AF*, 2:117f. and in Wadding, *Annales*, 6:172f., but addressed to the Saxon provincial in the former and the Tuscan provincial in the latter. If Cenci's dating is correct in "Le costituzioni," 513 and 525, such annual incomes had been officially accepted as late as the 1304 Assisi general chapter to provide *suffragii* for a deceased Franciscan bishop. Alvarus Pelagius, *De planctu ecclesiae* (Venice, 1560), 2:75rb, praises Gonsalvo highly.
92. Fussenegger, "Statuta provinciae Alemaniae," 238f. offers a concrete instance. Indirect evidence for reform is available but inconclusive. For example, see A. G. Little and R. C. Easterling, *Franciscans and Dominicans of Exeter* (Exeter, 1927), 27, for the 1307 surrender of yearly rent from a mill.

CHAPTER 6

Some Possible Explanations

Review

Having traced the *usus pauper* controversy from its apparent beginning in 1279 through the outbreak of persecution after Olivi's death, we can now make some generalizations. Before around 1279, there was no *usus pauper* controversy in the theoretical sense. There was a practical problem of how much poverty was enough but no continuing argument as to whether restricted use was part of the vow.

Debate on the latter question probably began around 1279 as a dispute among lectors in southern France. From then until the end of 1282 the opposing sides traded arguments and appealed for aid outside the province. When that aid finally came, it tended to support Olivi's opponents. From 1283 through 1285, Olivi suffered a temporary setback when the commission of seven censured him, his writings were banned, and he was removed from his teaching position. *Usus pauper* was only one of the many issues involved, however, and there was nothing final about the decision. By 1285 (the first time we hear of Olivi as head of a "sect") those in authority were evincing some interest in further investigation of the "Olivi question," which was essentially in limbo from then until 1287.

From 1287 until at least 1295 there was conflict in the order, but no suppression of Olivi's position regarding *usus pauper*. By 1290 the rigorists in southern France had developed a radical wing. It was disciplined in 1292, but Olivi and his stance remained safe. This is the major significance of the confessions extracted from Olivi from 1287 on. They show him cleaving to his position. If he was reinstated in 1287, it was not because the Montpellier general chapter had heard him recant his earlier views on *usus pauper*. If he emerged unscathed from the trouble of 1290–92, it was not because he had backed down at the Paris general chapter.

There is a parallel here with Olivi's stance regarding other problems concerning which he was censured in 1283. For example, he clung tenaciously to his view that marriage was not a sacrament in precisely the same sense as the other six sacraments and in a revision of his work made only minor adjustments to an argument which the commission had described as "heretical."[1] Nevertheless, however resilient his position on marriage may have proved, it presumably did not constitute a public issue as the *usus pauper* problem did. He may have continued to say the same thing about marriage, but he was not asked to repeat it periodically before assembled Franciscan leaders.

In short, the combination of Olivi's confessions and the 1292 censure demonstrates that between 1287 and 1292 *usus pauper* continued to be a central issue; that pope, minister general, and provincial minister thought it necessary to draw a line; and that the line, once drawn, lay to Olivi's left, though not all that far to his left. The climate changed between 1295 and 1297, when new leadership at all levels from pope to provincial minister created an alignment that would eventually allow effective persecution of Olivi's adherents; yet the persecution was not unleashed until 1299, after Olivi's death. The main issue then was *usus pauper*, and Olivi's opinion was considered unacceptable.

Thanks to Olivi, the controversy can be defined from a doctrinal viewpoint. He tells us what each side believed and how it went about defending those beliefs. To be sure, his presentation of his opponents' position must be handled with caution. The danger is not primarily that he is caricaturing their views to make them look ridiculous. Undoubtedly he is presenting their views in somewhat more rebuttable form than they would have preferred, but his portrayal is probably more or less accurate. The more serious danger is that he is in effect homogenizing the opposition, ignoring differences among them and thus ascribing to a single group arguments that would lead to divergent conclusions. All things considered, however, we can be thankful for what we have.

Knowing what they believed and how they defended it is not the same as knowing why they believed it or thought it worth defending. The latter questions cannot be answered simply by repeating the arguments advanced. Certainly the arguments were important, but the *usus pauper* controversy was more than a *disputatio* held by scholars. To understand its meaning for the participants we would have to see its relation to the complex social context out of which it arose. That is admittedly more than can be accomplished here, but a few suggestions are possible.

Common Ground

The problem can be approached on a general and rather obvious level by pointing to what was said in the first chapter about changes within the order. It requires little imagination to envisage the tensions created when Franciscans adapted their own self-understanding to the new situation, because such adaptation did not proceed uniformly through the order. Nevertheless, some adaptation did occur in all quarters. After 1279, the contest was not between the original Franciscan vision and its recent corruption. Olivi did not reject the historical development which had led to the order as he knew it. Indeed, he seldom considered that development except in terms of his apocalyptic theology of history, and one finds little to work with there; yet what he did say suggests that he did not see the order as having strayed dangerously off course simply by receiving prestige and power. In fact, in his Apocalypse commentary, written at the end of his life, he looks forward to a day when the entire church will be ruled by men whose hearts are essentially Franciscan, whatever their organizational affiliation might be.[2]

Less apocalyptic utterances give the same impression. In the *Questions on Evangelical Perfection*, wrestling with the question of what Franciscans should or should not do, Olivi is as notable for what he does not question as for what he rejects. The Franciscan involvement with power is usually taken for granted. Olivi insists that Franciscan bishops are still bound by their vow of *usus pauper*, but he sees nothing anomalous about the existence of Franciscan bishops. This acceptance is occasionally tempered by a suggestion that Franciscan poverty and secular pursuits are incompatible, as when he remarks that law is a valuable area of study for prelates, but friars, who have renounced temporal concerns, should study something less worldly.[3] There is, then, a degree of unresolved tension in Olivi's view, but he never resolves it by suggesting that the order should turn back the clock and avoid ecclesiastical responsibilities.

Olivi's attitude toward scholarship is similar. He accepts without serious demur a Franciscan scholarly enterprise that would have astounded Saint Francis. One could argue that a degree of unresolved tension surfaces here, too, particularly in the letter to R, where he says he has feared "Parisian ambitions" and rejoices in Christ's decision to frustrate the world in its decision to elevate him to the *magisterium*. This is a very ex post facto judgment, however. Olivi is simply seconding a decision already made for him by Christ. Moreover, his words probably reflect his attitude toward the situation at Paris rather than toward learning in general.[4]

The same might be said about Olivi's attitude toward living conditions. Far from wanting the order to emulate those heroic early days at the Porziuncula, he assumes the essential legitimacy of the Franciscan convent as he knows it. He wants nourishing meals, adequate living quarters, and decent study facilities. These should not be excessive, but they should suffice to keep the friars healthy and productive so that they can fulfill the assignments providence has given them.

If the difference between Olivi and his opponents cannot easily be traced to conflicting attitudes toward the historical development of the order, neither can it be correlated with any clear-cut difference as to whether the order should practice *usus pauper*. Olivi insists that *usus pauper* is part of the vow and his opponents insist that it is not; yet when one attempts to explore the practical implications of that difference one finds them hard to delineate. While Olivi feels that the vow constrains Franciscans to use only what is necessary, he begins with a fairly moderate view of necessity, is flexible in allowing for adjustment to individual situations, and considers violation a mortal sin only when it is gross or repeated. Although his opponents deny that the Franciscan is thus limited by his vow, at least some of them acknowledge that the Franciscan life is of little value without *usus pauper* and that excessive use is against the intention of the rule. Thus one might ask whether an ideal convent as envisaged by Olivi would be strikingly different from one proposed by at least one faction among his opponents. Perhaps so, but such is not obvious from the arguments themselves. In short, the theoretical differences do not lead inevitably to practical differences so clear-cut as to seem worth fighting over. Why, then, were the two sides fighting?

Three Unhelpful Explanations

Several possible answers, not all of them mutually exclusive, present themselves. One is that we should never underestimate the charm of pure theory among scholars. If Olivi and his opponents were capable of wrangling over the nature of quantity, they were able to cross swords over *usus pauper* without seeing a single practical implication in the matter. Nevertheless, granting this much, one persists in believing that there was more involved.

Moving to the other end of the spectrum, one might argue that we should take Olivi seriously when he dismisses his opponents' praise of *usus pauper* as nothing more than a public relations ploy. It is at least possible that they were cynically and deliberately masking their betrayal of Franciscan ideals. Such is possible, but we have no reason to consider it probable. On the whole, it is safer to begin with the assumption that Olivi's adversaries were honest in presenting themselves as committed to the Franciscan life, including restricted use.

It is also safer to eschew any attempt at transposing the *usus pauper* battle into a vaguely Marxist key by relating the spirituals with the poor and the conventuals with the emerging urban bourgeoisie. Such an alliance has been suggested,[5] but there seems to be little evidence for it. Indeed, one could just as easily argue that a close relationship existed in Languedoc between the spirituals and the upper middle class.[6] Certainly it is difficult to see any sign in Olivi's writings of a bias toward (or even much interest in) what he would call the "involuntary poor." Moreover, far from feeling out of step with current economic developments, he offers as informed and sympathetic an interpretation of contemporary business practices as one can find among scholastics. A modern economic historian describes him as "one of the really brilliant economic minds of the Middle Ages."[7] Another comments that "no other medieval author before or after Olivi confronted economic argumentation so acutely and with such creative solutions."[8] Olivi's economic views may seem oddly at variance with his personal commitment to poverty or irreconcilable with his apocalyptic expectations, but that probably says more about modern preconceptions than about Olivi's consistency. The subject bears more analysis than it has received. On the whole, his economic writings have been studied by economic historians and his writings on the order by church historians, yet neither group has paid much attention to the other. Pending further conversation, there seems no obvious way of linking the *usus pauper* controversy with general economic developments.[9]

The Commission of Seven: Psychic Insulation

A fourth explanation would view the commission's stance on *usus pauper* as a sincere attempt to reduce the tension between old Franciscan ideals and new Franciscan functions. It is possible that the thing they were most eager to safeguard was not public approval but self-respect. Perhaps the group they most needed to convince of their probity was themselves.

To pursue this line of thought we might look a bit more closely at the only group of Olivi's antagonists about whom anything is known, the seven-man Parisian commission that censured him in 1283. The commission members criticized not only passages concerning *usus pauper* as part of the vow but statements on burial, procurators, and Franciscan bishops as well. Olivi had trouble deciding precisely what they found wrong with his views, and his confusion is understandable. The only statement on *usus pauper* in the *Letter of the Seven Seals* is nothing more than a negation of the Olivian passage linking *usus pauper* with extreme necessity. It manages to criticize Olivi without committing the commission to any particular opinion on *usus pauper* as part of the vow. This tactic would have a discernible effect on the subsequent history of the controversy. It concentrated attention on Olivi's definition of *usus pauper*. In the future, he would continually find himself explaining what he meant by the term.

In the cases of burial, procurators, and bishops, it is equally hard to decide precisely what the commission thought it was criticizing. The *Letter of the Seven Seals* defends burial in words so general that Olivi himself can agree with them. On the matter of bishops it simply negates without explanation one of Olivi's own statements. It says nothing at all about procurators. The *rotulus* presents Olivian passages concerning all three issues, garnishing them with marginal criticisms so vague as to communicate nothing more than an undefined disapproval. Olivi announces his confusion, and one is moved to second him.

We must be careful not to read too much into this situation. The statements regarding *usus pauper* constitute only a small part of what the commission chose to censure. The *Letter of the Seven Seals* contains twenty-two articles, several of them phrased as simple negations of something Olivi has said. In the *apologia*, in which Olivi mentions thirty-two topics included in the *rotulus* and examines twenty of them, his discussion suggests that the commission's marginal comments were cursory in the extreme, not only on poverty but on other issues as well. In the process of defending himself on other matters besides poverty, he occasionally suggests that the censured view is solid and held by a selection of *auctoritates*. On one such occasion, he expresses confusion as to what the commission finds wrong with his statement. Thus there are some significant parallels between the statements regarding poverty and those regarding philosophy and theology.

Nevertheless, there is also a significant difference. When we study the other censures we can normally identify a specific issue at stake, a particular point on which Olivi and the commission differ. Olivi himself usually seems to recognize where the problem lies. Having cited the offending passage and the commission's reaction, he goes to work on the task of defending himself, arguing that his view is true when taken in some special sense; that his words have been taken out of context by considering a brief excerpt; or that he was simply stating without assertion a view which he cannot refute. One senses little of the bewildered exasperation that characterizes his reactions regarding poverty.[10]

Thus there really is something special about the passages concerning *usus pauper.* The commission gives the impression of a group reacting to a problem that is relatively new yet has a great deal of emotional resonance. The commission members have no theoretical foundation on which to base a brief, succinct rebuttal, but they are quite sure that, for whatever reason Olivi may be wrong, he is definitely wrong. Thus they content themselves with reactions that express their general disapproval without committing them to a definite positive stance.

If they have not as yet thought their way through the problem of *usus pauper* as part of the vow, then why are they so confident that Olivi's view is incorrect? Obviously the sheer number of censured articles would produce a cumulative weight of suspicion, making it easier to consider any particular article dangerous; yet one is still faced with the question of why any particular idea should have been selected from the mass of Olivi's writings and subjected to scrutiny in the first place. At this point we must look again at Olivi's view of *usus pauper*, asking how it differs from the one apparently held by his original opponents. The two positions do not inevitably lead to two different practical programs, and neither view considers minor violations of restricted use to be mortal sins. If one is contemplating the possibility of gross violation, however, then one would do well to vote for the view offered by Olivi's antagonists.

To clarify this assertion, I must take the risk of either boring the reader or insulting his intelligence by looking one more time at some of the arguments in the debate. Olivi's opponents argue that violation of a vow entails mortal sin. Thus if one were to vow *usus pauper*, the slightest deviation from it would be mortal. A single chicken dinner or glass of white wine could mean falling from grace. The problem does not lie merely in the low standard of living implied by *usus pauper*, however. It also lies in the indeterminacy of that standard. There is no way of specifying precisely what the individual should eat, what he should wear, or where he should live in order to observe it. Thus anyone vowing *usus pauper* could never be sure whether he was observing it or not. Fortunately, Olivi's opponents argue, the pope has spared Franciscans anxiety on this score by announcing that they are bound only to what is included as a precept in the rule, and at no point in the rule are words like *praecipio* or *teneantur* used in connection with *usus pauper*.

Olivi counters by arguing energetically for an interpretation of the vow that would limit these dangers and allow for variation of practice within limits. Some things fall under the vow in such a way that the line between observation and violation is sharp and readily discernible. For example, one either owns property or one does not. Here violation of one's vow constitutes a mortal sin. Other things, including restricted use, fall under the vow indeterminately and therefore can exist in various degrees. Here the friar can observe his vows more or less perfectly. In this life most Franciscans observe their *usus pauper* imperfectly and thus with a generous admixture of venial sin. Given this situation, an occasional chicken *cacciatore* or glass of Orvieto *secco* will hardly damn them, although it will do them little spiritual good.

We are guilty of mortal sin only when the deviation from *usus pauper* is so great that, all things considered, our behavior should be called rich use (*usus dives*) rather than poor. There is nothing unique about restricted use in this respect. Temperance, for example, can be practiced with an admixture of venial sin up to the point at which the deviation is so great that one's conduct should be judged intemperate rather than the reverse, at which point one is guilty of mortal sin. Precisely where is that point? Olivi answers that it cannot be determined any more than it can in the case of talking with women, entertaining carnal thoughts, or disobeying a prelate. Here we see a strong parallel between the rule and the divine law, since it is equally impossible to determine the precise point at which pride, jealousy, or vainglory turn into mortal sins. Viewed in this way, the rule does not bind Franciscans to a series of precisely determinable actions. Instead, it commits them to life within a range of possibilities. Within this range, the vow acts as a signpost pointing brothers toward the highest possible achievement and encouraging them to attain a life of perfection insofar as they are capable of doing so.

As to the assertion that one is bound by precept only to those parts of the rule which contain words like *praecipio* or *teneantur*, Olivi observes that such a criterion would make nonsense of the Franciscan life, removing some of its most cherished elements from the realm of precept. In other words, he denies that the rule has been equipped with a set of explicit verbal cues separating precept from counsel.

Although Olivi manages to counter the charge that a single violation would mean mortal sin, he recognizes that his view offers no clear-cut line beyond which mortal sin is incurred. Instead, he acknowledges that there is an inevitable indeterminacy about such matters. However bearable such an outlook might have been to a lector in a southern French convent, it might have seemed less comforting to a friar whose dealings with the world brought him constantly into that shadowy region where the transition between venial and mortal sin could occur.

The commission of seven offers food for reflection in this regard. Of the seven, we know a good deal about six. All six were eventually masters of theology at Paris, the most prestigious university in Europe. One also taught at Oxford, another at the papal curia. Three and perhaps four of them became provincial ministers, while two eventually became ministers general. At least three had served on other important commissions during the preceding decade. At least two were employed on sensitive diplomatic missions. As a modern dean might say, all had solid records in teaching and administration.[11]

These were men who moved easily in the world. By conscious design or institutional election, they were destined to follow paths of power, paths littered with temptation, paths that enabled and occasionally required them to live in such a way as to raise the question of how close to mortal sin they were treading, granting Olivi's view of *usus pauper*. There is no reason to view them as indifferent toward poverty. On the contrary, what evidence is available concerning John of Murrovalle, who received the chance to show his intentions when he became minister general, suggests that John was sincere about reform. Information concerning Arlotto of Prato, the other commission alumnus who attained that position, is less plentiful; yet what little we have points more toward serious observance of the rule than toward relaxation.[12] If such men rejected Olivi's position and opted for an undemanding interpretation of *usus pauper*, we cannot assume that they did so simply to clear the way for unimpeded enjoyment of worldly pleasures. Perhaps it was largely to protect their consciences from undue anxiety as they performed their roles.

Olivi was somewhat better insulated from such anxiety. Perhaps he was insulated to some extent by his concrete institutional role as lector in a southern French convent. Presumably a lector in Narbonne had less occasion for easy living than did a Parisian master; yet one can hardly push this point too far, not only because little is known concerning the social habits of either, but also because we do know that lectors were normally given special privileges within the convent and shouldered a number of duties in relation to the outside world which might work to their advantage.[13]

In any case, if Olivi was at all insulated from temptation by his role as lector in a local convent, then he was doubly insulated by a personality which insured that he would never get out of that role. His early doctrinal difficulties, his feud with southern French colleagues, and the tone of his writings all mark him as a man who could not expect to move easily up the corporate ladder of his order. Instead of tact and diplomacy Olivi had charisma. Instead of sound doctrine he had a restless, inquiring mind that often led him not to the common wisdom of his time but to positions evocative of fourteenth-century nominalism, Reformation thought, or nothing else at all. Although these characteristics do not render institutional advancement impossible, they do not usually facilitate it either.

In effect, Olivi's opponents offered a view of *usus pauper* which allowed energetic Franciscans to function and even rise in the world with easy consciences. It let them praise *usus pauper* lavishly (thereby asserting their basic Franciscanism), practice it insofar as they could, and ignore it with no crisis of conscience when they could not.

In emphasizing the tensions inevitably produced by Franciscan activities, the preceding remarks obviously put the best possible face on Olivi's critics. There is, of course, more to it than that. As we have seen, assumption of new functions by the order encouraged entry of the type of person who wanted to fulfill those functions. Acceptance of power and prestige by the order meant people could become Franciscans in the hope of gaining such things. Moreover, the startling increase in size entailed an almost inevitable drop in quality, a situation mirrored by the recognition of diminished standards implicit in some of the arguments Olivi places in the mouths of his opponents. Thus, while Franciscans found themselves performing roles that made it both objectively and subjectively harder to pursue a rigorous poverty, within their own houses they were increasingly surrounded by brothers unlikely to reinforce their commitment to such rigor.

Faced with this situation, they could react in three ways. They could flatly reject thirteenth-century changes and withdraw to a hermitage, a choice that in itself represented modification in the face of change. This alternative proved attractive to some Italian spirituals, but, as Raoul Manselli has observed,[14] the southern French spirituals seem to have been too engaged with their society to accept it easily. Thus Olivi offered a second solution, one that accepted the new functions performed by his order and demanded a disciplined life in the station to which one was called. Finally, there was the solution of Olivi's opponents, who accepted the changes but rejected the tensions and consequent anxiety seemingly entailed in Olivi's view. They opted for a Franciscan ideology that reassured them. As the contemporary sociologist Peter Berger would say, they wanted assurance that they were living in an "okay world."[15]

Berger's work is relevant in a number of ways. In speaking of man's use of religion to reinforce "the notion that the world one lives in is essentially and ultimately all right," he comments that "in this function, again, religion contributes to bad faith, . . . for in reality man does not live an 'okay world' at all. He rushes toward his own death on a course marked by a darkness full of pain. He can become authentically human only if, in some way, he faces and comes to terms with this destiny. The 'okay world' prevents precisely that. . . . It is a Potemkin village erected to provide the illusion of safety, sanity and order." Later Berger says,

> In speaking deprecatingly of the "okay world" we also do not wish to suggest that there is something wrong about men's quest for order, for an intelligible cosmos or for a meaning to their fate. Order is something that men seek, passionately desire, try to construct precariously in their own lives. Order is not something given, self-evident, secure. The "okay world" gives the latter impression, which is not only illusory but which effectively stops the search for order before it has even started—in the illusion of already sitting safely in an oasis men abandon the search for paths through the wilderness.

These words illuminate a striking difference between Olivi and his opponents. Neither side in the *usus pauper* controversy can be identified precisely with the views of Saint Francis; yet in one sense Olivi catches the spirit of early Franciscanism as his opponents do not. His approach is more faithful to the spirit of adventure found in Franciscan legend. When a young Franciscan vows the rule, he embarks on a spiritual quest. The vow points him toward a goal and encourages him to travel in that direction. It does not offer a cookbook religion in which all the necessary ingredients are measured out to the nearest quarter-teaspoon. The boundary between venial and mortal sin, between bending the vow and breaking it, remains unmapped. Nor can it ever be charted. It is beyond simplistic human measurement. The Franciscan life is thus challenging and exiting, but these qualities are purchased at the cost of some uncertainty and thus some anxiety.

In stark contrast, the life offered by Olivi's opponents seems less susceptible to uncertainty and anxiety, but it is as adventurous as lunch at a modern fast-food restaurant. The cost is reduced to a set price, and it is a price everyone feels he can afford; yet the value received is scaled down accordingly. The result is predictable but not very exciting.

One might suggest in passing—the matter is too complex to do more—that Olivi's more adventurous approach to Franciscan living reflects a pervasive quality of his thought which differentiates him from his antagonists and provides some clue as to how one might link the various propositions censured in 1283. On the whole, granting that little is known about the theological and philosophical views held by most of the commission members, it is probably safe to assume that theirs were more conventional than Olivi's, an assumption lent weight by their reactions to what they found in his writings. Of course the commission was not dominated by the leading minds of the age,[16] but it is likely that, whatever group of thirteenth-century theologians we chose to compare with Olivi, the point would hold. Although his animus toward Aristotle and to a lesser extent toward Thomism might seem to place him among the conservatives in his order, he was by no means the sort of person who clings to old formulations through a need for familiar, clear answers. On the contrary, he was probably more comfortable with uncertainty than were most theologians of his time, more willing to live with open questions, and more adventurous. He also displayed a noteworthy independence in deciding what should be accepted or rejected. This independence marked his attitude not only toward Aristotle and Thomas but toward his fellow Franciscans as well.

On the other hand, it is dangerous to overestimate the distance between Olivi and his detractors. He was, after all, a product of the same educational system. Thus Ubertino da Casale may have been exaggerating when he claimed that Gonsalvus of Spain held most of Olivi's views while lecturing on the *Sentences* at Paris, but it would hardly be suprising to find substantial continuity.[17] Anything said on this subject must ultimately be construed as little more than passing suggestions for someone's future research. Until that work is carried out we will not be able to speak intelligently about Olivi's relation to his contemporaries (and particularly to his antagonists in the *usus pauper* controversy) on a broad range of philosophical and theological issues.

Some Difficulties

At any rate, one could argue with some success that the *usus pauper* controversy is explicable as a predictable response to the tensions produced by increased Franciscan involvement in worldly affairs. Nevertheless, handy as such an argument might be, it faces certain difficulties. An obvious one is that, in seeking to explain the mentality of a group, it underplays individual differences. The commission of seven may have written *communiter falsum* in the margin next to Olivi's statement on *usus pauper*, but its members subsequently behaved in different ways toward him. One of the two who later became minister general, Arlotto of Prato, was apparently willing to hear Olivi out, although death prevented him from doing so. The other, John of Murrovalle, led the order in a thorough persecution of Olivi's adherents.

Mention of John's name reminds us that in a story like this one, individuals can have an important impact. If Raymond Geoffroi had managed to stay in office, the persecution of 1299 would not have occurred. John of Murrovalle came to power and it did. Throughout the controversy, certain people can be identified as major protagonists. Certainly Olivi and Raymond Geoffroi belong in that category, as do John of Murrovalle and Arnold of Roquefeuil.

One might object that, since Franciscan ministers were elected, their actions must reflect opinion within the order. Thus individual actions can be traced back to general sentiment, at least in a rough sense. The problem with such an argument is obvious. Although the persecution of 1299–1309 probably did reflect general opinion—no crackdown could be carried out that openly, that fiercely, and that long against anything but a definite minority, albeit a significant one[18]—the fact remains that the change of leadership which allowed it to take place at all depended heavily on papal influence. Nor is there any reason to assume that the pope's interference was primarily motivated by his views concerning the *usus pauper* question, let alone the general sentiment of the order in that regard.

This observation reminds us that not only individuals but significant alignments of them are important. The occurrence and the parameters of the 1292 investigation reflect the combined impact of Nicholas IV and Raymond Geoffroi. The more extensive goals of the 1299 persecution depended not only on a John of Murrovalle being willing to establish such goals but on a Boniface VIII being willing to support him. When the persecution ground to a temporary halt in 1309, it was because another pope had decided to impede it, whatever the leadership of the order might have had in mind.

The explanation offered so far suffers from a second difficulty. In concentrating on the differences between Olivi and the commission of seven, it overlooks the fact that the controversy seems to have begun in southern France and that Olivi's original opponents were supporters of another lector whose position in the order must have been analogous to Olivi's. The words *must have been* are significant. The truth is that we know nothing about the people whom Olivi originally opposed.

A third difficulty offered by the argument is that it does not explain why the controversy surfaced precisely when it did and immediately assumed serious proportions. Can we simply describe it as an intellectual equivalent of spontaneous combustion? Was the problem ready to flame up at any moment and did it just happen to do so then? Was the world simply waiting for someone like Olivi to come along and formulate the issue? Or was there some hidden element that made the issue particularly delicate at that moment?

Usus Pauper and the *Correctorium* Controversy

Thus we arrive at another possible explanation which merits attention. It is arguable that the *usus pauper* controversy was related to another current debate, the *correctorium* controversy. It is significant that Olivi defends his position by appealing not only to Bonaventure and Pecham but to William de la Mare's *Correctorium fratris Thomae*.[19] In the *Correctorium*, which was written before August 1279, William criticizes two passages from Thomas Aquinas dealing with vows.[20] In one, taken from the *Summa theologiae*, Thomas asks whether someone who takes a vow sins mortally in transgressing against anything contained in it. He replies that those who profess a rule do not vow to observe everything in it, but rather vow the regular life, which consists of poverty, chastity, and obedience. Some orders are more prudent inasmuch as they vow not to observe the rule but to live according to it so that the rule becomes an exemplar after which they can pattern their lives. Other orders are even more prudent and vow obedience according to the rule so that only what is against the precept of the rule constitutes a mortal sin, all other transgressions or omissions being venial. "In one religion, however, namely the order of Preaching Brothers, such transgressions or omissions [against anything other than a precept] by their nature do not entail either mortal or venial guilt, but only that one should sustain the punishment meted out."

In the other question, taken from the *Quodlibeta*, Thomas asks whether one who intends to vow everything in the rule sins mortally in transgressing any part of it. He replies that if one were obliged by vow to obey everything in the rule, the religious state would be *in laqueum peccati mortalis*, for the vower would incur mortal sin by breaking any part of it. Moreover, he suggests that anyone who vows to observe the rule seems to oblige himself to obey everything in it and therefore apparently exposes himself to precisely such a danger. Thus the *sancti*, when they instituted orders, saved people from the snares of damnation by having them promise not observance of the rule but obedience according to the rule.

In both cases, Thomas is arguing that Dominicans take the wisest possible course in vowing obedience according to the rule; yet where does that leave the Franciscans, who must vow "to observe the rule throughout my whole life"[21] and whose rule itself speaks of "promising . . . to observe the rule," announcing that "the rule and life of the friars minor is . . . to observe the holy gospel"?[22] It seems to leave them, in Thomas's happy phrase, in the snares of damnation. One can see why William de la Mare found these passages irritating.[23]

William replies that anyone professing a rule should intend to conform himself with it according to the intention of its author. No author intends to produce a rule that binds people to all of its parts equally. That would be stupid and dangerous. Such is particularly obvious in the case of the Franciscan rule, which distinguishes between precepts and admonitions. Citing papal decisions on the matter, William argues that in vowing to observe the gospel Franciscans are bound only to those things which are expressed in the rule *praeceptorie vel inhibitorie*.

The *Correctorium* represents one chapter in a history of tension between two orders that often seemed very alike to contemporaries yet very unlike to one another. Writing in 1246–47, Thomas of Celano tells how the two founders saluted each other in brotherly love,[24] and close to a century later Dante describes Aquinas and Bonaventure performing a similar ritual in heaven;[25] yet even the passage from Celano contains a denunciation of existing conflict.[26] By the time Dante wrote, the two orders had been bickering for a century over such worldly prizes as space and membership. Whichever group arrived first in a city often did what it could to bar the other from establishing itself.[27] Competition for members was stiff, and each order criticized the other for its recruitment of the young, just as the secular clergy criticized both.[28] This competition contributed to the need for an obligatory one-year novitiate, which in turn became a source of tension.[29]

During the second half of the century, remaining fraternal ties were strained by continuing competition in the cities, by Franciscan involvement in the scandal of the eternal gospel,[30] and by varying postures in the crisis over Aristotelian philosophy from the 1270s on. The secular-mendicant controversy united them against a common foe, but by the late 1270s victory on that front seemed assured and the two orders were free to turn upon one another.

Well before that, leaders were trying to hold the line. John of Parma's generalate apparently saw a serious effort to insure amity. This is most clearly displayed in the joint letter issued by John and the Dominican master Humbert of Romans in 1255.[31] This document begins with an allusion to the joint apocalyptic destiny of the two orders.[32] Such a calling, it says, must not be thwarted by fraternal bickering. The two leaders then settle down to the task of compiling a list of things their members must not do. They are specific enough to offer, in effect, a tour of the battlefield.

Some of the problems involve the struggle for space. The orders are enjoined not to build too close to one another's houses, nor to snatch up building sites which they hear the other hopes to acquire. The scramble for benefactors is also reflected. Friars are directed not to criticize the other order before laymen with an eye to deflecting alms to their own group, or to try stopping bequests already made to the other order. Prospective members are also at issue. Brothers are told to stop discouraging those who intend to join the other order.

We also find reflected in this document the fact that both orders were dedicated to preaching. They addressed a genuine need but competed in fulfilling it. The friars are enjoined not to impede one another's sermons or steal either their listeners or the sermons themselves.

Beyond these efforts to deal with very practical issues, we see an attempt to stop the general war of words. The friars are told not to extoll their own saints and life in such a way as to denigrate those of the other order. They are enjoined to stop speaking ill of the other order, not merely in public but even in private. If they know of some wickedness perpetrated by a member of the other group, they are to denounce him to his own leaders or reproach him privately, not spread it abroad where it will do no good. When they hear that members of the other order are saying evil things about their own, they should not accept the news too readily or increase hostility by repeating it to their colleagues. If someone is actually injured by a member of the other order, he should show patience and avoid reacting in such a way as to inflame his confreres. If one of his own brothers is guilty of such an offense, he should correct him or report him instead of simply concealing his fault.

The effort to secure amity—as well as its limitations—is also seen in Bonaventure's *Letter Concerning Three Questions*, which was probably written during John of Parma's generalate.[33] It has been suggested that the addressee could have been a Franciscan zealot.[34] If so, then Bonaventure would have been dealing with a very alienated zealot indeed, one whose quarrel was with common Franciscan practice from the 1220s on and to some extent with the rule itself. It seems safer to look for some other recipient.

Even if we ignore the final passage of the letter (found in a single manuscript and printed in the Bonaventure *Opera* as an appendix), the work has a familiar ring to anyone who approaches it by way of Pecham's defense against the Dominicans, which will be examined in a moment. Bonaventure refutes precisely the same charges concerning receipt of money, and he does so in much the same way.[35] His discussion of books and houses contains a basic introduction to the theoretical underpinnings of Franciscan practice.

The final passage, which is probably genuine,[36] erases any doubt as to the source of the criticism Bonaventure intended to counter. He assures his reader that the critic who has been poisoning the reader's mind is not speaking for his group, since "the greater and better among them" claim to hold the highest opinion of the Franciscan order. Thus if they tell the reader otherwise, they are lying either to him or to Bonaventure and are untrustworthy in any case. The only hardened critic among them known to Bonaventure is "a certain whited sepulcher" who, Bonaventure believes, was severely punished by his order. At any rate, the Franciscan provincial minister of England spoke to the master of the slanderer's order concerning the matter and was assured that the slanderer had spoken without either the authority or the approval of the master. Use of the title *magister ordinis* lends credence to the belief that Bonaventure is speaking of Dominicans.

In other words, we are confronting an example of the tactics condemned in the joint letter of 1255. Presumably, a promising candidate for the Franciscan order, temporarily confused by a Dominican disinformation campaign, has sought clarification from the eminent Franciscan master of theology at Paris, Bonaventure of Bagnoreggio. It seems likely that critic and inquirer were both located in England. One could go on to try assigning names—Roger Bacon and John Pecham have been offered as candidates—but there is no need do so.

While Bonaventure's letter represents Franciscan self-protection in the face of Dominican attack, such sniping may have been motivated at least partly by Dominican defensiveness, as we learn from an unintentionally humorous document describing a quarrel between the two orders at Oxford in 1269.[37] Written by an Oxford Franciscan, it chronicles his colleagues' obsessive struggle to satisfy their wounded honor after a Dominican had accused them of hiding behind a subterfuge in receiving money through middlemen while claiming not to receive it at all. Redress was eventually sought in several quarters, including the original offender, the local Dominican house, the provincial prior, and finally a commission of secular scholars. In the process, what originally seemed the private whim of an individual Dominican was revealed to be the general sentiment of his order. Asked why they continued their criticism, the Dominicans replied that they were tired of being compared unfavorably with the Franciscans because they accepted money. They wanted to show the world that there was in fact no difference.

England also furnishes perhaps the most disquieting example of such tension, John Pecham's open letter to Robert Kilwardby in 1271 or 1272. After returning to his native land as regent master at Oxford, Pecham somehow discovered a letter which Kilwardby, the Dominican provincial, had addressed to novices. It praised the Dominican rule and mission through invidious (though implicit) comparison with the Franciscans. Pecham struck back hard.

What is so disturbing about Pecham's letter, beyond the jarring discord between its tone and Pecham's insistence on addressing the recipient as *karissime*, is the degree of alienation between the two orders it suggests. At times Pecham and Kilwardby seem to be not so much debating as squabbling like small boys. Kilwardby asserts that Dominicans are better fitted to preach the gospel because they wear shoes. Thus they enjoy greater mobility in the winter, when barefoot preachers would be impeded from traveling about, and offer a better example in the summer, when going unshod would involve self-indulgence. This is obviously a ridiculous argument, and one might expect a man of Pecham's intelligence to note as much, but he does not. Instead, he answers in kind, protesting that Franciscans get around just fine in the winter and are in fact allowed to wear shoes when conditions so require. Besides, hot summer ground is harder on the feet than cold winter ground.[38]

Despite the bickering, some very important issues are raised. In noting that Christ and his disciples carried a purse, Kilwardby questions the Franciscan claim to practice evangelical poverty.[39] He also seems to have questioned whether the Franciscans were in fact without possessions. This is less clear since Pecham—our only source for Kilwardby's letter—simply quotes a passage in which Kilwardby acknowledges the Franciscan claim to absolute poverty, then announces that, not wishing to be contentious, he will concede that matters are as they say. Nevertheless, Pecham replies by refuting objections based on Franciscan receipt of gifts and legacies through procurators, as well as the argument that would eventually prove so attractive to John XXII, that *usus* cannot be distinguished from *dominium* in things consumed through use.[40] He never actually attributes these objections to Kilwardby, but someone must have offered them and this is clearly the same problem that divided Oxford mendicants two or three years earlier. Thus it is safe to assume that Pecham is answering Dominican arguments, though perhaps not Kilwardby's.

The debate had a profound effect on Pecham, who went on answering the same charges throughout his later writings.[41] How much good these replies may have done is another problem. If any single motive for Kilwardby's attack emerges from the attack itself as filtered through Pecham, it is the Dominican's desire to defend his order against what he interprets as arrogant Franciscan claims to superiority. Without mentioning the Franciscans, Kilwardby speaks of those who prefer themselves to others and belittle others.[42]

This was hardly a private whim on Kilwardby's part. A similar motivation underlay the Oxford Dominicans' criticism. Nor was it a bit of group paranoia suffered by English Preachers, or even a misunderstanding. The Franciscans did identify their rule with the height of evangelical perfection. They always had done so. The idea is implicit in the opening lines of the rule. This is not to say that every minorite since Francis himself was equally likely to offend Dominican sensibilities. It is one thing to pursue evangelical perfection in all humility and quite another to claim it in a spirit of self-congratulation or self-advertisement. Even claiming it can produce different reactions, depending on whether one does so from the Portiuncula in 1221 or from Greyfriars, London, in 1272, but that is another matter. The important point is that in the 1272 context, the claim was almost inevitably offensive to those who found themselves competing with the Franciscans.

The tension was hardly limited to England.[43] During the same period, Olivi's own province was the scene of several unfortunate incidents. Before 1245, in every town where both orders settled, the Dominicans arrived before the Franciscans. After that date the Franciscans expanded rapidly and were usually the first to appear.[44] Trouble came not only from the standard problems of establishment and recruitment but from involvement in the Inquisition, with each order getting in the other's way when it exercised inquisitorial duties.[45]

Despite the example of Pecham and Kilwardby, the worst tension in the 1270s seems to have stemmed from local rivalries. Franciscan and Dominican leaders recognized that the conflict was debilitating. Their attempt to stifle it appears in several minor incidents,[46] but preeminently in the common letter published in 1274 by John of Vercelli, master of the Dominicans, and Jerome of Ascoli, minister general of the Franciscans.[47] It not only demanded that local disputes be settled at the provincial level but forbade meddling with the Inquisition, attempts to influence choice of burial places by the laity, mutual criticism, and discussion concerning the relative perfection of each order.

Obviously the incidents continued. After 1277, conflict was promoted to the philosophical sphere by the Paris condemnation and consequent controversy over Thomism. In 1279 the Franciscans were able to take their case to the highest level possible. In May of that year, Pope Nicholas III asked the general chapter at Assisi what he could do to help the order.

A delegation consisting of the new minister general (Bonagratia of San Giovanni in Persiceto), some provincial ministers, and various brothers journeyed to Soriano where the pope was spending the summer. The result was the bull *Exiit qui seminat.*[48]

Exiit was promulgated, in the words of one Franciscan source, "to settle questions about the rule and to curb certain people who were springing and snapping at it."[49] The bull itself refers to those who "snap at the brothers and tear at their rule with doggy barks."[50] It would be overstating the case to argue that those biting dogs were all *domini canes*. Some of the issues addressed by *Exiit* had also been raised in the secular-mendicant controversy, and some antedate even that conflict.[51] Nevertheless, it is hard to read *Exiit* without recognizing it as an answer to certain claims advanced by Aquinas, Kilwardby, and other Dominicans at Franciscan expense.[52]

In *Exiit*, Nicholas acknowledges that the Franciscan vow to observe the gospel "might seem to ensnare the soul of the vower," since such a promise, taken absolutely, could not be kept. He replies that the words must be taken according to Francis's intention. In his rule, some evangelical counsels are, in effect, promoted to the status of precepts because they are demanded *praeceptorie vel inhibitorie* or by equivalent expressions. Other counsels remain counsels because they are recommended in the rule only through words of admonition, exhortation, and advice. By virtue of his status, the Franciscan is more committed to pursue those counsels than the average Christian would be; yet he is not committed to them as he is to precepts.

William de la Mare and Nicholas III were hardly breaking new ground when they tried to protect Franciscans from sin and consequently from the Dominicans by limiting their vow to what was stated in the rule *praeceptorie vel inhibitorie*. Gregory IX had said something similar in 1230 and Innocent IV in 1245. By the 1270s the idea had worked its way into some commentaries on the rule and even into the secular-mendicant controversy.[53] Nevertheless, Nicholas did make an important contribution to the discussion through addition of the words "or by equivalent expressions." The phrase created an ambiguity that would not be removed until three decades later at the Council of Vienne when Clement V consented to furnish a list of these expressions.

In any case, Nicholas's words were duly noted by the Dominicans. By the end of 1279 their general master, John of Vercelli, had written to inform his order that it was now dangerous to argue with the Franciscans about their rule.[54] When the Dominican superior in the province of Provence forwarded this document to his flock in January 1280, he added his own covering letter observing that "it is the intention of the high pontiff and the will of the general master that we speak cautiously on matters pertaining to the Franciscan rule" and warning them to be careful lest they incur excommunication.[55] Thus Dominican leaders were quite aware that, whoever else *Exiit* may have had in mind, it was certainly aimed at them.

The pope's opinion was also duly noted by Olivi. In late 1279 he wrote his question on "whether one vowing the gospel or some rule simply and without determination must observe everything in it in such a way that he always sins mortally in transgressing it."[56] Aimed at Thomas and echoing William de la Mare, it is clearly an installment in the *correctorium* controversy. The early part of the question follows an outline provided by William's *Correctorium*. The latter part uses elements from William but forges them into a characteristically Olivian argument.

Olivi follows William in arguing that no legislator binds his subjects to all elements of his law equally; yet he adopts a different criterion for determining the differences. Whereas William argues that the rule itself distinguishes between precepts and counsels, Olivi talks about degrees of obligation based on a hierarchy of ends. When someone vows a rule, he binds himself to all those things which are substantial parts of it, things without which the rule would not be itself. The *cultus dei* is the supreme end of all rules and therefore the principle thing one vows. Training of the soul and spiritual union with Christ and one's confreres constitute penultimate goals. Below this level are external acts of poverty and chastity. Lower still come things like clothing, fasting, and silence. Beneath all these are what Olivi calls "ornaments and compliments," which are not substantial elements at all.[57]

Thus Olivi does not throw away the idea of precepts and counsels, but he does dismiss the idea that one can find them neatly labeled as such. One must identify as precepts not only those passages of the rule in which the words *praecipio* and *teneantur* are used but all those things that are necessary to the substantial integrity of the rule. Only in this context can Olivi ratify the views of Gregory IX and Nicholas III: "Thus Gregory and Nicholas . . . speak well in saying that we are not bound to all the evangelical counsels, but only to those which the ruler intends to prescribe," namely "all those counsels which are substantial and necessary elements of the apostolic state."[58]

Within the category of precepts, Olivi draws his usual distinction between those proffered precisely, which cannot be violated without mortal sin, and those given indeterminately, violation of which is mortal only if the offense is great, since only a great offense will substantially damage the apostolic state. He is quite aware that his view leaves room for uncertainty. How does one determine the point at which what is prescribed indeterminately becomes mortal sin? Olivi simply refers the reader to his question on *usus pauper*. How can one recognize which demands in the rule are precepts and which are counsels? It is hard, he says, but at least we can be sure that, whenever we encounter words like *consulo, moneo*, or the like we are dealing with counsels.[59]

One can imagine how some of Olivi's colleagues must have reacted to these statements. The *correctorium* controversy had sensitized them to the charge that the Franciscan rule was dangerous. They had worked out an answer to that charge and were suspicious of theories that undermined their answer. Olivi did just that. He rejected the notion of a distinction between precept and counsel based entirely upon the language of the rule. In doing so, he contradicted William de la Mare and three popes. In place of this explicit distinction, which seemed to be serving the order so well, he offered an implicit one based upon the substantial integrity of the Franciscan state, a vague notion at best. He cheerfully acknowledged that it was hard to say what was precept and what counsel, and he granted that in the case of his indeterminate precepts there was no way of determining the point at which violation ceased to be venial and became mortal. One can see why some of his brethren were alarmed.

This is not to say that they were alarmed only because they saw Olivi as compromising a good defense against Dominican criticism. Like William de la Mare, they shared more of Thomas's assumptions than Olivi did. Thus their opposition stemmed not only from a desire to protect their flank against a rival order but also from a pastoral desire to protect tender consciences by avoiding vague or impossibly high standards. Here as elsewhere, Olivi was less bound by current notions and was perhaps more intellectually adventurous than his opponents.

This picture of Olivi's opponents as sharing more of Thomas's assumptions is corroborated by the polemic against "Brother Ar" and his supporters. Although the work as we have it deals with scholastic theology and philosophy rather than with Franciscan poverty, it is likely that Brother Ar and his friends can be identified as Olivi's opponents in the *usus pauper* controversy. Seven times in this polemic Olivi notes that his opponents have gone wrong because they are following Thomas Aquinas.[60] Four times he cites William de la Mare against them.[61] The total picture he paints is one of himself as defender of the Franciscan tradition against a group that has granted too much to Thomism.

That picture is not entirely accurate. Olivi is always correct in noting that William de la Mare disagrees with Olivi's opponents, but he sometimes tactfully avoids acknowledging that William would disagree with his position as well. Thus his strategy here is analogous to that pursued in the *usus pauper* controversy when he cites William and Nicholas III against his opponents, yet ignores his own divergence from both William and Nicholas on the critical issue of how one determines what is precept and what counsel in the rule. Here again is evidence of Olivi's notable independence, not only from Thomas, but from Franciscan authorities and even from the pope.

That, of course, is substantially more independence than Olivi could have been expected to acknowledge. Had he been able to do so, he might also have reversed the equation and recognized the significant common ground he shared with Aquinas.[62] Both tended to think of the religious as vowing to move toward an end rather than to do a specific number of things. Both posited a hierarchy of ends, although they described these ends differently and applied diverse yardsticks for judging when a vow is violated. On the latter score Thomas preferred to think in terms of the distinction between pursuing the rule and treating it with contempt; yet even here there are parallels in Olivi and in other Franciscans as well, including Hugh of Digne. They, too, had read Saint Bernard. The similarities are so notable that Olivi might well have acknowledged them had he not encountered Thomas in the polemical context created by Dominican-Franciscan tension and reacted strongly to Thomas's lower evaluation of poverty.

In any case, Olivi's confrontation with his own order seems clear enough. William de la Mare had countered Dominican criticism of the Franciscan rule by developing a criterion for separating precept from counsel. That criterion had been suggested by two previous popes and was accepted by still another in 1279. Neither William nor the popes agonized over how the criterion would affect *usus pauper*. It was a question they simply did not consider seriously.

Olivi and his opponents considered it very seriously indeed. His opponents argued with some force that a strict application of the criterion would eliminate *usus pauper* from the Franciscan vow. Faced with that choice, they elected to keep the criterion and cut *usus pauper* loose from the vow while nevertheless emphasizing its centrality for the Franciscan life. Olivi chose precisely the opposite course. He retained *usus pauper* as a part of the vow, but to do so he had to develop a different criterion for separating precept from counsel, one many of his colleagues must have found hopelessly vague.

Having said so much, are we in any position to say that we have isolated the reasons why the *usus pauper* controversy began around 1279 in southern France? Of course not. There is nothing obviously incorrect or even manifestly questionable about what has been said in this chapter. A number of important suggestions have been made. On one level, we find a crisis of conscience produced by the tension between old Franciscan ideals and new Franciscan functions, a tension exacerbated by changes stemming from rapid growth and the influx of persons attracted by the new functions. On another level, we see a defensive element stemming from Franciscan desire to protect the rule against not only secular critics but fellow mendicants. On still another level, we encounter personal antagonisms engendered by the ingenious and charismatic Olivi, a man apparently born to polarize opinion.

To say that there is nothing manifestly false about these suggestions is not to call them true, however. Lacking hard facts, we must be satisfied with a few working hypotheses.

Notes

1. See Burr, *Persecution*, 44–46.
2. *Rev.*, 75ra.
3. *De perf.*, q. 3, in Aquilinus Emmen and Feliciano Simoncioli, "La dottrina dell'Olivi sulla contemplazione, la vita attiva e mista," *SF* 61 (1964): 158.
4. *Letter to R*, 51(63)v. See my comments in *Persecution*, 32f.
5. For example Peck, *Fool of God*, esp. ch. 4; Frederick Antal, *Florentine Painting and Its Social Background* (New York, 1975), ch. 3.
6. Jean-Louis Biget, "Autour de Bernard Délicieux," in *Mouvements franciscains et société française, XIIe-XXe siècles* (Paris, 1984), 75–93.
7. Odd Langham, *Price and Value in the Aristotelian Tradition* (Bergen, 1979), 153.
8. Amletto Spicciani, *La Mercatura e la formazione del prezzo nella riflessione teologica medioevale* (Rome, 1977), 185. See also Giacomo Todeschini, *Un trattato di economia politica francescana* (Rome, 1980). For a valid critique of Todeschini's analysis see Julius Kirshner and Kimberly Lo Prete, "Peter John Olivi's Treatises on Contracts of Sale, Usury and Restitution: Minorite Economics or Minor Works?" *Quaderni fiorentini* 13 (1984):233–86.
9. The Kirshner–Lo Prete article makes some valuable suggestions. For general treatment of economic development and the mendicants see Lester Little, *Religious Poverty and the Profit Economy in Medieval Europe* (Ithaca, 1978); but see the valid critique of such approaches in d'Avray, *Preaching of the Friars*, ch. 4.
10. See the issues examined in Burr, *Persecution*, 44–61.
11. The six members in question are Simon of Lens, Droco of Provence, John of Wales, Arlotto of Prato, Richard of Middleton and John of Murrovalle. For their careers see Palémon Glorieux, *Répertoire des maîtres en théologie de Paris au XIIIe siècle* (Paris, 1933–34), nos. 320–24, 326, 331.

12. See his 1286 letter in *Chronologia historico-legalis* (Naples, 1650), 1:34.
13. For privileges and power within the convent see Delorme, "Explanationes constitutionum generalium narbonensium," 519 and 521; Bihl, "Statuta generalia ordinis," 57; Little, "Statuta provincialia provinciarum Aquitaniae et Franciae," 478; Ubertino da Casale, *Rotulus*, 102f.; Ubertino, *Sanctitas vestra*, 73, 80; Jacopone da Todi, *Laude, lauda* 31. These include dining privileges, closed rooms, special medical attention, and a degree of freedom from the guardian's control. For an example of outside duties see Giordani, "Acta," 261.
14. Raoul Manselli, "Divergences parmi les mineurs d'Italie et de France méridionale," in *Les Mendiants en pays d'Oc au XIIIe siècle* (Toulouse, 1973), 355–74.
15. Peter Berger, *The Precarious Vision* (Garden City, 1961), 121.
16. Richard of Middleton and perhaps John of Wales might be considered exceptions, but Richard was a bachelor of theology in 1283 and thus presumably not a leader in the commission's work.
17. Ubertino da Casale, *Sanctitati apostolicae*, 383. Ephrem Longpré, "L'oeuvre scolastique du cardinal Jean de Murro," 467 and 482 emphasizes the continuity between Olivi and John of Murrovalle.
18. Writing in 1311, Ubertino da Casale, *Declaratio*, 192, says the order has disciplined more than three hundred spirituals. Others probably shared the spirituals' views to some degree.
19. *Tractatus*, 26vb. The following paragraphs are heavily dependent upon my article "The *Correctorium* Controversy and the Origins of the *Usus Pauper* Controversy," *Speculum* 60 (1985): 331–42.
20. *Le Correctorium Corruptorii "Quare,"* 302–308, 405–407. See Aquinas, *Summa theologiae*, 2a 2ae, q. 186, a. 9; *Quodlibet* I, a. 20.
21. The formula given in the constitutions of Narbonne begins "Ego, frater N., voveo et promitto Deo et B. Mariae Virgini et B. Francisco et omnibus sanctis et tibi, pater toto tempore vitae meae servare regulam fratrum minorum." See Bihl, "Statuta generalia ordinis," 40.
22. *Regula*, cc. 1 and 12.
23. For explicit mention of the charge that the Franciscan rule is a *laqueus* see William de la Mare, *Correctorium*, 406; the anonymous *Determinationes quaestionum*, 354f.; Olivi, *Tractatus*, 24vb–25ra; and as we shall see, Nicholas III, *Exiit qui seminat*. The term exercised a continuing fascination for Franciscans. See Richard of Conington, *Tractatus de paupertate fratrum minorum*, 344, 360; and *Beatus vir*, in *AFH* 42 (1949): 221, 232.
24. Thomas of Celano, *Vita prima, vita secunda et tractatus de miraculis*, in *AF*, 10:109.
25. *Paradiso*, XI–XII.
26. Nor is other evidence lacking. See Matthew Paris, *Chronica* (London, 1872–84), 1:474–76.
27. Other powers often joined in the battle. See W. A. Hinnebusch, *History of the Dominican Order* (Staten Island, 1965), 161, for instances of papal and episcopal intervention.
28. See ibid., 296 and 322, for relevant papal bulls.
29. Eccleston, *De adventu*, c. 13 reveals the Dominican effort to protect nov-

ices from Franciscan poaching. See also *BF*, 1:327f., 345f.; 2:50, 129, 130; 3:160f. See Gilles Meersseman, *Ordo fraternitatis* (Rome, 1977), 1:379–86 for examples of rivalry over control of lay confraternities in the late 1280s and 1290s.

30. See the suggestive discussion of changing apocalyptic awareness in the two orders offered by Stanislao da Campagnola, "Dai 'viri spirituales' di Gioacchino da Fiore ai 'fratres spirituales' di Francesco d'Assisi," 24–52.

31. In Wadding, *Annales*, 3:380–83.

32. Analyzed by Marjorie Reeves, *Influence of Prophecy in the Later Middle Ages* (Oxford, 1969), 144f.

33. Three manuscripts contain the notice that Bonaventure wrote the letter before he became minister general, while he was regent master at Paris (*Epistola de tribus quaestionibus*, in *Opera*, 8:336). If so, it must have been written by February 1257.

34. Esser, "Zu der 'Epistola de tribus quaestionibus' des hl. Bonaventura," 159.

35. *Epistola de tribus quaestionibus*, 332.

36. The *Opera* editors (p. 331, note 1) offer a plausible explanation of why it is found only in the oldest manuscript. When the letter was eventually made public, the identity of the critic was suppressed by eliminating this section.

37. Included as an appendix in A. G. Little, *The Grey Friars of Oxford* (Oxford, 1892), 320–35.

38. *Contra Kilwardby*, in *Tractatus tres de paupertate* (Aberdeen, 1910), 129f.

39. Ibid., 131.

40. Ibid., 136–40.

41. See his comments on the relative discomforts of summer and winter for barefoot friars in *Canticum pauperis*, 190f., and *Expositio super regulam* in Bonaventure, *Opera*, 8:403. Though not discussed by Harkins, "The Authorship of a Commentary on the Franciscan Rule," these passages support his ascription of the *Expositio* to Pecham and his suggested chronology of Pecham's writings. See also *Registrum epistolarum* (London, 1886), 3:867, where Pecham criticizes Dominicans for bragging that the truth flourishes more in their order than in others.

42. *Contra Kilwardby*, 142.

43. See *BF*, 3:117, for evidence of Franciscan attempts to block Dominican establishment in southern Italy and papal lamentation concerning the hostility between the orders.

44. M.-H. Vicaire, "La Province dominicaine de Provence," in *Les Mendiants en pays d'oc au XIIIe siècle* (Toulouse, 1973), 48f.; Richard Emery, *The Friars in Medieval France* (New York, 1962).

45. See Yves Dossat, "Les origines de la querelle entre Prêcheurs et Mineurs provencaux: Bernard Délicieux," in *Les Franciscains d'oc, Les spirituels, 1280–1324* (Toulouse, 1975), 315–54; and *BF*, 3:82–86. See also *BF*, 3:90 for evidence of acrimony in Olivi's territory, but not involving the Inquisition.

46. See the case cited by Pierre Amargier, "Prêcheurs et mentalité universitaire dans la province de Provence au XIIIe siècle," in *Les Universites du Languedoc au XIIIe siècle* (Toulouse, 1970), 130. The Dominican prior at

Montpellier was removed from office in 1270 for his poor reception of the visiting Franciscan minister general. The 1260 constitutions of Narbonne, in Bihl, "Statuta generalia ordinis," 58, enjoin Franciscans to treat any Dominican staying at their convent in kindly and loving fashion, as if he were a member of their own order.

47. *Monumenta ordinis fratrum praedicatorum* (Rome, 1898–1900), 5:100–104. See also *Chronica XXIV generalium*, 365. Note the dating problem involved.

48. On *Exiit* see Fidelis Elizondo, "Bulla 'Exiit qui seminat' Nicolai III (14 Augusti 1279)," *Laurentianum* 4 (1963): 59–119.

49. *Chronica XXIV generalium*, 369.

50. *Corpus iuris canonici*, 1110. Pecham's *Expositio super regulam*, 437, refers to *detractores lacerantes*. The *Meditatio pauperis*, 13, speaks of those who slander the Franciscans like barking dogs and hopes they will be set right by *Exiit*. Olivi's letter to Conrad of Offida, 372, says the rebels are providing ammunition for enemies of the rule who *latraverunt et latrant* that it is unobservable. Angelo Clareno, *Historia septem tribulationum*, 148f., says that when the Dominican inquisitors gained possession of Bernard Délicieux they acted *sicut canes* that *lacerant* whatever beast they catch. To show that he is not above punning, he offers a bad one on "Délicieux." Shortly after, apparently still referring to the Inquisition, he says they attacked "seculars, beguines or fraticelli, men or women," *imitantes canes et lupos rabidos*; yet in the middle of this denunciation he says they also condemned Olivi's thought "at their general chapter meeting." He seems to mean the 1319 Franciscan general chapter. Thus dog imagery is not exclusively anti-Dominican.

51. Some, like the problems connected with vowing to observe the gospel, were already addressed in 1231 by *Quo elongati*.

52. Beyond the issues to be discussed here, *Exiit* agrees with the Franciscans in seeing absolute poverty as the apostolic pattern and in arguing away the purse held by the disciples. In these cases Dominican critics were essentially in harmony with secular masters. Nicholas could combat both at once with arguments already used in Bonaventure's *Apologia pauperum*. On the relationship between *Exiit* and the *Apologia pauperum* see Venantius Maggiani, "De relatione scriptorum quorumdam S. Bonaventurae ad Bullam 'Exiit' Nicholai III (1279)," *AFH* 5 (1912):3–21; Lambert, *Franciscan Poverty*, ch. 6.

53. Gregory IX, *Quo elongati*, in *BF*, 1:68; Innocent IV, *Ordinem vestrum*, in *BF*, 1:400; *Expositio quattuor magistrorum*, 125f.; Hugo de Digna, *Rule Commentary*, 95; Pecham, *Tractatus pauperis*, c. 9. It is also found in Guilelmus Petrus de Falgar, *Quodlibet* II, q. 16, MS Paris, Bibl. Nat. lat. 14305, 158va, which probably dates from the early 1280s.

54. B. M. Reichert, *Litterae encyclicae magistrorum generalium*, in *Monumenta ordinis fratrum praedicatorum historica* (Rome, 1900), 5:116. The letter also mentions certain subjects which must be avoided; yet these relate to the Franciscan claim of absolute poverty and not to the problem of the vow.

55. Ibid., 116.

56. Edited by Delorme, "Fr. P. J. Olivi quaestio de voto regulam aliquam prof-
    itentis," *Antonianum* 16 (1941): 131–64. It is question 17 of the *Qq. de
    perf. evang.* in MS Vat. lat. 4986.
57. Q. 17, 158.
58. Q. 17, 162. He quotes Nicholas in a slightly different way on p. 161.
59. Pecham's *Expositio super regulam*, 436, is similar, since it points the
    reader toward words explicitly denoting counsel rather than those explic-
    itly denoting precept; yet its general argument is different. It suggests that
    one should take as precept everything not expressly qualified as counsel. It
    then distinguishes three types of precept, one of which is not explicitly
    labeled as such in the rule.
60. *Impugnatio*, 44r, 46r–v, 47v. Elsewhere (for example, 45v) he links
    Brother Ar with a Thomist view without mentioning Aquinas.
61. *Impugnatio*, 44v–45r, 46v–47r. For the impact of these passages on a
    dating of the *Correctorium* see Valens Heynck, "Zur Datierung des 'Cor-
    rectorium fratris Thomae' Wilhelms de la Mare," *Franziskanische Studien*
    49 (1967):1–21.
62. On the following see Aquinas, *Summa theologiae*, IIa IIae, q. 186, aa. 2
    and 9.

CHAPTER 7

Some Long-Term Problems

The preceding chapter was devoted to reasons why Olivi's view of *usus pauper* may have been contested. This one will continue the discussion by exploring two underlying issues which seem to have gained importance as the debate progressed: obedience and apocalyptic expectation.

Obedience to Superiors

The *Questions on Evangelical Perfection* treat the first issue at length. Olivi says very little about it through question ten, but he says a great deal thereafter. To be sure, this is primarily due to the organization of the *Questions*. The fifth deals with vows, the sixth and seventh with chastity, the eighth, ninth and tenth with poverty. Thus he is just getting around to the vow of obedience by question eleven. Nevertheless, he devotes all the remaining questions to that subject.[1] In the process, he deals with three different types of obedience: to superiors, to the pope, and to the rule.

In question eleven, Olivi asks whether it is a part of evangelical perfection to vow obedience in things which are contrary neither to the soul nor to the evangelical rule. He concludes that it is and presents a series of arguments based upon scripture and reason. Obedience, he says, is valuable in the pursuit of poverty, chastity, humility, and other virtues. Citing Aristotle, Olivi argues the value of living within a united group and the necessity of order in such a group.[2]

Having said so much, he immediately turns to a consideration of the threefold limit placed upon evangelical obedience. First, one should never obey an order which clearly entails sinning. This applies both to mortal and to venial sin, unless it is a question of some action which loses its character as a sin by the very fact of having been commanded, as, for example, some conversation which might be idle in itself yet lose its idle nature when called for by a superior. Thus, Olivi concludes, they have spoken falsely who said that any venial sin should be committed for the sake of obedience when it is commanded by a superior. Sin is sin and it is always wrong, no matter who orders it.[3]

If one has reasonable doubt as to whether the action is sinful, the command should be obeyed. The doubt must be rational, however. There is no excuse for ignorant incertitude concerning something generally recognized to be sinful. Olivi manages to suggest that connection with the vow of obedience makes a sin even graver than it would otherwise be, and he argues explicitly that obeying a superior in opposition to divine law smacks of heresy, because it implies that one prefers the former to the latter.[4]

The second limitation on obedience is that one must never obey if doing so would endanger one's own salvation, and the third is that one must do nothing that compromises the purity of evangelical perfection. The latter requirement has some interesting ramifications. Since leadership roles have been instituted in the Franciscan order for the purpose of helping brothers to observe the rule, it is impossible that anyone should be required to obey an order that works in the opposite direction. Moreover, the superior's power is derived from the rule, and it is impossible that the rule could give him any power to command its transgression.[5]

Francis inserted these limitations into the rule itself. When speaking of the obedience owed a superior, he explicitly excludes anything contrary to the rule and to our souls, thus teaching us that evangelical obedience is principally ordained to observance of the rule. He also warns superiors not to command anything contrary to the rule or harmful to the brothers' souls and tells the brothers that if they find they cannot observe the rule spiritually—"that is," Olivi says, "in its purity, simplicity and spiritual perfection"—then "they should not immediately challenge their superiors' control" but should instead go to them and explain the problem. Moreover, "lest it should be believed that the ministers have legitimate control over the brothers everywhere in such cases, [Francis] immediately adds that [the superiors] should treat them so familiarly that [the brothers] can speak and act as lords do with their servants." Thus Paul resisted Peter to his face, and Peter, although he was Paul's highest superior, reacted as if Paul were the lord and he the servant.[6]

Olivi sees no limitations on obedience beyond these three. It is required not only in matters explicitly included in the rule but in those implicitly included. Thus, he says, it is wrong to argue that a superior cannot order fasting beyond what is stipulated in the rule. In fact, Olivi seems to imply

that the superior can even compel his subordinates to engage in missionary activity among the Saracens.[7]

His discussion of appeals to higher authority follows much the same
pattern. If they are fraudulent or prejudicial to regular discipline, they
are contrary to evangelical perfection as well as to canon law. They are
legitimate only when launched to protect the purity of the rule, the truth
of the catholic faith, or the spiritual good and peace of the community.
In these cases, however, an appeal is not only legitimate but obligatory.[8]

Olivi was hardly revolutionary in placing limits on obedience to Franciscan superiors. The rule itself supplied him with the notion that obedience could not be demanded in matters that harmed the soul or infringed
upon the rule.[9] A long tradition of interpretation insisted that the first
category included not only sins but whatever provided incentive to sin,
while the latter comprised not only violations of what is prescribed by
the rule but also violations of those statutes instituted to safeguard the
purity of the rule.[10] The same tradition acknowledged that the passage in
the rule about inability to observe the rule *spiritualiter* could be construed as referring not only to defects within the individual but to defec-
tive environments as well, although Olivi does seem to give the passage a
novel interpretive twist in the way he reads guidelines for disobedience
into it.[11] He also parts company with extant rule commentaries in the
sheer amount of space he devotes to the limitations on obedience. Of
course he is not in fact writing a rule commentary, and when he did
produce one it came closer to displaying the traditional lineaments;[12] yet
his emphasis here is intriguing nonetheless.

At any rate, it worth noting that even John of Murrovalle, who seems
to appear at strategic moments in the story and play Inspector Javert to
Olivi's Jean Valjean, is on record as arguing that the vow of obedience
has its limits. In a question written during roughly the same period as
Olivi's,[13] John emphasizes that the subordinate is excused from obedience
not only in those things which are contrary to the rule, but also in those
which are *contra indulgentias regulae*. Thus the Franciscan can ride a
horse in case of necessity, even if ordered not to do so by his superior.

In other words, both Olivi and John speak of limitations on obedience,
but John speaks of situations in which a superior contravenes the rule
through excessive rigor and Olivi concentrates on situations in which he
violates it through excessive laxity. It is tempting to read a great deal into
this difference; yet we must remember that in John's case we are dealing
with a single extant question by a young *sententiarius* who may well have
altered his emphasis when he found himself running the order over a
decade later. Thus, though the contrast may shed some light on the con-

frontation between the young Olivi and the young John in the censure of 1283, it is less helpful in gauging John's attitude toward the deceased Olivi and his supporters after 1298.

Obedience to the Pope

What about higher authority? Olivi asks whether the pope can dispense from vows,[14] and replies that absolution from vows is impossible, but dispensation is not. Vows are ordained to the divine *cultus* and to the vower's own salvation. A vow that worked toward these ends when it was made may well promote something more ominous as circumstances change. The papal power of dispensation is nothing more than an authority to make the necessary corrections in this regard, commuting the obligation to some more expedient requirement if the situation causes the vow to militate against its own proper ends. There is one area in which this reasoning cannot apply, however. In no case can the pope dispense from evangelical vows. They could only be commuted to lesser vows and to a status less advantageous to the church as well as the individual, all of which is impossible.

Olivi goes on to ponder the limitations of ecclesiastical power. Four criteria should be noted, he says. First, it cannot be used for destruction but only for edification, not against the truth but only for it. Second, it depends upon Christ's power and is thus subject to his laws and statutes. Third, it cannot diminish itself, which would occur if a professor of evangelical vows (subject to the pope in the counsels as well as the precepts) were made a nonprofessor (subject only in the latter). Finally, it does not extend to areas in which God wishes men to be free and thus cannot cancel the free act by which we give ourselves and our property to God through evangelical vows.

Very well, the supreme pontiff cannot commute evangelical vows. What should be done if he tries to do so anyway? Olivi replies that any pope persisting in this attempt need not be obeyed but should be cut off as a schismatic and a heretic.[15] Those are strong words, but Olivi uses even stronger language in another (unfortunately quite undatable) question dealing with whether it would be licit for the Franciscans to be supported by regular income from possessions entrusted to procurators. One of the arguments offered for the affirmative suggests that the pope has authority to arrange such matters as he thinks expedient, and if he were to decide on this course, the Franciscans would be obliged to accept it. Olivi replies that the pope certainly has power to order what is best and most expedient; yet where (let it never occur!) he audaciously and pertinaciously wishes to introduce some profane novelty in opposition to the counsels and examples of Christ and the apostles; and in opposition to the testimonies most worthy of belief, the regular statutes, and the examples of the angelic man Francis, who was sealed in christiform fashion with the sacred stigmata; and in subversion of the whole evangelical state; then in this case he would not act as the vicar of Christ but as the noonday devil, and he should by no means be obeyed but rather resisted with all one's powers as Lucifer and the noonday devil.[16]

It is important to recognize the limits of Olivi's originality in making such a statement. The order had a long history of anxiety on the subject of papal dispensations. Early rule commentaries expressed reservations about them[17] and a series of general chapters from 1251 through 1260 tried to lessen the impact of certain papal privileges. Even in the 1270s and 1280s Franciscan legislation displayed a degree of ambivalence in this area.[18]

Moreover, there was nothing particularly outlandish about the suggestion that the pope could not dispense from evangelical vows. From the middle of the thirteenth century on, a number of respectable scholastics discussed this matter in *Sentence* commentaries and quodlibetal questions. Some of them were willing to draw the line at least at chastity, which canon law and Ecclesiasticus 26:20 both seemed to place beyond papal authority.[19] Hugh of Digne went farther, rejecting the pope's right to dispense from evangelical vows of either continence or poverty. Some scholars have wished to see him as father of the spirituals for precisely this reason,[20] but his associations seem a good deal more respectable. Bonaventure, in his *Sentence* commentary, raises the question of whether the pope can dispense from evangelical vows.[21] He refuses to assert any opinion on the matter but clearly prefers and eloquently defends the negative view, which he explicitly affirms elsewhere.[22] Even in the *Sentence* commentary he suggests that, if the pope cannot dispense from chastity, then he certainly cannot dispense from poverty.[23]

To be sure, even in the mid-thirteenth century some scholars were willing to allow for papal dissolution of evangelical vows in order to attain some notable common good. In *Sentence* commentaries and quodlibets this question was normally raised concerning the vow of chastity. The standard scenario was a kingdom that could avert war by a diplomatic marriage involving the king's daughter, a nun; or a Christian people that could escape persecution only by acceding to the infidel ruler's unexplained desire to marry a sworn virgin.[24] By the final decades of the century, dissolution of a vow in such circumstances was accepted by several major scholars, including Richard of Middleton;[25] yet it was still possible to remain theologically respectable while defending the opposite thesis.[26] Even those who defended the pope's power to dispense found it hard to avoid placing some limitation on that power, albeit inconspicuously. Richard is typical. He argues that the pope can dispense from all vows of supererogation if there is rational cause to believe that greater good will ensue or greater evil be avoided. Otherwise it would be not *dispensatio* but *dissipatio*.[27]

Olivi does seem to be breaking new ground in the way he formulates the problem. He is not simply inquiring whether Franciscans should politely forbear to take advantage of privileges extended by generous popes. Nor is he simply defining the boundaries of papal prerogative. He is asking what should be done when one is torn between two conflicting authorities, the pope and the rule, both of which demand obedience. That is a question preceding Franciscan scholars did not care to broach quite so explicitly.

Some Franciscans were discussing the matter during the decade before Olivi wrote, but not in a scholarly context. The debate seems to have begun in response to a rumor that spread through the March of Ancona in 1274, during the Council of Lyons. Franciscans heard that the pope would soon order them to own property, and they soon found themselves arguing over what should be done in that case. Most of the brothers said they would obey, but a few insisted that they would have to follow the rule. The debate continued long after it became clear that the rumor was false. Those who (theoretically) declined to obey the pope were eventually disciplined.[28] Thus Olivi's discussion does have an immediate ancestry, but hardly an encouraging one.

Whatever fate may have befallen those stiff-necked brothers in Ancona, the notion that one should disobey the pope in certain situations was not always subject to disciplinary action in the thirteenth century, nor was it limited to a radical fringe. Olivi's words are certainly no bolder than those uttered by Robert Grosseteste when, as bishop of Lincoln, he refused to admit Pope Innocent IV's nephew to a canonry there in 1253. Grosseteste wrote the pope saying,

> After the sin of Lucifer, which is the same as that of Antichrist to appear at the end of time, there can be no sin so contrary to the doctrine of the apostles, . . . so hateful, detestable and abominable to the Lord Jesus Christ himself, and so ruinous to man, as that of destroying souls (which should be enlivened and healed

by pastoral care) through the corruption of the pastoral office. It is impossible that the most holy apostolic see, to which has been handed down . . . all manner of power, according to the apostle, for edification and not for destruction, can command . . . anything verging upon this kind of sin. . . . For this would be evidently a falling off and corruption and abuse of its most holy and plenary power. . . . No faithful subject of the Holy See, no man who is not cut away by schism from the body of Christ and the same Holy See, can submit to mandates, precepts or any other demonstrations of this kind, no, not even if the author were the supreme order of angels. He must necessarily repudiate them and rebel against them with all his strength. Thus, reverend lord, because of the very debt of obedience owed by me, I obediently disobey, contradict and rebel.[29]

One is immediately struck by the similar apocalyptic and demonological allusions. Both Olivi and Grosseteste mention Lucifer. Olivi, too, discusses the sin of Antichrist in this context. Olivi identifies his erring pope with Lucifer and the sin of Antichrist, whereas Grosseteste rates his a close second, but that difference somehow seems less significant than the comparison itself.

More important, perhaps, is the common yardstick both apply to papal actions. The supreme pontiff acts in conformity with Christ and the apostles for the edification of the church. If the man who happens to wear the papal tiara acts in contradiction to the example of Christ and the apostles and in such a way as to destroy the church, then not only need he not be obeyed, he must not be obeyed. Obedience itself calls for rebellion.

Grosseteste and Olivi were hardly alone in this belief. As Brian Tierney demonstrated more than three decades ago,[30] the obligation to disobey was acknowledged by various canonists in the thirteenth century and even by Innocent IV, the pope whom Grosseteste was disobeying. As a canonist, Innocent offered an extreme theory of papal power yet acknowledged that monks commanded to act in violation of their vows should not obey, even if ordered to do so by the pope himself.[31]

Obedience and the *Usus Pauper* Controversy

In short, Olivi is eager to praise obedience but equally anxious to establish that, when the purity of the rule is at stake, one is obliged by his vow to appeal all the way up to the pope if necessary. If the pope himself orders violation of its purity, then the pope must be resisted. A Franciscan's primary loyalty is always to the rule. Olivi is careful to avoid encouraging ignorant, willful opposition. When there is reasonable doubt, one's superior should be obeyed. In his *Rule Commentary* he notes that the brothers should recur to their ministers when they know they cannot observe the rule spiritually, not when they merely think so.[32] Nevertheless, he also says in the same work, characteristically, that they not only can but must recur to the minister in such cases.

Olivi's argument takes on a distinct coloration when we remember that he considers *usus pauper* to be a part of the vow and therefore one of the things a friar must observe despite any commands to the contrary. It is easy to see the effect such an assertion must have had on discipline once it was accepted by a significant minority, many of whom felt that the order had strayed from its original purity. Restricted use was a sensitive and highly controversial issue, but lack of ownership was not. It was an odd combination of circumstances that managed to produce an argument about ownership in the March of Ancona. As Angelo Clareno acknowledges, even on that occasion the argument refused to die precisely because the participants had serious differences on the question of use as well.

In other words, once *usus pauper* was included by some of the more rigorous Franciscans as an issue on which their vows bound them to a course of action, the order faced a serious discipline problem. Those who found themselves living in what they considered excessively lax houses could not simply register a modest protest and then conform for the sake of the obedience owed their superiors, as they might have done if *usus pauper* was not part of the vow. Instead, obedience to the vow pointed them in precisely the opposite direction. True, they also had promised to obey their superiors, but the latter's authority was oriented toward fulfillment of the rule and thus, in effect, disappeared when they commanded anything that compromised its observance. The same applied to the pope. Thus we see another reason why recognition of *usus pauper* as part of the vow would not have appealed to leaders of the Franciscan order. It turned a controverted issue into a crisis of conscience and in the process undercut duly constituted authority. The problem was not that Olivi postulated a loyalty beyond that owed to institutional superiors but that he placed that loyalty where a sizable number of Franciscans were sure to stumble over it, a place where it got in the way of orderly administration.

When did leaders of the order realize that inclusion of *usus pauper* in the vow created an intolerable discipline problem? It was abundantly clear to John XXII, who became pope in 1316, and to Michael of Cesena, elected minister general in the same year. Their repression of the spirituals during the following years concentrated heavily on establishing the necessity of obedience to one's superiors.[33] The discipline problem had already been exploited at the Council of Vienne, where the community consistently depicted the spirituals as an anarchic group who wished to break loose from duly constituted authority and obey the *regula nuda*, interpreting it however the mood struck them.[34]

On the other hand, there is no evidence that this problem weighed heavily—or indeed at all—with Olivi's original opponents. It is not reflected in their arguments, at least insofar as Olivi reports them. Nor do the brief, enigmatic comments of the Parisian commission show any such concern. It is understandable that the problem of discipline should have played no role at this early stage, because Olivi was not challenging the leadership of the order or even explicitly disagreeing with it. It may seem odd that Olivi's adversaries, in their search for incriminating evidence, could have perused his *Questions on Evangelical Perfection* without noticing some of his stronger statements in questions eleven, fourteen, and sixteen, but there is no way of establishing that these questions were even available to them.

In any case, the theoretical basis of the problem was present by the early 1280s in Olivi's writings. Another element, a discernible Olivi faction, was present by 1285, when Arnold of Roquefeuil characterized Olivi as a sower of discord and head of a superstitious sect.[35] Nevertheless, it was Arnold rather than Olivi who lost this round, and Olivi spent the rest of his life as spokesman for a licit and entirely respectable position. One may wonder what would have happened if Olivi had not been rehabilitated in the late 1280s and his supporters had remained at odds with official policy, thus fulfilling a third requirement for serious trouble.

What did happen was more complex. Various shades of opinion emerged among the zealots, and Olivi was left standing distinctly to the right of the more radical elements. By the 1290s, leaders of the order were forced to take action against what they viewed as disruptive minorities acting out their consciences in southern France and Italy. In southern France at the beginning of the decade, the papacy intervened and demanded action against a group "causing schism." It would be nice to know more about this episode, but we do not.

In Italy the papacy was inevitably involved when some Franciscan zealots denied the legitimacy of Boniface's election. Of course, it was not only Franciscan zealots who did so, Olivi was not personally implicated in these events, and there is no solid evidence that the events themselves were a major cause of the crackdown from 1299 on. Nevertheless, it is easy to imagine Boniface deducing that the new Franciscan minister general should be encouraged to put a tighter, shorter leash on his order. In the resultant new environment, any notable dissent might be regarded as a threat. Nor is it unthinkable that some of the more disruptive elements in the 1290s actually appealed to Olivi's authority. Angelo Clareno reports that the Tuscan spirituals who seized control of their houses in 1312 did so,[36] and Ubertino da Casale's *Arbor vitae* is evidence that even in 1305 Italian spirituals more radical than Olivi were making use of him. Olivi's impact on the Italian spirituals dates from at least 1287, when Ubertino came to know him at Florence. Perhaps it dates from 1279. Of course, as we see from Ubertino and Angelo, the Italian spirituals made odd use of Olivi; yet, however much they may have distorted him, however orderly Olivi's own behavior, and however vehement his complaint to Conrad of Offida, any Franciscan leader who took the trouble to read his work could see that he resembled the rebels in his insistence that defying authority on the matter of *usus pauper* was not simply a right but a sacred duty when the purity of the rule was at stake.

Olivi's Apocalyptic Program

In short, although the impact of Olivi's view of *usus pauper* on discipline within the order does not seem to have been a factor in the debate during the early 1280s, it became one in time. Something similar might be said of his apocalyptic thought. Olivi's commentary on Revelation, completed shortly before his death in 1298, has received the most attention, because it played an important role in posthumous attacks on him; yet his early apocalyptic thought is more relevant to the subject at hand. It is found not only in the *Questions on Evangelical Perfection* but in what may have been his three earliest Bible commentaries, those concerning Matthew, Job, and Isaiah, all of which stem from the period 1279–82.[37]

The apocalyptic program found in these earlier works does not differ strikingly from that contained in his Revelation commentary. Olivi divides world history into six *etates* with a seventh in eternity and also into fourteen periods, seven of the Old Testament and seven of the church.[38] He sees his own time as one of transition between the fifth and sixth periods of the church. The fifth was a time of *condescensio* in which the church came to terms with the world in a way that allowed it to expand and gain power, but at the price of moral decline. The sixth period is one of rebirth, when new wisdom and increased evangelical poverty will lead first to persecution, temptation, and the reign of Antichrist, then to the final, seventh period of peace and contemplation.

This pattern is complemented by a threefold division of history into ages of Father, Son, and Holy Spirit. The first extended from creation through the birth of Christ; the second stretches rrom Christ through the fifth period of church history; and the third will be commensurate with the sixth and seventh periods of church history. The first was characterized by a *velamen figurarum* in which spiritual things were concealed under apparently temporal promises.[39] In the second the veil was partly torn away by Christ. The church, searching beneath the *figurae* of the Old Testament, discovered the spiritual senses of the law and prophets.[40] Even in the second age, however, the temporal possessions of the church and religious orders veiled some deeper knowledge.

In the third age, the harbingers of which are Joachim of Fiore and Francis of Assisi, the perfect life of Christ will be established.[41] That life will feature apostolic poverty and an *intelligentia spiritualis* exceeding all prior knowledge. Such new wisdom involves a deeper understanding of scripture though discovery of its spiritual meanings, but it also includes a *suavitas et iocunditas contemplationis* in which the secrets of the contemplative life will be opened through an affective experience given directly by Christ.[42]

Much of this is not new. The sixfold division of world history went back to Augustine and beyond, while the sevenfold division of church history was a commonplace of thirteenth-century exegesis. Olivi's decision to place himself at the beginning of the sixth period rather than in the early fifth put him at variance with most Franciscan scholars but in line with Bonaventure and Joachim. Explicit acceptance of Joachim of Fiore's three *status* was rarer still. Even Bonaventure had avoided it.[43]

Other elements seem uniquely Olivian; yet even the most apparently idiosyncratic elements often prove at least tangentially linked with his Franciscan formation. His expectation of a "higher knowledge" in the seventh period was foreshadowed by Bonaventure's celebration of Francis in the *Collationes in Hexaemeron*, and his description of the third age as Christ's second advent may also have been anticipated there.[44] His emphasis on the affective elements of that knowledge is probably related to his characteristically Franciscan insistence that contemplation, which includes both conceptual understanding and love, is principally in the will rather than in the intellect.[45]

In the final analysis, perhaps the most striking aspect of Olivi's theology of history is not any specific pattern such as the seven periods, three *status*, or two advents, but the strongly progressive reading of history which underlies all these patterns. For that, too, there is a precedent. Like Bonaventure before him, Olivi stands Dionysius the Areopagite on his side, reading history in terms of hierarchy.[46] No one who understands Dionysius, he argues, would expect all periods of church history to be uniform. They would expect inequality, with one period superior to another. They would expect some relation to an end, which is final cause of the entire sequence.

For Christians, the end is a state of beatitude in which the truth is revealed. Olivi grants that the end of history is transhistorical, heavenly bliss, but he also insists on identifying some stage of history that will witness "a clarification of faith, an inundation of divine delights, and a banishing of all errors insofar as such is possible in this life."[47] Only if such occurs can God's power and goodness be fully displayed.

Inherent Dangers

Is there anything particularly subversive about this vision of history? Ever since Olivi's time there have been churchmen (and then historians) willing to argue the affirmative, but they have been less than unanimous on precisely where the danger should be sought. On the whole, there has been a powerful suspicion abroad that the logic of the Joachite threefold pattern must lead one to expect a new era superseding the Christian dispensation. Such suspicions are more easily entertained than proved. Olivi does not expect Christ, church, or scripture to be abolished in the third age. The perfection attained by *viri spirituales* in the third age will be evangelical perfection or the perfect life of Christ, their poverty will be apostolic poverty, and their sufferings will be an imitation of Christ's passion. The carnal church will fall and the spiritual church will triumph; yet these two entities are seen not as separate institutions but as elements within a single church enduring from Christ until the eschaton. The *intellectus spiritualis* of the new age will involve a new way of reading the Bible, not a new Bible. Even the direct contemplative knowledge of that age will not be entirely new. Olivi has heard about Pentecost. He knows that contemplative experience has been enjoyed throughout history. He simply expects it to be enjoyed more generally and more fully in the third age.[48]

If there is an inherent danger in Olivi's apocalyptic thought, it lies not in any purported supersession of the New Covenant but in Olivi's progressive reading of it. It is not the notion of progress itself but the sort of progress anticipated that constitutes the main difficulty. Advancement in knowledge was hardly an unsupportable notion in Olivi's time. Scholars recognized that dogma came into being when church councils made explicit what was merely assumed in the Bible and by the church fathers. Duns Scotus announces that he accepts the doctrine of transubstantiation because it is established in a decree of the Fourth Lateran Council, "in which the truth of some things to be believed is set out more explicitly than in the . . . creeds."[49] Scholars were even prepared to acknowledge that the Holy Spirit could be involved in such advances. Thus Scotus notes that, although he cannot find transubstantiation in the Bible, he follows the council on this matter, knowing that it was guided by the same spirit that presided over the writing of holy scripture. In fact, some scholars were willing to entertain, at least in unguarded moments, the notion that the Holy Spirit could announce to the church truths completely absent from scripture.[50]

Olivi goes substantially farther. He foresees a more generous endowment of the Holy Spirit in the third age. It will speak directly to a great many people, at times perhaps without benefit of Bible, *sancti*, or discursive reasoning.[51] It will speak not simply to duly constituted authorities like the pope or a general council but to *viri spirituales*. In short, the Holy Spirit will not be routed through official channels.

Even here Olivi is not entirely unique, since the same ideas might be deduced from Bonaventure's *Collationes in Hexaemeron*; yet anyone who reads both authors will notice a difference. It lies partly in Olivi's greater sense of immediacy. He and Bonaventure both see the new age as having dawned with Francis, but Olivi is more anxious to read contemporary Franciscan history in that context. He talks about it more volubly and in the process offers a fuller account of the apocalyptic timetable.

Olivi is never very specific on this subject and is even less so in the early works than at the end of his life in the Revelation commentary, but in the latter work he reduces all the great controversies of his day to a single battle between the dawning new age and its opponents. Nor does he expect an easy victory for the new age. He anticipates that in the future an already decadent church will continue to deteriorate until leadership from the pope down, including that of the Franciscan order, is controlled by carnal men. Ecclesiastical leaders will persecute spiritual men until the carnal church is destroyed by non-Christian forces. Babylon thus having fallen, pious survivors will undergo the persecution of the great Antichrist. Only when he is destroyed by Christ will they be able to enter fully into the contemplative joys of the third age.[52]

The earlier works do not yield as neat a schedule, but it is instructive to note how often Olivi underscores a parallel between persecution of

Christ by carnal scribes, pharisees, *prelati*, *rectores*, and *seniores* of the synagogue and persecution of spiritual men in the dawning sixth period of church history.[53] In expositing Matthew 16:18–21, he offers a contemporary application of the passage, one that combines both positive and negative elements.

> Just as, during Christ's first advent in the flesh, there were various opinions about him, but the disciples truly and solidly confessed the truth and Christ's church was founded upon them; so, in Christ's second advent in the spirit, there are and will be various opinions concerning Christ's life, but on those disciples solidly confessing its sublimity will be founded the spiritual church, against which the gates of Hell—that is, the hellish sects of Antichrist—will not prevail. In fact, it will have the highest power to open the secrets of scripture . . . and of the contemplative state and close them to the unworthy. Note, however, that once they are solid in the aforesaid confession, the life of Christ (or Christ in the spirit of his life) will openly tell them that they and he must go to Jerusalem and be reproved by the scribes and elders of the carnal church.[54]

In his early works, Olivi never says precisely where these scribes and elders will be encountered, but it seems likely that here, as in the Revelation commentary, he assumes that they will eventually dominate the church hierarchy and the Franciscan order. One could deduce as much from the model provided by Christ's passion, from the weight of persecution and subtlety of temptation constantly identified with the spirituals' "passion" in the dawning sixth period, and from Olivi's anticipation of a future domination by Antichrist. After the great Antichrist the church will be ruled by good shepherds, but before him spiritual men must face increasing persecution by their own leaders.

Thus we arrive at what may be the most significant question to be asked about Olivi's apocalyptic scenario: did it subvert established authority by encouraging believers to defy their leaders? There is little doubt that it eventually did just that in the 1320s, when spiritual Franciscans and Beguins in southern France, applying Olivian apocalyptic to the world around them, renounced the hierarchy because they believed that by condemning Olivi's thought it had revealed itself as the carnal church. It is another matter to argue that Olivi's theology of history already had some impact on the *usus pauper* controversy as early as the 1280s. Here we must really answer two different questions. The first is whether Olivi himself saw any connection, the second whether his opponents saw any.

Apocalyptic Expectation and the *Usus Pauper* Controversy

Certainly Olivi saw some connection. In the eighth of his *Questions on Evangelical Perfection* he crowns his argument for poverty with an explanation of its apocalyptic significance.[55] This section is more important than its size (around 7 percent of the entire question) might suggest, because it states explicitly what is implicit elsewhere. Nevertheless, this observation must be balanced with two others.

The first observation is that anyone reading question eight will be struck by its generally optimistic tone. The Antichrist appears on several occasions, often in company with Aristotle. On at least two occasions Olivi identifies excessive valuation of wealth as the principal root of the error of Antichrist, and he observes at another point that the principal beliefs associated with the temptation of Antichrist are already being sown in the world. He also contends that the church will decay around the end of the fifth period and all but a few will err in the time of Antichrist.[56] Thus stated, his message sounds grim. If one merely counted the number of times Olivi alludes to Antichrist, one might argue that he is very much on Olivi's mind.

Nevertheless, the total impression one gets from question eight is not that of an embattled minority reeling under persecution. Far from being disowned by the ecclesiastical hierarchy, the new age has been embraced by the papacy. Here as in his selection of patristic authorities, Olivi follows a recognizably Minorite line of attack. Franciscan *novitas* "was initiated and validated, not by human means, but by the divine spirit and by the authority of the supreme pontiff and the Roman seat." The pope has ratified not only the existence of the order but its self-understanding as well. "Thus in privileges and letters it is frequently called 'the highest poverty' and 'evangelical poverty.' "[57]

Moreover, Olivi's negative comments must be viewed in context. Thirteenth- and early fourteenth-century mendicant commentaries on the Apocalypse tended to divide church history into seven periods. They saw the sixth as dominated by the temptation of Antichrist, and they were very likely to see the fifth as characterized by the precursors of Antichrist. Some of them were vigorous in condemning contemporary life and placing it within the early fifth period.[58] Olivi heightens the apocalyptic tension by placing himself in the sixth period, but so does Bonaventure in the *Collationes in hexaemeron*. Like Bonaventure, Olivi alters the contours of the sixth period by identifying it not only with the temptation of Antichrist but with a remarkable leap forward in doctrinal and spiritual history. In this respect, the tone of question eight is remarkably similar to that of the *Collationes*. The negative elements are there, but one is primarily struck with the positive claims being made.

The second observation to be made is that question eight is in any case a chapter in the secular-mendicant controversy, not the *usus pauper* controversy. Its intention is to argue the value of poverty, not the centrality of restricted use within Franciscan poverty. That honor belongs to question nine, in which Olivi defends his position by invoking all the arguments used to defend poverty in question eight. In some cases he recalls the arguments at length, showing their application to the present question. When he arrives at the apocalyptic section, however, he simply notes that the comments made there are applicable to *usus pauper* and drops the matter.[59] Nor does he say substantially more in the *Treatise on Usus Pauper*. Olivi begins that work by placing the *usus pauper* controversy within a history of Satan's attempts to thwart evangelical poverty in the latter days and closes it with a suggestion that the current attack on *usus pauper* is a preparation for the sect of Antichrist.[60] The rest of the work is almost devoid of apocalyptic allusions.

If Olivi's works on *usus pauper* contain only scant reference to his theology of history, the reverse is equally true. The Matthew, Job, and Isaiah commentaries are rich in apocalyptic speculation yet largely innocent of allusions to the *usus pauper* controversy, even though it was in full swing when they were being composed. The only passage relating to it in the Matthew commentary[61] lacks any apocalyptic dimension. Undoubtedly Olivi is thinking of the *usus pauper* controversy when he speaks of carnal oppositon to evangelical renewal in the sixth period, just as he is thinking of the secular-mendicant controversy and Dominican criticism of the Franciscan rule,[62] but he never says so.

What, then, are we to make of the emphasis on persecution of spiritual men, the prediction that spiritual men must go to Jerusalem and be reproved by the scribes and elders? The real question is not whether he expects these things to occur—he does—but when he expects them to occur. In other words, are these events scheduled for the indefinite future or does Olivi think he will be called upon to make his witness in the present controversy?

Here again, the early works are less receptive to such questions than is the Revelation commentary, and the latter is none too obliging. The most recent attempt to wring dates from the Revelation commentary concludes that it places the destruction of the carnal church and subsequent reign of the great Antichrist between around 1300 and 1340.[63] That is hardly a precise timetable, but it suggests that Olivi must have been watching the signs rather anxiously by 1298, the year of his death. On the other hand, there is no evidence that, like Ubertino in 1305, he saw Boniface VIII as the mystical Antichrist. In fact, there is no reason to assume that Olivi would have seen Boniface's election as a greater disaster than Celestine's. Unlike Angelo and his associates, he had little sympathy for Celestine's willingness to split the order and no vested interest in seeing Celestine remain.[64]

The early commentaries offer little to work with on this matter, but the documents of the *usus pauper* controversy are instructive in the attitude toward authority they project. Olivi is very explicit in asserting that one must not obey a papal order (or for that matter an order from any superior) if it entails violation of one's vows, yet he makes no suggestion that such is actually occurring. On the contrary, in defending *usus pauper* he appeals confidently to the words of contemporary popes and ministers general. He may or may not recognize that he has to stretch those words occasionally to make them fit, but he certainly considers it worth trying. Nor does Olivi hesitate to present his case to the minister general. He even seems open to the possibility that he will win that case. In short, he does not act like a man who thinks that the very godliness of his position will insure its rejection by the authorities.

Even when the tide began to turn against him in the early 1280s, Olivi avoided drawing apocalyptic conclusions. In the letter to R and his associates, Olivi defends his apocalyptic thought but does not apply it to his present situation.[65] He announces that he is being conformed with Christ's suffering but presents this conformity as an individual purification process rather than as the result of his allegiance to evangelical perfection.[66] Later, in his letter to the commission that had censured him in 1283, Olivi describes his reaction. He thinks the process against him was marred by procedural errors, not to mention an unfortunate conclusion, and he chronicles his unsuccessful efforts to set the record straight. The letter represents one more attempt to do so.[67] Here again he acts like a man who considers it possible to do more than simply suffer for the truth.

Obviously, none of these considerations is conclusive; yet taken together, they encourage the hypothesis that insofar as Olivi was influenced in the early 1280s by his apocalyptic expectations, it was primarily by the positive rather than the negative side of those expectations. His stance was in some ways similar to that adopted by Bonaventure in his declining years.[68] Both saw slippage in their own day but at least acted as if they thought it could be arrested or even reversed. The amount of decay seen by each was limited by the fact that both saw the developments from Francis's time to their own not as a fall from original innocence but as a progression. The order had changed remarkably during those decades, accumulating a large membership, new responsibilities, and a great deal of power. Instead of bewailing these alterations, Bonaventure and Olivi both accepted them as positive accomplishments. Thus they sought, not a return to the original standards of Rivo Torto and the Porziuncula, but the maintenance of a modest yet salubrious existence within a well-administered community, allowing the brothers to fulfill their responsibilities in the world while edifying it with their behavior. Far from impeding this attitude, Olivi's theology of history probably facilitated it, since his apocalyptic perspective encouraged a tolerance for change and discouraged identification of evangelical perfection with primitive Franciscanism.

Nevertheless, Olivi's positive expectations probably did encourage him to remain steadfast on certain issues that might have seemed less critical to those unblessed with apocalyptic insights. If Francis and his rule were harbingers of the new age, then the pristine purity of the rule had to be defended. The stakes were high. Thus Olivi pursued the *usus pauper* question vigorously.

These positive expectations also gave an odd twist to some of Olivi's arguments. He defended positions shared by others with arguments those others might have found vaguely alarming. For example, the idea that Franciscan bishops should observe *usus pauper* has its own logical integrity quite apart from Olivi's theology of history, but Olivi seems to suggest that Franciscans should practice *usus pauper* because all bishops should do so.[69] This position is comprehensible when viewed in light of his suggestion in the Revelation commentary that the pontificate "was usefully and rationally commuted to a state possessing temporals from the time of Constantine until the end of the fifth period" but will return in the end to its original apostolic state of poverty.[70] His apocalyptic expectations encouraged him to see the Franciscan life not merely as one option within the church but as a pattern for future ecclesiastical leadership. A Franciscan bishop who failed to observe *usus pauper* would thus betray not only his vow but the future itself.

The question remains whether Olivi's opponents saw any subversive apocalyptic dimension in his position. Certainly they showed little interest in the matter through 1283. The censure visited upon him during that year never even touched upon his apocalyptic views. This aspect of his thought had not gone unnoticed, however. The earliest allusion to it as a problem is in a letter he wrote to a group of friends sometime before the censure of 1283. Apparently they had seen the list of charges sent to the minister general by his opponents and had written Olivi asking him to comment. His reply briefly discusses his apocalyptic thought even though, as he observes, his friends did not inquire about it. He is volunteering the information, he says, "because some people accuse me of following dreams and fantastic visions like a soothsayer, and of rashly busying myself with the prediction of future events."[71] As for dreams and visions, Olivi offers a set of ground rules for testing the spirits. The overall impression they convey is that he does have an interest in visions and does accept some in his own time as valid, although there is no evidence that he thinks of himself as a visionary. His attitude is understandable in view of his expectation of new wisdom in the dawning third age.[72]

He then turns to predictions, by which he obviously means apocalyptic speculation. He protests that he has avoided specificity. Never has he asserted "that this would happen during that day or year, or this or that person would do this or that thing." He holds as certain that the Franciscan order, after being purged by innumerable temptations, will reform divine worship throughout the world, but he does not presume to offer a detailed description of how this will come about.

The passage, combined with our knowledge of the 1283 censure, suggests that some of Olivi's early opponents denounced his apocalyptic enthusiasms but failed to convince the authorities that the subject was worth pursuing. It would be interesting to discover what they thought unsettling about his theology of history, but that information has disappeared along with a great deal else.

When did those in power become anxious, if not in 1283? Certainly there was a concerted attack under John XXII. John appointed the commission that read and censured Olivi's Revelation commentary in 1318,[73] and in the same year he attacked Italian spiritual apocalyptic views in the bull *Gloriosam ecclesiam*.[74] Leaders of the Franciscan order were concerned before that date and included Olivi's apocalyptic speculation among the charges made against him at the Council of Vienne. Anticipating the commission of 1318, Olivi's detractors at Vienne pictured him as "calling the church a great whore and dogmatizing many other things in disparagement of the church;"[75] yet this was not one of the issues they chose to emphasize, and there was no discernible reaction from Pope Clement V.

Nevertheless, here again the 1290s might be considered a watershed period. The antagonism between spirituals and conventuals escalated noticeably. There is no evidence as to whether the French spirituals punished in 1292 were motivated by apocalyptic expectation, but we do know that in 1299 a provincial council at Béziers complained of certain educated men from approved orders who were stirring up *beguini seu beguinae*, telling them, among other things, that the end of the world was near and the time of Antichrist had begun, "or just about."[76] Olivi remarks that the Italian spirituals who opposed Boniface VIII from 1295 on were citing the line from Revelation, "come out of her, my people," as a call to separate from the carnal leadership of church and order.[77] Boniface's various letters also suggest a degree of apocalyptic awareness on the rebels' part.[78]

Of course, Olivi managed to distance himself from all such phenomena, and there would be little reason to believe that either French or Italian troublemakers in the 1290s saw him as an important influence were it not for evidence that, on the orders of Boniface VIII, Giles of Rome undertook a refutation of Olivi's Revelation commentary.[79] What is important is that from the 1290s on fractious elements within the order were offering an apocalyptic justification for resistance to authority.

After Olivi's death, what had hitherto been a tension in the order over the practice of poverty turned into a repression of dissidents by those in power. In the process, Olivi's writings were confiscated and his supporters persecuted. In southern France, conditions were now ripe for both sides to see the battle in terms of Olivian apocalyptic. The community could see it as the *secta fratris Petri Iohannis* rebelling against legitimate authority as Olivi had advised, while the embattled spirituals could read the attack on them and on Olivi's works as a validation of those works, a fulfillment of precisely what Olivi himself had predicted in them.

We cannot say when and where Olivi's writings were first given this twist in southern France, but Ubertino da Casale's *Arbor vitae*, written in 1305, offers sobering evidence of what an Italian spiritual could do with them. Ubertino combines generous borrowing from Olivi's Revelation commentary with precisely the sort of specificity Olivi wanted to avoid.[80] The point is not that Ubertino made specific historical applications but Olivi did not. Both did so, as did most late thirteenth-century Franciscan commentaries on Revelation, although in varying degrees. For example, Francis was identified with various apocalyptic angels. Ubertino was more willing to try his hand at negative applications (for example, concerning the mystical Antichrist, the beast from the sea, the beast from the earth, and so on), but even this was hardly new. Apocalyptic name-calling was a common element in polemical literature. Participants in the secular-mendicant controversy were addicted to it,[81] and

Olivi's opponents apparently branded him as the Antichrist.[82] The important point is that Ubertino's specific applications were such as to undermine confidence in the presiding ecclesiastical authorities. It is one thing to speak of the mystical Antichrist and quite another to suggest—as Ubertino does—that he has ruled the church in the persons of the last two popes.

In short, Olivi's apocalyptic speculation did contain certain elements which, in the right situation, would encourage defiance of ecclesiastical authority. The situation was right after 1294 and was even more so after 1318; yet it was not at all right in 1279. Although Olivi's theology of history did have some influence on his stance in the *usus pauper* controversy and was criticized by his opponents, it was not seen by those in authority as an important factor, let alone an imminent danger to good order, during most of his lifetime.

Notes

1. Q. 13 (whether the pope can resign) is an exception, but it was written much later and inserted between two other questions dealing with the pope.
2. Q. 11, MS Florence, Bibl. Laur. 448, 101vb–103ra.
3. Q. 11, 103va: "Patet igitur quod nullum peccatum mortale vel veniale propter imperium praelati est agendum nisi sit talis actio a qua superveniens imperium tollat rationem peccati. . . . Falsum est igitur quod quidam simplices aliquando dixerunt, quod, scilicet, omne peccatum veniale erat a subditis quando eis imperabatur propter bonum obedientiae agendum. . . . Propterea constat quod omne peccatum inquantum tale est purum malum et maxime hoc est verum in illis quae sic per se sunt mala quod non possunt esse aut cogitari sine malitia de quorum numero sunt multa venialia." Olivi quotes extensively from Bernard of Clairvaux.
4. Q. 11, 103vb–104rb. Olivi concludes: "Propterea gravius est contempnere divinam legem quam preceptum praelati, immo praeferre praeceptum praelati divinae legi et aestimare se magis astringi ad servandum praeceptum praelati quam ad praeceptum divinae legis sapit haeresim valde periculosam."
5. Q. 11, 104va: "Cum enim praelati regularis imperium ad observantiam regulae ordinetur propter observantiam enim regulae tamquam propter finem suum principalem sunt praelati in religionibus instituti, impossibilis est quod eius praeceptum obliget ad aliquid quod puritatem regulae diminuat vel labefaciat."
6. Q. 11, 104va–vb, concluding: "In omnino simili autem casu Paulus in facie restitit Petro summo praelato suo. Unde et Petrus recepit tunc verba illius sicut servus a domino suo." See *Regula*, c. 10.
7. Q. 11, 107vb–108rb, where he notes: "Fuerunt tamen quidam qui hanc distinctionem non attendentes dixerunt quod ad illa quae regula Francisci

nos licentiat non possimus cogi per ministros nostros utpote ad ieiunandum in illis temporibus de quibus regula dicit: Aliis autem temporibus non teneantur fratres, etc. Vel ubi de quadragesima Christi dicit: Et qui nolunt non sint astricti. Vel ubi dicit: Si qui fratres voluerint ire inter sarracenos petant, id est, licentiam etc. . . . . Quando autem regula dicit quod aliis temporibus non teneantur, etc., non vult aliud dicere nisi quod ex ipso statuto regulae per se et immediate ad hoc non teneantur non autem quin praelatus cui summam potestatem imperiandi in aliquo capitulo donant possit ad hoc cum sibi videbitur eos alligare." On missionary activity see *Regula*, c. 12.

8. Q. 11, 108rb–109rb, which again cites the rule on what to do when one cannot observe the rule *spiritualiter*. Olivi also contests Aquinas's denigration of poverty in favor of obedience, as he does in the Matthew commentary in the passage edited by d'Alverny, "Un Adversaire de Saint Thomas," 217–18.

9. *Regula*, c. 10.

10. This point is argued in *Expositio quatuor magistrorum*, 165, and echoed in subsequent commentaries. On these commentaries see Flood's introduction to *Olivi's Rule Commentary*, 92–103.

11. However this passage was originally intended, it was the only part of the 1223 rule relevant to the matter. The more explicit call for fraternal initiative in *Regula non bullata*, c. 5, had been removed. Angelo Clareno, *Le due prime tribulazioni* (Rome, 1908), 58–60 and *Expositio regulae* (Quaracchi, 1912), 205f., offers an intriguing though unsubstantiated report that *Regula*, c. 10, originally gave brothers permission to observe the rule literally even if ministers tried to prevent it, but the passage was altered to its present form by the pope in the interests of good order. For the strong element of individual freedom and responsibility in *Regula non bullata* see Desbonnets, *De intuition à l'institution*, 60–63.

12. Flood, *Olivi's Rule Commentary*, 185–87.

13. Published by Longpré, "L'oeuvre scolastique," 472–74.

14. Q. 14, MS Bibl. Laur. 448, 115va–124vb.

15. Q. 14, 120ra–rb: "Si enim omnis subversor ecclesie et boni communis eius debet censeri non solum scismaticus set plus quam scismaticus, multo magis hoc esset in eo qui cum deberet habere rationem capitis et pastoris potestative statum ecclesie confunderet et contra bonum eius commune publice tyrannice exerceret. . . . Unde non dubito quod ex quo pertinaciter in hoc facto persisteret quod ei non esset obediendum tanquam pape, immo esset tanquam scismaticus et tanquam hereticus precisus et tanquam lupus a fidelibus totaliter evitandus."

16. Burr and Flood, "Peter Olivi," 58: "Ubi quod absit contra Christi et apostolorum consilia et exempla et contra angelici viri Francisci sacris stigmatibus christiformiter consignati fide dignissima testimonia et regularia statuta dogmata et exempla in subversionem totius evangelici status audaciter et pertinaciter vellet aliquid attemptare et tam profanam novitatem inducere, quia in hoc non ut Christi vicarius sed ut daemon meridianus procederet, nequaquam esset sibi obediendum immo tanquam lucifero et

meridiano daemoni totis viribus resistendum." In Vat. lat. 4980 it is question 16.

17. *Expositio quatuor magistrorum*, 164; Hugo de Digna, *Rule Commentary*, 91.

18. See the *definitiones* of the Lyons 1274 chapter in Bonaventure, *Opera*, 8:467; or those of the 1282 Strasbourg general chapter in Fussenegger, "Definitiones capituli generalis Argentinae," 135; or *definitio* 23 of the Milan 1285 general chapter in Callebaut, "Acta capituli generalis Mediolani celebrati an. 1285," 289. On Franciscan avoidance of papal declarations see Harkins, "Authorship of a Commentary," 181–85. On the date of the Lyons statutes see Abate, "Memoriali," *CF* 33 (1933): 15, seconded by Harkins.

19. See, for example, Thomas Aquinas, *Summa theologiae*, IIa IIae, q. 88, a. 11; Albertus Magnus, *Commentarii in quartum librum sententiarum*, IV, d. 38, a. 16 in *Opera* (Paris, 1894), vol. 30; Alexander Halensis, *Glossa in quattuor libros sententiarum* (Quaracchi, 1957), IV, d. 38, 7.

20. For example, Claudia Florovsky in her introduction to the "De finibus paupertatis," *AFH* 5 (1912): 279.

21. *Commentarius in I, II, III, IV librum sententiarum*, IV, d. 38, a. 2, q. 3 in *Opera*, 4:822–29.

22. *Sermo VI de assumptione B. Virginis Mariae*, in *Opera*, 9:706.

23. *Sent.*, IV, d. 38, a. 2, q. 3 ad 4.

24. E.g. Petrus de Tarantasia, *In IV libris sententiarum commentaria* (Toulouse, 1652), IV, d. 38, q. 2, aa. 3–5; Gerardus de Abbevilla, *Quodlibet* IV, q. 13, MS Paris, Bibl. Nat. lat. 16405, 51rb–va.

25. *Super quattuor libros sententiarum* IV, d. 38, a. 9, q. 1. See also Godefridus de Fontibus, *Quodlibet* IV, q. 18, in M. de Wulf and A. Pelzer, eds., *Les quatres premiers quodlibets de Godefroid de Fontaines* (Louvain, 1904); Henricus a Gandavo, *Quodlibet* V, q. 28, in *Quodlibeta* (Venice, 1613), vol. 1; R. de Atrabato, *Quodlibet* II, q. 2, MS Paris, Bibl. Nat. lat. 15850, 30va–31ra; Simon de Guiberville, *Quodlibet* I, q. 4, MS Paris, bibl. Nat. lat. 15850, 38va; Gervasius de Mont Saint-Eloi, *Quodlibeta*, q. 41, MS Paris, Bibl. Nat. lat. 15350, 277vb–278ra.

26. Raymundus Rigaldi, *Quodlibet* V, q. 35, MS Todi, Bibl. Comm. 98, 29ra, does so. Durandus de Sancto Porciano, *Quodlibet* II, q. 11, MS Paris, Bibl. Nat. lat. 14572, 7rb, written ca. 1312–13, treats it as an open question but announces that he himself believes the pope cannot dispense from the vow of continence.

27. Richard is echoing Bernard of Clairvaux, *De consideratione*, c. 23, a passage quoted by others as well.

28. Angelo Clareno, *Historia septem tribulationum*, 301–4.

29. *Epistolae* (London, 1861), letter 128, partly translated in W. A. Pantin, "Grosseteste's Relations with the Papacy and the Crown," in *Robert Grosseteste* (Oxford, 1955), 189f.

30. Brian Tierney, "Grosseteste and the Theory of Papal Sovereignty," *Journal of Ecclesiastical History* 6 (1955): 1–17.

31. Innocentius IV, *In quinque libros decretalium commentaria* (Venice, 1570),

ad V, iii, 34; yet if Matthew Paris, *Chronica maior*, 392f. is correct, Grosseteste escaped disciplinary action only through the intervention of sympathetic cardinals.

32. Flood, *Olivi's Rule Commentary*, 186.

33. *BF*, 5:130. For the repression see Lambert, *Franciscan Poverty*, ch. 10. Bernardus Guidonis, *Practica inquisitionis*, 265, explicitly includes Olivi's "treatise on dispensations" among the works treasured by the Beguins.

34. *Sapientia aedificavit*, in *Archiv*, 3:99.

35. Raymundus de Fronciacho, *Sol ortus*, 14: "Concorditer asserunt illi fratres, et fratrem P[etrum] Jo[hannis] esse caput supersititiose secte et divisionis et plurium errorum in eodem provincia Provincie."

36. *Epistole*, 121–31.

37. On the Apocalypse commentary see Raoul Manselli, *La "Lectura super Apocalypsim" di Pietro di Giovanni Olivi* (Rome, 1955); Burr, *Persecution*, chs. 3 and 11. For the dating of the earlier commentaries see Burr, "The Date of Petrus Iohannis Olivi's Commentary on Matthew," as corrected in ch. 2 of this work.

38. For his description of these periods in *Rev.* see Burr, *Persecution*, 18f. His description of individual periods varies notably in the early works, but most of this variation seems due to the problems encountered in imposing a pattern on the particular material he is expositing. See *Lectura super Iob* (hereafter *Job*), MS Florence Bibl. Laur. Conv. sopp. 240, 55va, 55vb, 56rb, 57ra, 67rb; *Mtt.*, 86rb.

39. *Lectura super Isaiam* (hereafter *Isa.*), MS Paris Bibl. Nat. nouv. acq. 774 (hereafter BN), 44r; *Job*, 41va; *Mtt.*, 35ra, 87vb.

40. *Mtt.*, 87vb, 100rb, 101va, 155rb–va.

41. *Job*, 55rb, 56va, 57ra, 97ra; *Mtt.*, 86rb. On the roles of Joachim and Francis see David Burr, "Olivi, Apocalyptic Expectation, and Visionary Experience," *Traditio* 41 (1985): 273–88.

42. *Isa.*, MS Padova Univ. 1540 (hereafter PU), 45ra, BN 44r, 58v; *Job*, 56va, 57ra; *Mtt.*, 87vb, 101va, 107rb–vb, 155rb–va. Sometimes he follows Joachim in seeing the new understanding of scripture as analogous to the double procession of the Holy Spirit: after the letter of the Old and New Testaments, there will follow a *concordia* and spiritual interpretation of both. See *Mtt.*, 107vb, as well as *Isa.*, BN 58v; *Mtt.*, 58va.

43. For the sevenfold pattern of church history see Robert Lerner, "Refreshment of the Saints," *Traditio* 32 (1976): 97–144. For Bonaventure's relation to Joachim see Joseph Ratzinger, *Die Geschichtstheologie des heiligen Bonaventura* (Munich, 1959), cited here in its English translation, *The Theology of History in St. Bonaventure* (Chicago, 1971); and Bernard McGinn, *The Calabrian Abbot* (New York, 1985), Part III. For Olivi and Bonaventure see David Burr, "Bonaventure, Olivi and Franciscan Eschatology," *CF* 53 (1983): 23–40.

44. It is anticipated in the version published by Ferdinand Delorme, *Collationes in Hexaemeron et Bonaventuriana quaedam selecta* (Quaracchi, 1934), visio III, collatio IV, p. 185. The distinction between Christ's two advents is linked to another between the first John the Baptist, who came to reveal the person of Christ, and the second (Francis), who came to re-

veal the life of Christ. Sometimes the pattern is expanded into a threefold one involving Christ's advents in flesh, spirit, and judgment. See q. 8, 29a; *Isa.*, PU 2vb; *Job*, 13ra; *Mtt.*, 107rb–va. See also *Lectura super Genesim* (hereafter *Gen.*), MS Florence, Bibl. Naz. Conv. Sopp. G 1.671, 85va; *Lectura super prophetas minores* (hereafter *Minor Prophets*), MS Paris, Bibl. Nat. lat. 507, 21rb, 22vb-23ra, 24rb, 26va, 28vb, 35vb; *Rev.*, 7vb.

45. *De perf. evang.*, qq. 1 and 2, in *SF* 60 (1963):382–445; 61 (1964): 108–40.

46. Ratzinger, *Theology of History*, 92, makes this observation about Bonaventure.

47. Bibl. Laur. 448, 33ra: "Non plene apparet Dei condescensio et magnificatio circa ecclesiam suam, si saltem in uno tempore eius non fieret clarificatio fidei et inundatio divinarum deliciarum et evacuatio omnium errorum, prout est possibile in hac vita."

48. I argue these points at greater length in "Apokalyptische Erwartung und die Entstehung der Usus-pauper Kontroverse," *Wissenschaft und Weisheit* 47 (1984): 84–99.

49. Johannes Duns Scotus, *Opus Oxoniense*, IV, d. 11, q. 3, in *Opera* (Lyons, 1639), 8:618f.

50. See Bonaventure on the form of baptism in *Commentarius in I, II, III, IV librum sententiarum*, IV, d. 3, p. 1, a. 2, q. 1, in *Opera*, 4:71.

51. For Olivi's interest in prophecy and visions see Burr, "Olivi, Apocalyptic Expectation, and Visionary Experience."

52. See Burr, *Persecution*, ch. 3.

53. For example, *Job*, 57va, 69rb; *Mtt.*, 107rb–va, 113ra, 116vb, 140va, 153ra.

54. *Mtt.*, 107rb–va: "Sicut in primo adventu Christi qui fuit in carnem, fuerunt in plebe varie opiniones de Christi persona, discipulis tamen vere et solide confitentibus veritatem propter quam ecclesia fundata est in eis; sic in secundo adventu qui est in spiritu, sunt et erunt varie opiniones de vita Christi, sed in discipulis eius fundabitur ecclesia spiritualis, contra quam porte inferni, idest secte infernales Antichristi, non prevalebunt, immo habebit summam potestatem aperiendi archana scripturarum et gratiarum et secreta contemplativi status et claudendi ea indignis. Nota tamen quod ex quo erunt solidi in prefata confessione, ex tunc vita Christi seu Christus in spiritu sue vite aperte dicet eis, quod tam ipsum quam ipsos oportet ire in Ierusalem et reprobari a scribis et senioribus ecclesie carnalis."

55. Q. 8, 29va–34va.

56. See especially 12vb–16ra, 19vb, 30va–31ra, 34rb, 40rb. The final passage connects Aristotle with Antiochus (the image of Antichrist) via Alexander and sets up an equation: the doctrine of Plato is to the heresy of Arianism as the doctrine of Aristotle is to the heresy of Antichrist. See also *Quodlibet* II, q. 5, in *Quodlibeta*, 12v; *Quaestiones in secundum librum sententiarum*, q. 5, 1:98.

57. Q. 8, 29rb: "Modus etiam renovationis est omni fide dignus: tum quia non humano modo fuit inventus aut acceptus, sed divino spiritu et auctoritate summi pontificis et Romanae sedis. . . . Unde in privilegiis et epistolis apostolicis vocatur frequenter paupertas altissima et evangelica."

58. These observatons are based on fourteen mendicant Apocalypse commentaries from the period, all but four of them Franciscan. Detailed analysis must await another occasion; yet for all the characteristics noted here see the commentary published under the name of Alexander Halensis, *Commentarii in apocalypsim* (Paris, 1647), and the one found in MS Assisi 66. Vital du Four may have authored the latter. See the evidence in Dionisio Pacetti, "L'"Expositio super Apocalypsim' di Mattia di Svezia," *AFH 54* (1961): 297–99. Who wrote the former? It is clearly Franciscan.

59. Q. 9, 84ra–rb.

60. *Tractatus*, 10ra, 31vb. The opening paragraph can be called apocalyptic only in the weakest sense of that term. In fact, there are vague parallels in a series of unlikely places, such as Pecham, *Registrum epistolarum*, 3:952, or Aquinas, *De perfectione spiritualis vitae*, c. 13 in *Opera*, 41:B–81.

61. See Chapter 2 of this work.

62. See *Tractatus*, 10ra, for mention of all three.

63. David Burr, "Olivi's Apocalyptic Timetable," *Journal of Medieval and Renaissance Studies* 11 (1981), 237–60.

64. See his reference in *Rev.*, 84ra to "the novelty of the election of Pope Celestine and his successor and other presently worsening matters." On Ubertino see note 80 below.

65. *Quodlibeta*, 53(65)r.

66. Ibid., 51(63)v, 53(65)r.

67. *Responsio* II, 132–35.

68. On the following see Burr, "Bonaventure, Olivi and Franciscan Eschatology," 23–40.

69. See Chapter 4 above. Olivi discusses the problem in q. 9.

70. *Rev.*, 7va–7rb. *De perf.*, q. 9, refers enigmatically to the existence of various *status ecclesiae*.

71. Letter to R., 53(65)r.

72. See Burr, "Olivi, Apocalyptic Expectation and Visionary Experience."

73. Stephanus Baluze, *Stephani Baluze Miscellaneorum* (Paris, 1678), 213–67.

74. *BF*, 5:137–42.

75. Raymundus de Fronciacho and Bonagratia de Bergamo, *In nomine domini*, in *Archiv*, 2:371. Refuted by Ubertino da Casale, *Sanctitati apostolicae*, 407.

76. Johannes Mansi, *Sacrorum conciliorum nova et amplissima collectio* (Venice, n.d.), 24:1216.

77. Olivi, *Epistola ad Conradum de Offida*, in Livarius Oliger, "Petrus Iohannis Olivi de renuntiatione papae Coelestini V quaestio et epistola," *AFH* 11 (1918): 273.

78. See Chapter 5. It is tempting to place Jacopone da Todi's apocalyptically oriented *lauda* 50 in this period.

79. Leon Amorós, "Aegidii Romani impugnatio doctrinae Petri Ioannis Olivi an. 1311–12, nunc primum in lucem edita," *AFH* 27 (1934): 403; Edith Pásztor, "Le Polemiche sulla 'Lectura super apocalypsim' di Pietro di Giovanni Olivi fino alla sua condanna," *Bulletino dell'Istituto Storico Italiano per il Medio Evo e Archivio Muratoriano* 70 (1958): 321 note 2.

80. *Arbor vitae*, 454r–469r. On Ubertino see Gian Luca Potestà, *Storia ed escatologia in Ubertino da Casale* (Milan, 1980).

81. See Penn Szittya, *The Antifraternal Tradition in Medieval Literature* (Princeton, 1986), ch. 1.

82. Raymundus de Fronciacho, *Sol ortus*, 10.

Conclusion

During Olivi's lifetime the *usus pauper* controversy was centered in two major areas. North-central Italy was the scene of controversy over concrete practice. There was trouble in Ancona as early as the 1240s, but evidence concerning its nature comes largely from Angelo Clareno and must be treated with caution. In the 1270s and 1280s another quarrel resulted in imprisonment for a few dissidents. This time Angelo probably can be trusted, since he was one of those dissidents; yet he tells us disappointingly little. It would seem that the battle was originally over what ought to happen if the order was told to accept possessions, but it soon broadened to include current practice. The Anconan zealots set a course that would be followed by many later Italians, including Ubertino da Casale at the Council of Vienne. Their criticism of current practice called into question very basic changes that had transformed the order in the thirteenth century. They questioned current Franciscan educational methods and settlement patterns. Perhaps Ubertino reflected several decades of Italian zealots when he envisaged an order that would emulate Saint Francis himself by being less interested in worldly wisdom, less protected by privileges, and less closely bound to secular urban society.

While it would be folly to insist that no one in southern France offered such a radical critique of current Franciscan life, there is no evidence that anyone did so. Certainly Olivi did not. He refers enigmatically to those who wish to split off and lead an eremitical life, but he neglects to say where these people can be found. He might well be referring to Italians.

On the other hand, controversy on the southern French front offered something unencountered in the early stages of the Italian campaign, a debate over whether *usus pauper* was an essential part of the vow. In fact, our evidence suggests that the *usus pauper* controversy in southern France began around 1279 as a difference of opinion among lectors over just this issue. Almost from the beginning, however, its practical implications were apparent if ill-defined. Early in the contest, Olivi suggested that his opponents were trying to free themselves for easy living. The opponents themselves argued that their theoretical position was vindicated by official acceptance of laxity within the order. By the 1290s, the practical aspect had become important. The quarrel had moved out of the lecture room and into the rest of the convent.

The debate over practice seems more comprehensible than that over *usus pauper* and the vow. The latter surprises not so much because of its content as because of its intensity. After all, one side argued that Franciscans vowed restricted use, but did so indeterminately and thus could adjust practice to concrete circumstances. The other side insisted that *usus pauper* was not an essential part of the vow, but was so important that Franciscan life was useless without it. Was there really all that much difference between these two positions?

Southern French lectors thought so, and Parisian masters soon agreed. Those who defended an essential connection could argue with some justification that they were defending Franciscan tradition. They could appeal to Franciscan theologians, papal bulls, and even Francis himself. Bonaventure, Pecham, and Nicholas III did not explicitly espouse the Olivian view. One could hardly expect them to have done so, for it would have entailed answering a question no one had yet thought to ask. Nevertheless, they did seem to assume that the Franciscan *professio* committed friars to lack of possessions and limited use. The same could be said of Francis. Here again it was a question not of explicit statements but of general implication. It was hard to imagine Francis thinking that he and his brothers were not bound as tightly to *usus pauper* as they were to lack of ownership.

Supporters of an essential connection could also appeal to general lay opinion. Olivi correctly predicted what the man in the street might say if he heard a Franciscan arguing the opposite view. For Olivi and for that lay observer, denial of any essential connection between the vow and limited consumption opened the order to the charge of gross hypocrisy. It would be only too easy to conclude—as many did—that Franciscan poverty had become an empty charade. More was at stake than the opinion of outsiders, however. Severing the bond between vow and use did not remove all restraints on consumption, but it did make excess easier on the conscience and therefore more likely. Olivi saw that much quite clearly.

When we inquire what concerns motivated Olivi's adversaries, we may be tempted to conclude that they were moved by a desire for easy living. The suspicion is probably a sound one as far as it goes. There is no reason to believe that all of Olivi's opponents were conscious of such a motivation or even that they all shared it, but it is hardly coincidental that the faction which denied an essential connection between *usus pauper* and the vow also found itself rationalizing existent relaxations.

Nevertheless, Olivi's opponents also rejected his view because they thought it would lead to spiritual dangers. Franciscans busy with the Lord's work as assigned by popes and secular leaders would find their consciences troubled. It was not simply a question of moving close to the line where laxity meant violation of the rule and therefore mortal sin. It was also a question of being unable to determine where that line lay. Such a situation reopened Franciscans to the old charge that their rule was a "snare of sin." By 1279 the order had evolved an answer to the charge. Its response was enshrined in rule commentaries, polemical works, and papal declarations. Olivi's argument implicitly swept that answer aside. In this sense he was thoroughly out of step with Franciscan tradition and papal decrees. Nicholas III, for example, may have assumed that the vow bound Franciscans to restricted use, but he also assumed that if the vow was not to be a snare, there could be nothing indeterminate about it.

There were other dangers in Olivi's view, although his opponents did not cite them at first. His position could have unfortunate implications for discipline within the order. It turned disputes over practice into crises of conscience. Those who accepted his argument found it necessary to ask whether life in the convent was consistent with their notion of *usus pauper*. If they were certain that it was not, they were bound to protest. Moreover, Olivi's apocalyptic program suggested that such a confrontation was more or less inevitable.

The resultant situation was not a happy one for those entrusted with the smooth, harmonious operation of the order. At best it encouraged the more "spiritual" brethren (or the more stiff-necked, self-righteous brethren, depending on one's perspective) to criticize their colleagues' conduct, thus producing considerable ill-will. At worst it led such people to demand their own convents or even their own order. When their demands went unheeded, they felt justified in pursuing various forms of rebellion including the seizure of convents and defection from the order.[1] There is no evidence that Olivi's opponents recognized these implications during the early years of the controversy; yet they did eventually see them and the implications had been there from the beginning.

Olivi himself was no rebel. This was perhaps at least partly a matter of temperament, but it was also because he cherished a fairly moderate view of *usus pauper*. He probably did not see daily life in the Narbonne convent as stunningly inconsistent with his vow. He undoubtedly thought there was room for criticism, but that is not the same as being confronted with a situation in which one must disobey in order to avoid sinning against one's conscience. Nevertheless, however safe Olivi's position may have been for Olivi, it could have a much different effect upon anyone who decided that the order had gone seriously awry. Ironically enough, official disapproval of Olivi's position would eventually spur his supporters toward just such a conclusion.

Before that occurred, a long development had to take place. Several distinct phases can be isolated along the way. In the 1280s there was debate on the question of *usus pauper* and Olivi was momentarily bested, but the question remained unsettled. By the end of the decade, Olivi was teaching again and Raymond Geoffroi was governing the order. In Italy what seems to have been a nasty but relatively localized persecution took place in the 1280s, but it was seriously impeded by Raymond's election.

The 1290s were a watershed period. Apparently the French zealots developed a radical faction that was disciplined by the order. Then the election and resignation of Celestine V encouraged some Italian zealots to rebel against the new pope, Boniface VIII. Although moderates like Olivi withheld their blessing from such enormities, they were compromised nonetheless. Those in authority increasingly saw zealots of whatever stripe as a threat to discipline. By the end of the decade, pope and minister general were combining to suppress Olivi's views and supporters.

This repressive stage persisted until 1309, when Pope Clement V decided that the zealots deserved a hearing and opened the second major round of debate on *usus pauper*. The result was another spate of polemical writings in which the theoretical issue of *usus pauper* as part of the vow remained important, but practical abuses were also discussed at length. These led to *Exivi de paradiso* (May 1312) and a series of concrete actions aimed at settling the problem once and for all.[2]

On a theoretical level, Clement's solution endorsed neither spirituals nor community, but rather the papal position already enshrined in *Exiit qui seminat* and its ancestors: since a vow must fall *sub certo*, the Franciscan vow bound one by precept only to those aspects of *usus pauper* specifically demanded in the rule by precept, prohibition, or equivalent words. Clement saw that this position had its conceptual difficulties, because no one took every single imperative in the rule as a precept and no one had an easy formula for identifying "equivalent words." Thus he offered a list of items that should be taken as precepts.

Perhaps the most significant thing about Clement's list is that it differed from the one compiled by a fourteen-man commission charged with advising him.[3] Moreover, the report of that commission makes it clear that its own members differed among themselves. The proceedings at Vienne showed that the traditional formula of "precept, prohibition, or equivalent words" did not automatically provide a set of requirements acceptable to all. Thus the ultimate sanction of Clement's list lay in Clement's own authority.

Clement's solution contained another difficulty. Olivi's opponents had argued that restricted use could not be a part of the vow because there was no way of locating the exact point at which violation would occur. They agreed with Clement that a vow must fall *sub certo*. When the pope included elements like vile clothing among his chosen precepts, he seemed to defy that requirement. He solved the problem by placing determination of such matters in the hands of Franciscan superiors. The brothers need only obey and their consciences would be clear.

In short, Clement told the order that vile clothing was a precept because the pope had told them it was such, and that they must adopt a certain level of vileness because their superiors told them it was the proper level. Such a solution shifted the weight of authority from rule to leaders and thus made it harder to oppose the latter in the name of the former. There was little place in such a world for Olivi's notion that the friar had a responsibility to disobey superiors if they demanded violation of the rule. Unfortunately, a number of Franciscans found Olivi's view hard to abandon.

Their difficulty would not have been so obvious if Clement's settlement had succeeded on the practical level, but it did not. The factions were soon at war again, and the fight continued until 1317. During this phase the theoretical argument over *usus pauper* as part of the vow remained virtually undiscussed, and most of the contestants' attention was focused on the issue of obedience. This stage in turn came to an end in 1317, when John XXII inaugurated still another one by siding with the community and embarking upon a suppression of dissent. John was not the first to brand the spirituals as heretics, but he went about it more systematically than anyone before him had done. In the process he orchestrated the final great attack on Olivi's reputation. In 1318 Olivi's tomb at Narbonne, now a popular pilgrimage center, was destroyed and his body removed to an undisclosed location. In 1319 his Apocalypse commentary was censured by a papal commission and by a Franciscan general chapter.[4]

The net effect was to confront the spirituals with a clearer, less palatable set of options than they had faced so far: knuckle under or openly defy pope and order. Some, like the four who died at Marseilles, chose martyrdom. Others simply fled. Still others found that the choice could be evaded at least temporarily through the obscurity of an Italian hermitage or the patronage of a powerful supporter. Still others undoubtedly conformed, awaiting better days.

One is tempted to characterize this controversy as a major turning point in Franciscan history. Perhaps it was, but its significance should not be exaggerated. Here we return to the thesis of the first chapter. However much the original Franciscan vision might have been compromised by decreasing standards of poverty, it was compromised by other changes as well, and perhaps in more important ways. An order that could lock up its members under inhumane conditions and eventually acquiesce in burning a few might have puzzled the Poverello. A rebellious, self-righteous minority willing to defy pope and minister general in the name of regular observance might have proved just as problematic to him.

Inevitably we return to the idea of *minoritas*. Francis saw poverty as part of a more encompassing attitude based ultimately on the imitation of Christ. Whether he could run an order on that basis was another question. He seems to have opted for coercive power relationships in internal administration, but he conceived them as entailing a different sort of leadership than that found in the world at large. He took the word *fraternitas* seriously. Leaders were to be kindly servants of their flocks. The flocks were to have substantial responsibility for internal discipline, including a degree of surveillance over their leaders; yet the duty of obedience was also stressed. The result was a degree of tension in the roles of superior and subordinate alike. Francis saw the relation of his order to the outside world in somewhat simpler terms. Here, it seemed, Franciscans could be consistently *minor*.

By the time of Francis's death, the ideal was being modified in two ways. Internally Franciscan government was being brought more into line with prevailing hierarchical leadership patterns in the church. Externally, Franciscans were acquiring significant coercive power over those outside the order. Francis himself (perhaps unwittingly) encouraged this development almost from the start by accepting papal protection, but even if he had not done so there was little he could have done to stop it. The paradox of *minoritas* as Francis conceived it is that one can maintain it only if allowed to do so by those in power. In the thirteenth century the pope, the supreme power, decided otherwise. He decreed that the Franciscans should exercise some of his power for him. Their acceptance of it had an incalculable effect on the original Franciscan ideal of *fratres minores* pursuing the way of Christ. It is arguable that the poverty so bitterly debated in the later thirteenth century was, in effect, what was left of the original ideal after much of the rest had been lost. Had the rest not been lost, the Franciscans might still have found themselves differing over *usus pauper*, but not with such rancor and such results.

Notes

1. In 1312 Tuscan zealots seized the convents in Arezzo, Asciano, and Carmignano, and in 1315 French zealots took over the convents at Narbonne and Béziers. See Angelo Clareno, *Historia septem tribulationum*, 138–42; Raymundus de Fronciacho, *Sol ortus*, 26f.; Ehrle, "Die Spiritualen," *Archiv*, 4:52–63; Anna Maria Ini, "Nuovi documenti sugli spirituali di Toscana," *AFH* 66 (1973): 305–77.
2. For *Exivi* see *Corpus iuris canonici*, 2:1193–1200. For his actions see Lambert, *Franciscan Poverty*, chs. 7–9.
3. In Geroldus Fussenegger, "Ratio commissionis in concilio Viennensi institutae ad decretalem 'Exivi de paradiso' praeparandum," *AFH* 50 (1957): 155–77.
4. Edith Pásztor, "Le Polemiche sulla 'Lectura super Apocalipsim,'" 365–424.

BIBLIOGRAPHY

In listing unpublished works, I include only the manuscripts cited in the notes, although in most cases they were compared with others. My choice of manuscripts should not be taken as a final critical judgment. The many sources published by Franz Ehrle in the course of his articles in *Archiv* are listed here by *incipit*.

Works by Olivi

Epistola ad Conradum de Offida. In Oliger, Livarius. "Petri Iohannis Olivi de renuntiatione papae Coelestini V quaestio et epistola." *AFH* 11 (1918): 309–73.

Epistola ad R. In Petrus Iohannis Olivi. *Quodlibeta*. Venice, 1509.

Epistola ad regis Siciliae filios. In *Archiv*, 3:534–40.

Expositio super regulam. In Flood, David. *Olivi's Rule Commentary*. Wiesbaden, 1972.

Impugnatio XXXVII articulorum. In Petrus Iohannis Olivi. *Quodlibeta* (Venice, 1509), 42r–49v.

Lectura super apocalypsim. MS Rome, Bibl. Ang. 382.

Lectura super genesim. MS Florence, Bib. Naz. Conv. sopp. G 1.671.

Lectura super Ioannem. MS Florence, Bibl. Laur. Plut. 10 dext. 8.

Lectura super Iob. MS Florence, Bibl. Laur. Conv. sopp. 240.

Lectura super Isaiam. MSS Padua, Univ. 1540 and Paris Bibl. Nat. nouv. acq. 774.

Lectura super Lucam. MS Rome, Vat. Ottab. lat. 3302.

Lectura super Marcum. MS Rome, Vat. Ottab. lat. 3302.

Lectura super Mattheum. MS Oxford, New College 49.

Lectura super prophetas minores. MS Paris, Bibl. Nat. lat. 507.

Quaestio quid ponat ius vel dominium. In Delorme, Ferdinand. "Question de P. J. Olivi 'Quid ponat ius vel dominium' ou encore 'De signis voluntariis.'" *Antonianum* 20 (1945): 309–30.

Quaestiones de perfectione evangelica (as numbered in MS Rome, Vat. lat. 4986).

1. *An contemplatio sit melior ex suo genere quam omnis alia actio.*
2. *An contemplatio principalius sit in intellectu quam voluntate.*
3. *An studere sit opus de genere suo perfectum.*
4. *An aliquod opus vitae activae praeter regimen animarum et praedicationem sit melius ex suo genere quam studium.* Questions 1–4 published

in Emmen, Aquilinus, and Feliciano Simoncioli. "La dottrina dell'Olivi sulla contemplazione, la vita attiva e mista." *SF* 60 (1963): 382–445; 61 (1964): 108–67.

5. *An sit melius aliquid facere ex voto quam sine voto.* In Emmen, Aquilinus. "La dottrina dell'Olivi sul valore religioso dei voti." *SF* 63 (1966): 88–108.

6. *An virginitas sit simpliciter melior matrimonio.* In Emmen, Aquilinus. "Verginità e matrimonio nella valutazione dell'Olivi." *SF* 64 (1967): 11–57.

7. *An votum vitandi suspectum consortium vel colloquium implicetur in consilio evangelico.* MS Rome, Vat. lat. 4986.

8. *An status altissime paupertatis sit simpliciter melior omni statu divitiarum.* MS Florence, Bibl. Laur. 448.

9. *An usus pauper includatur in consilio seu in voto paupertatis evangelice, ita quod sit de eius substantia et integritate.* MS Rome, Vat. Borgh. 357.

10. *An pauperibus evangelicis sit perfectius et convenientius victum suum adquirere per mendicitatis questum aut per manuale opus seu laboritium.* MS Florence, Bibl. Laur. 448.

11. *An vovere alteri homini obedientiam in omnibus, que non sunt contraria anime et evangelice regule seu perfectioni sit perfectionis evangelicae.* MS Florence, Bibl. Laur. 448.

12. *An romano pontifici in fide et moribus sit ab omnibus catholicis tanquam regule inerrabili obediendum.* In Maccarone, Michele. "Una questione inedita dell'Olivi sull'infallibilità del Papa." *RSCI* 3 (1949): 309–43.

13. *An papa possit renuntiare papatui.* In Oliger, Livarius. "Petri Iohannis Olivi de renuntiatione papae Coelestini V quaestio et epistola." *AFH* 11 (1918): 309–73.

14. *An papa possit in omni voto dispensare et specialiter in votis evangelicis.* MS Florence, Bibl. Laur. 448.

15. *An vivere de prebendis vel quibuscunque redditibus vel vivere de possessionibus absque vendicatione cuiuscunque dominii vel iuris possit esse licitum pauperibus evangelicis.* MS Florence, Bibl. Laur. 448.

16. *An professio paupertatis evangelice et apostolice possit licite ad talem modum vivendi reduci, quod amodo sufficienter vivat de possessionibus et redditibus a papa certis procuratoribus commissis.* In Burr, David, and David Flood. "Peter Olivi: On Poverty and Revenue." *FS* 40 (1980): 18–58.

17. *An vovens evangelium vel aliquam regulam simpliciter et absque determinatione teneatur observare omnia, que in eis sunt contenta.* In Delorme, Ferdinand. "Fr. P. J. Olivi quaestio de voto regulam aliquam profitentis." *Antonianum* 16 (1941): 131–64.

Quaestiones in secundum librum sententiarum. Quaracchi, 1921–26.

Quaestiones quatuor de domina. Quaracchi, 1954.

Quod regula fratrum minorum excludit omnem proprietatem. In *Firmamentum trium ordinum*, 4:107vb–111rb. Paris, 1511.

Quodlibeta. Venice, 1509.

Responsio P. Ioannis ad aliqua dicta per quosdam magistros Parisienses de suis quaestionibus excerpta. In Laberge, Damasus. "Fr. Petri Ioannis Olivi, O.F.M., tria scripta sui ipsius apologetica annorum 1283 et 1285." *AFH* 28 (1935–36): 130–55, 374–407.

Responsio quam fecit P. Ioannis ad litteram magistrorum praesentatam sibi in Avionione. In Laberge, Damasus. "Fr. Petri Ioannis Olivi, O.F.M., tria scripta sui ipsius apologetica annorum 1283 et 1285." *AFH* 28 (1935–36): 126–30.

Tractatus de usu paupere. MS Assisi 677.

Works by Others

Abate, Giuseppe. "Memoriali, statuti ed atti di capitoli generali dei fratri minori." *MF* 33 (1933): 15–45; 34 (1934): 248–53; 35 (1935): 101–6, 232–39.

Alatri, Mariano d'. *Eretici e inquisitori in Italia* (Rome, 1986–87).

———. *L'Inquisizione francescana nell'Italia centrale nel secolo XIII.* Rome, 1954.

———. "San Bonaventura, l'eresia e l'inquisizione." *MF* 75 (1975): 305–22.

Albertus Magnus. *Opera.* Paris, 1894.

Alexander Halensis (?). *Commentarii in apocalypsim.* Paris, 1647.

Alexander Halensis. *Glossa in quattuor libros sententiarum.* Quaracchi, 1957.

———. *Summa theologica.* Venice, 1575.

Alvarus Pelagius. *De planctu ecclesiae.* Venice, 1560.

Alvernay, Marie-Thérèse d'. "Un Adversaire de St. Thomas: Petrus Johannis Olivi." In *St. Thomas Aquinas, 1274–1974*, 2:179–218. Toronto, 1974.

Amargier, Pierre. "Prêcheurs et mentalité universitaire dans la province de Provence au XIIIe siècle." In *Les Universités du Languedoc au XIIIe siècle*, 119–44. Toulouse, 1970.

Amorós, Leo. "Aegidii Romani impugnatio doctrinae Petri Ioannis Olivi an. 1311–12, nunc primum in lucem edita." *AFH* 27 (1934): 399–451.

———. "Series condemnationum et processuum contra doctrinam et sequaces Petri Ioannis Olivi." *AFH* 24 (1931): 495–512.

Analecta franciscana. Quaracchi, 1885–1941.

Angelo Clareno. *Le due prime tribulazioni.* Rome, 1908.

———. *Epistole.* In *Angeli Clareni Opera*, vol. 1. Rome, 1980.

———. *Expositio regulae.* Quaracchi, 1912.

———. *Historia septem tribulationum.* In *Archiv*, 2:108–327.

Antal, Frederick. *Florentine Painting and Its Social Background.* New York, 1975.

Auw, Lydia von. *Angelo Clareno et les spirituels italiens.* Rome, 1979.

Baluze, Stephanus. *Stephani Baluze Miscellaneorum.* Paris, 1678.

Baratier, Edouard. "Nominations et origines des évêques des provinces d'Aix et Arles." In *Les évêques, les clercs, et le roi*, 115–48. Toulouse, 1972.

Batany, Jean. "L'Image des Franciscains dans les 'revues d'états' du XIIIe au XVIe siècle." In *Mouvements franciscains et société française, XIIe–XXe siècles*, 61–74. Paris, 1984.

Beatus vir. *AFH* 42 (1949): 213–35.

Berg, Dieter. *Armut und Wissenschaft*. Dusseldorf, 1977.

Berger, Peter. *The Precarious Vision*. Garden City, 1961.

Bernardus Claravallensis. *Opera*. Rome, 1957–63.

Bernardus Guidonis. *Practica inquisitionis heretice pravitatis*. Paris, 1886.

Biget, Jean-Louis. "Autour de Bernard Délicieux." In *Mouvements franciscains et société française, XIIe–XXe siècles*, 75–93. Paris, 1984.

Bihl, Michael. "Statuta generalia ordinis edita in capitulis generalibus celebratis Narbonae an. 1260, Assisii an. 1279 atque Parisiis an. 1292." *AFH* 34 (1941): 13–94, 284–358.

Biscaro, Gerolamo. "Eretici ed inquisitori nella marca trevisana (1280–1308)." *Archivio veneto* 62 (1932): 148–72.

Boase, T. S. R. *Boniface VIII*. London, 1933.

Bonaventura. *Collationes in Hexaemeron et Bonaventuriana quaedam selecta*. Quaracchi, 1934.

———. *Opera*. Quaracchi, 1882–1902.

Brady, Ignatius. "The Writings of Saint Bonaventure Regarding the Franciscan Order." *MF* 75 (1975): 89–112.

Brooke, Rosalind. *Early Franciscan Government*. Cambridge, 1959.

———, ed. *Scripta Leonis*. Oxford, 1970.

Bullarium franciscanum historicum. Rome, 1759–1904.

Burr, David. "Apokalyptische Erwartung und die Entstehung der Usus-pauper Kontroverse." *Wissenschaft und Weisheit* 47 (1984): 84–99.

———. "Bonaventure, Olivi and Franciscan Eschatology." *CF* 53 (1983): 23–40.

———. "The *Correctorium* Controversy and the Origins of the *Usus Pauper* Controversy." *Speculum* 60 (1985): 331–42.

———. "The Date of Petrus Iohannis Olivi's Commentary on Matthew." *CF* 46 (1976): 131–38.

———. "Olivi, Apocalyptic Expectation, and Visionary Experience." *Traditio* 41 (1985): 273–88.

———. "Olivi's Apocalyptic Timetable." *Journal of Medieval and Renaissance Studies* 11 (1981): 237–60.

———. *The Persecution of Peter Olivi*. Philadelphia, 1976.

Callaey, Frédégand. *L'Idéalisme franciscain spirituel au XIVe siècle*. Louvain, 1911.

Callebaut, Andreas. "Acta capituli generalis Mediolani celebrati an. 1285." *AFH* 22 (1929): 272–91.

Carlini, Armandus. "Constitutiones generales ordinis fratrum minorum anno 1316 Assisii conditae." *AFH* 4 (1911): 269–302; 508–36.

Cenci, Cesare. "Le costituzioni padovane del 1310." *AFH* 76 (1983): 505–88.

———. "Ordinazioni dei capitoli provinciali umbri dal 1300 al 1305." *CF* 55 (1985): 5–31.

Chiappini, Anicetus. "Communitas responsio 'Religiosi viri' ad rotulum fr. Ubertini de Casale." *AFH* 7 (1914): 654–75; 8 (1915): 56–81.

Chronologia historico-legalis. Naples, 1650.

Chronica XXIV generalium. In *AF*, vol. 3.

Corpus iuris canonici. Graz, 1959.

Le Correctorium Corruptorii "Quare." Le Saulchoir, 1927.

Damiata, Marino. *Guglielmo d'Ockham*. Florence, 1978.

Daniel, E. Randolph. *The Franciscan Concept of Mission in the High Middle Ages*. Lexington, 1975.

D'Avray, D. L. *The Preaching of the Friars*. Oxford, 1985.

Delorme, Ferdinand. "Constitutiones provinciae Provinciae (saec. XIII–XIV)." *AFH* 14 (1921): 415–34.

———. "Diffinitiones capituli generalis Narbonnensis." *AFH* 3 (1910): 502–4.

———. "Explanationes constitutionum generalium Narbonensium." *AFH* 18 (1925): 511–24.

———. "Notice et extraits d'un manuscrit franciscain." *MF* 15 (1945): 5–91.

Denifle, Heinrich. "Die Denkschriften der Colonna gegen Bonifaz VIII." In *Archiv*, 5:509–15.

Denifle, Heinrich, and Franz Ehrle. *Archiv für Literatur- und Kirchengeschichte des Mittelalters*. Berlin, 1885–1900.

Desbonnets, Théophile. *De intuition à l'institution*. Paris, 1983.

Digard, George. *Philip le bel et le Saint-Siège de 1285 à 1304*. Paris, 1936.

Dossat, Yves. "Les origines de la querrelle entre Prêcheurs et Mineurs provencaux: Bernard Délicieux." In *Les Franciscains d'oc: Les Spirituels, 1280–1324*, 315–54. Toulouse, 1975.

Douie, Decima. *Archbishop Pecham*. Oxford, 1952.

———. *The Nature and the Effect of the Heresy of the Fraticelli*. Manchester, 1932.

———. "Olivi's Postilla super Matthaeum." *FS* 35 (1975): 66–92.

Durandus de Sancto Porciano. *Quodlibeta*. MS Paris, Bibl. Nat. lat. 14572.

Ehrle, Franz. "Die Spiritualen, ihr Verhaltniss zum Franciscanerorden und zu den Fraticellen." In *Archiv*, 1:509–69; 2:106–64, 249–336; 3:553–623; 4:1–190.

———. "Petrus Johannis Olivi, sein Leben und seine Schriften." In *Archiv*, 3:409–552.

———. "Zur Vorgeschichte des Concils von Vienne." In *Archiv*, 2:353–416; 3:1–195.

Elizondo, Fidelis. "Bulla 'Exiit qui seminat' Nicolai III (14 Augusti 1279)." *Laurentianum*, 4 (1963): 59–119.

Emery, Richard. *The Friars in Medieval France*. New York, 1962.

———. *Heresy and Inquisition at Narbonne*. New York, 1941.

Esser, Cajetan. *Origins of the Franciscan Order*. Chicago, 1970.

Esser, Kajetan. "Zu der 'Epistola de tribus quaestionibus' des hl. Bonaventura." *Franziskanische Studien* 27 (1940): 149–59.

Expositio quatuor magistrorum super regulam fratrum minorum. Rome, 1950.

Felder, H. *Geschichte des wissenschaftlichen Studien im Franziskanerorden bis um die Mitte des 13. Jahrhunderts*. Freiburg im Br., 1904.

Finke, Heinrich. *Aus den Tagen Bonifaz VIII*. Munster i. W., 1902.

Flood, David. *Olivi's Rule Commentary*. Wiesbaden, 1972.

Franchi, Antonio. "Il concilio di Lione II (1274) e la contestazione dei Francescani delle Marche." *Picenum seraphicum* 11 (1974): 53–75.

Francis of Assisi. *Opuscula*. Grottaferrata, 1978.

Fussenegger, Geroldus. "Definitiones capituli generalis Argentinae celebrati anno 1282." *AFH* 26 (1933): 127–40.

————. "'Littera septem sigillarum' contra doctrinam Petri Ioannis Olivi edita." *AFH* 47 (1954): 45–53.

————. "Ratio commissionis in concilio Viennensi institutae ad decretalem 'Exivi de paradiso' praeparandum." *AFH* 50 (1957): 155–77.

————. "Statuta provinciae Alemaniae superioris annis 1303, 1309 et 1341 condita." *AFH* 53 (1960): 233–75.

Galletti, Anna Imelde. "Insediamento e primo sviluppo dei frati minori a Perugia." In *Francescanesimo e società cittadina*, 1–44. Perugia, 1979.

Gerardus de Abbevilla. *Quodlibeta*. MS Paris, Bibl. Nat. lat. 16405.

Gervasius de Mont Saint-Eloi. *Quodlibeta*. MS Paris, Bibl. Nat. lat. 15350.

Giordani, Bonaventura. *Acta franciscana e tabulariis bononiensibus deprompta*. In *AF*, vol. 9.

Glassberger, Nicholas. *Chronica fratris Nicolai Glassberger*. In *AF*, vol. 2.

Glorieux, Palémon. "Maîtres franciscains régents à Paris." *Recherches de théologie ancienne et médiévale* 18 (1951): 321–32.

————. *Répertoire des maîtres en théologie de Paris au XIIIe siècle*. Paris, 1933–34.

Godefridus de Fontibus. *Quodlibeta*. In M. de Wulf and A. Pelzer, eds., *Les quatres premiers quodlibets de Godefroid de Fontaines*. Louvain, 1904.

Gonsalvus Hispanus. *Quaestiones disputatae et de quodlibet*. Quaracchi, 1935.

Gratien de Paris. "Une lettre inédite de Pierre de Jean Olivi." *Etudes franciscaines* 29 (1913): 414–22.

Guilelmus Petrus de Falgar. *Quodlibeta*. MS Paris, Bibl. Nat. lat. 14305.

Guillemain, Bernard and Catherine Martin. "Les origines sociales, intellectuelles et ecclésiastiques des évêques de la province de Narbonne entre 1219 et 1317." In *Les évêques, les clercs, et le roi*, 91–106. Toulouse, 1972.

Harkins, Conrad. "The Authorship of a Commentary on the Franciscan Rule Published Among the Works of St. Bonaventure." *FS* 29 (1969): 157–248.

Henricus a Gandavo. *Quodlibeta*. Venice, 1613.

Herde, Peter. *Colestin V*. Stuttgart, 1981.

Heynck, Valens. "Zur Datierung des 'Correctorium fratris Thomae' Wilhelms de la Mare." *Franziskanische Studien* 49 (1967): 1–21.

Heysse, Albanus. "Descriptio codicis bibliothecae Laurentianae Florentinae, S. Crucis plut. 31 sin. cod. 3." *AFH* 11 (1918): 251–69.

————. "Fr. Richardi de Conington, O.F.M., tractatus de paupertate fratrum minorum." *AFH* 23 (1930): 57–105, 340–60.

————. "Ubertini de Casali opusculum 'Super tribus sceleribus.'" *AFH* 10 (1917): 103–74.

Hinnebusch, W. A. *History of the Dominican Order*. Staten Island, 1965.

Hugo de Digna. "De finibus paupertatis." In *AFH* 5 (1912): 277–90.

————. *Rule Commentary*. Grottaferrata, 1979.

Infrascripta dant. In *Archiv*, 3:141–60.

Ini, Anna Maria. "Nuovi documenti sugli spirituali di Toscana." *AFH* 66 (1973): 305–77.

Innocentius IV. *In quinque libros decretalium commentaria*. Venice, 1570.

Jacopone da Todi. *Laude*. Bari, 1974.

Jean de Joinville. *Histoire de Saint Louis*. Paris, 1874.

Johannes Duns Scotus. *Opera*. Lyons, 1639.

Johannes Pecham. *Canticum pauperis*. In *Biblioteca franciscana ascetica medii aevi*, 4:131–205. Quaracchi, 1908.

———. *Contra Kilwardby*. In *Tractatus tres de paupertate*, 91–147. Aberdeen, 1910.

———. *Expositio super regulam*. In Bonaventure, *Opera*, 8:391–438.

———. *Registrum epistolarum*. London, 1886.

———. *Tractatus pauperis*. Chapters 1–6 in *Tractatus pauperis* (Paris, 1925); cc. 7–9 in *SF* 29 (1932): 47–62, 164–93; cc. 10 and 16 in *Tractatus tres de paupertate* (Aberdeen, 1910), 21–87; cc. 11–14 in *CF* 14 (1944): 84–120; and c. 15 in *Fratris Riccardi de Mediavilla quaestio disputata* (Quaracchi, 1925), 79–88.

Kirshner, Julius, and Kimberly Lo Prete. "Peter John Olivi's Treatises on Contracts of Sale, Usury and Restitution: Minorite Economics or Minor Works?" *Quaderni fiorentini* 13 (1984): 233–86.

Koch, Joseph. "Philosophische und theologische Irrtumslisten von 1270–1329." In *Mélanges Mandonnet*, 309–29. Paris, 1930.

———. "Die Verurteilung Olivis auf dem Konzil von Vienne und ihre Vorgeschichte." *Scholastik* 5 (1930): 489–522.

Lambert, Malcolm. *Franciscan Poverty*. London, 1961.

Landini, Lawrence. *The Causes of the Clericalization of the Order of the Friars Minor*. Chicago, 1968.

Langham, Odd. *Price and Value in the Aristotelian Tradition*. Bergen, 1979.

Langlois, Ernest. *Les registres de Nicholas IV*. Paris, 1886.

Larner, John. *The Lords of Romagna*. Ithaca, 1965.

Le Goff, Jacques. *La Naissance du purgatoire*. Paris, 1981.

Lerner, Robert. "Refreshment of the Saints." *Traditio* 32 (1976): 97–144.

Little, A. G. *The Grey Friars of Oxford*. Oxford, 1892.

———. "Statuta provincialia provinciae Franciae et marchiae tervisinae (saec. XIII)." *AFH* 7 (1914): 447–65.

———. "Statuta provincialia provinciarum Aquitaniae et Franciae (saec. XIII–XIV)." *AFH* 7 (1914): 466–501.

Little, A. G., and R. C. Easterling. *Franciscans and Dominicans of Exeter*. Exeter, 1927.

Little, Lester. *Religious Poverty and the Profit Economy in Medieval Europe*. Ithaca, 1978.

Longpré, Ephrem. "L'ouvre scolastique du cardinal Jean de Murro, O.F.M." In *Mélanges Augustin Pelzer*, 467–92. Louvain, 1947.

———. "Le quolibet de Nicolas de Lyre, O.F.M." *AFH* 23 (1930): 42–56.

Maggiani, Venantius. "De relatione scriptorum quorumdam S. Bonaventurae ad Bullam 'Exiit' Nicholai III (1279)." *AFH* 5 (1912): 3–21.

Maier, Annaliese. "Per la storia del processo contro l'Olivi." *RSCI* 5 (1951): 326–39.

Manselli, Raoul. "Divergences parmi les mineurs d'Italie et de France méridionale." In *Les Mendiants en pays d'Oc au XIIIe siècle*, 355–74. Toulouse, 1973.

———. *La "Lectura super Apocalypsim" di Pietro di Giovanni Olivi*. Rome, 1955.

————. *Spirituali e beghini in Provenza*. Rome, 1959.

Mansi, Johannes. *Sacrorum conciliorum nova et amplissima collectio*. Venice, n.d.

Martin, Hervé. *Les Ordres mendiants en Bretagne*. Paris, 1975.

Matthew Paris. *Chronica*. London, 1872–84.

McGinn, Bernard. *The Calabrian Abbot*. New York, 1985.

Meersseman, Gilles. *Ordo fraternitatis*. Rome, 1977.

Migne, J.-P. *Patrologiae cursus completus, series latina*. Paris, 1844–66.

Monumenta ordinis fratrum praedicatorum historica. Rome, 1898–1900.

Pacetti, Dionisio. "L'"Expositio super Apocalypsim' di Mattia di Svezia." *AFH* 54 (1961): 273–302.

Pagnani, Giacinto. *I fioretti di San Francesco*. Rome, 1959.

Pantin, W. A. "Grosseteste's Relations with the Papacy and the Crown." In *Robert Grosseteste*, 178–215. Oxford, 1955.

Pásztor, Edith. "Le Polemiche sulla 'Lectura super Apocalipsim' di Pietro di Giovanni Olivi fino alla sua condanna." *Bullettino dell' Istituto Storico Italiano per il Medio Evo e Archivio Muratoriano* 70 (1958): 365–424.

Paul, Jacques. "Le Commentaire de Hugues de Digne sur la règle franciscaine." *Revue d'histoire de l'église de France* 61 (1975): 231–41.

————. "Hugues de Digne." In *Franciscans d'Oc*, 69–97. Toulouse, 1975.

Péano, Pierre. "Les Ministres provinciaux de la primitive province de Provence (1217–1517)." *AFH* 79 (1986): 3–77.

————. "Ministres provinciaux de Provence et spirituels." In *Franciscains d'Oc: Les Spirituels, 1280–1324*, 41–68. Toulouse, 1975.

————. "Raymond Geoffroi ministre général et défenseur des spirituels." *Picenum seraphicum* 11 (1974): 190–203.

Peck, George. *The Fool of God*. University, Ala., 1980.

Pelegrino da Bologna, *Chronicon abbreviatum de successione ministrorum*. In Thomas of Eccleston. *De adventu fratrum minorum in Angliam*, Appendix II. Paris, 1909.

Pellegrini, Luigi. "Gli insediamenti francescani nella evoluzione storica degli agglomerati umani e delle circoscrizioni territoriali dell'Italia del secolo XIII." In *Chiesa e società dal secolo IV ai nostri giorni*, 195–237. Rome, 1979.

————. *Insediamenti Francescani nell'Italia del duecento* (Rome, 1984).

Pelster, Franz. "Nikolaus von Lyra und seine Quaestio de usu paupere." *AFH* 46 (1953): 211–50.

Petrus de Tarantasia. *In IV libris sententiarum commentaria*. Toulouse, 1652.

Potestà, Gian Luca. *Storia ed escatologia in Ubertino da Casale*. Milan, 1980.

Poulenc, Jerome. "Hugues de Digne." *Dictionnaire de spiritualité*, 7.1:876–79. Paris, 1932–69.

R. de Atrabato. *Quodlibeta*. MS Paris, Bibl. Nat. lat. 15850.

Ratzinger, Joseph. *Die Geschichtstheologie des heiligen Bonaventura*. Munich, 1959. English translation, *The Theology of History in St. Bonaventure*. Chicago, 1971.

Raymundus de Fronciacho. *Sol ortus*. In *Archiv*, 3:7–32.

Raymundus de Fronciacho and Bonagratia de Bergamo. *Infrascripta dant*. In *Archiv*, 3:141–60.

Raymundus Rigaldi. *Quodlibeta*. MS Todi, Bibl. Comm. 98.

Reeves, Marjorie. *Influence of Prophecy in the Later Middle Ages*. Oxford, 1969.

Reichert, B. M. *Litterae encyclicae magistrorum generalium, monumenta ordinis fratrum praedicatorum historica*. Rome, 1900.

Richardus de Mediavilla. *Super quattuor libros sententiarum*. Brescia, 1591.

Robertus Grosseteste. *Epistolae*. London, 1861.

Ryan, James. "Nicholas IV and the Evolution of the Eastern Missionary Effort." *Archivum historiae pontificiae* 19 (1981): 79–95.

Salimbene da Parma. *Cronica*. Bari, 1966.

Sbaralea, J. H. *Supplementum ad scriptores trium ordinum S. Francisci*. Rome, 1908–36.

Schiff, Otto. *Papst Nikolaus IV*. Berlin, 1897.

Simon de Guiberville. *Quodlibeta*. MS Paris, Bibl. Nat. lat. 15850.

Sisto, Alessandra. *Figure del primo francescanesimo in Provenza*. Rome, 1975.

Spicciani, Amletto. *La Mercatura e la formazione del prezzo nella riflessione teologica medioevale*. Rome, 1977.

Stanislao da Campagnola. "Dai 'viri spirituales' di Gioacchino da Fiore ai 'fratres spirituales' di Francesco d'Assisi." *Picenum seraphicum* 11 (1974): 24–52.

Szittya, Penn. *The Antifraternal Tradition in Medieval Literature*. Princeton, 1986.

Testimonia minora saeculi XIII de S. Francisco Assisiensi. Quaracchi, 1926.

Thomas Aquinas. *Opera* (Rome, 1882–).

Thomas of Celano. *Vita prima, vita secunda, et tractatus de miraculis*. In *AF*, vol. 10.

Thomas of Eccleston. *De adventu fratrum minorum in Angliam*. Paris, 1909.

Thomson, Williell. *Friars in the Cathedral*. Toronto, 1975.

Tierney, Brian. "Grosseteste and the Theory of Papal Sovereignty." *Journal of Ecclesiastical History* 6 (1955): 1–17.

Todeschini, Giacomo. *Un trattato di economia politica francescana*. Rome, 1980.

Ubertino da Casale. *Arbor vitae*. Venice, 1485 edition reprinted Torino, 1961.

———. *Sanctitas vestra*. In *Archiv*, 3:51–89.

———. *Sanctitati apostolicae*. In *Archiv*, 2:377–416.

Vicaire, M.-H. "La Province dominicaine de Provence." In *Les Mendiants en pays d'oc au XIIIe siècle*, 35–78. Toulouse, 1973.

Vitalis de Furno (?). *Expositio in apocalypsim*. MS Assisi 66.

Volpato, Antonio. "Gli spirituali e l'*intentio* di S. Francesco." *RSCI* 33 (1979): 118–53.

Wadding, Luke. *Annales minorum*. Rome, 1732.

INDEX

Abruzzi, 120
Alexander IV, 16, 34 n. 55, 100
Alexander of Hales, 72
Anagni, 125
Ancona: and issue of obedience, x; in 1240s, 16–17, 190; in 1290s, 108, 120, 124; in early 1300s, 127
Angelo Clareno: on Ancona, 16–17, 27–29, 37 n. 113, 108, 170; on Bernard Délicieux, 161 n. 50; on Bonaventure, 26–27, 30, 36 n. 108, 78; and Boniface VIII, 113, 116, 118–24; on Conrad of Offida, 117; on John of Parma, 17, 30; on Olivi, 39, 106–7, 172; on the rule, 184 n.11
Antichrist, 66, 124, 168–69, 173, 175–79, 182–83, 187 n. 56
Apocalyptic thought: Bonaventure, 25–26, 173; Italian zealots, 114–15, 124; John of Parma, 18; Olivi, 45–46, 52 n. 7, 65–66, 96, 115, 172–83, 192, 194
Aquitaine, provincial statutes, 9, 33 n. 41, 104 n. 30
Ar, Olivi's dispute with, 39–42, 49–50, 52 n. 9, 156–57
Aristotle: criticism of, 17, 41, 44, 146, 149, 177, 187 n. 56; positive use of, 25, 163
Arlotto of Prato: and Olivi, 52 n. 9, 88, 102 n. 9, 107, 143, 146
Armenia, 108
Arnold Galhardi, 39, 52 n.9

Arnold of Roquefeuil, 52 n. 9, 107, 125–26, 147, 171
Arnold of Villanova, 127, 134 n. 88
Assisi: basilica of St. Francis, 34 n. 55; general chapter (1279), 8–9, 39, 41, 60, 104 n. 30, 153; general chapter (1304), 128
Athens, 119
Attack on Brother R, 39–40, 49–50
Augustine: on desire and use, 77, 86 n. 65; on the sixfold division of history, 173
Auw, Lydia von, 37 n. 113, 116, 123
Avignon, 106

Beguins, 176, 182
Berger, Peter, 144–45
Bernard of Clairvaux, 18, 122–23, 36 n. 94, 58, 157
Bertrand de Sigotier, 109, 125, 129 n. 15
Besançon, 121
Béziers, 38, 182
Bishops, Franciscan, 93–96, 103 n. 23, 139–40, 180
Bologna, 11–12, 14
Bonagratia of San Giovanni in Persiceto: purported agreement with Olivi, 50–51; cited by Olivi, 58, 60, 79; criticism of order, 2, 29; role in *Exiit qui seminat*, 154; role in Olivi's censure, 40–42, 88, 106
Bonaventure: and apocalyptic speculation, 173, 175, 178–80; on

University of Pennsylvania Press
MIDDLE AGES SERIES
Edward Peters, General Editor

Edward Peters, ed. *Christian Society and the Crusades, 1198–1229*. Sources in Translation, including The Capture of Damietta by Oliver of Paderborn. 1971

Edward Peters, ed. *The First Crusade: The Chronicle of Fulcher of Chartres and Other Source Materials*. 1971

Katherine Fischer Drew, trans. *The Burgundian Code: The Book of Constitutions or Law of Gundobad and Additional Enactments*. 1972

G. G. Coulton. *From St. Francis to Dante: Translations from the Chronicle of the Franciscan Salimbene (1221–1288)*. 1972

Alan C. Kors and Edward Peters, eds. *Witchcraft in Europe, 1110–1700: A Documentary History*. 1972

Richard C. Dales. *The Scientific Achievement of the Middle Ages*. 1973

Katherine Fischer Drew, trans. *The Lombard Laws*. 1973

Henry Charles Lea. *The Ordeal*. Part III of Superstition and Force. 1973

Henry Charles Lea. *Torture*. Part IV of Superstition and Force. 1973

Henry Charles Lea (Edward Peters, ed.). *The Duel and the Oath*. Parts I and II of Superstition and Force. 1974

Edward Peters, ed. *Monks, Bishops, and Pagans: Christian Culture in Gaul and Italy, 500–700*. 1975

Jeanne Krochalis and Edward Peters, ed. and trans. *The World of Piers Plowman*. 1975

Julius Goebel, Jr. *Felony and Misdemeanor: A Study in the History of Criminal Law*. 1976

Susan Mosher Stuard, ed. *Women in Medieval Society*. 1976

James Muldoon, ed. *The Expansion of Europe: The First Phase*. 1977

Clifford Peterson. *Saint Erkenwald*. 1977

Robert Somerville and Kenneth Pennington, eds. *Law, Church, and Society: Essays in Honor of Stephan Kuttner*. 1977

Donald E. Queller. *The Fourth Crusade: The Conquest of Constantinople, 1201–1204*. 1977

Pierre Riché (Jo Ann McNamara, trans.). *Daily Life in the World of Charlemagne*. 1978

Charles R. Young. *The Royal Forests of Medieval England*. 1979

Edward Peters, ed. *Heresy and Authority in Medieval Europe*. 1980

Suzanne Fonay Wemple. *Women in Frankish Society: Marriage and the Cloister, 500–900*. 1981

R. G. Davies and J. H. Denton, eds. *The English Parliament in the Middle Ages.* 1981

Edward Peters. *The Magician, the Witch, and the Law.* 1982

Barbara H. Rosenwein. *Rhinoceros Bound: Cluny in the Tenth Century.* 1982

Steven D. Sargent, ed. and trans. *On the Threshold of Exact Science: Selected Writings of Anneliese Maier on Late Medieval Natural Philosophy.* 1982

Benedicta Ward. *Miracles and the Medieval Mind: Theory, Record, and Event, 1000–1215.* 1982

Harry Turtledove, trans. *The Chronicle of Theophanes: An English Translation of anni mundi 6095–6305 (A.D. 602–813).* 1982

Leonard Cantor, ed. *The English Medieval Landscape.* 1982

Charles T. Davis. *Dante's Italy and Other Essays.* 1984

George T. Dennis, trans. *Maurice's Strategikon: Handbook of Byzantine Military Strategy.* 1984

Thomas F. X. Noble. *The Republic of St. Peter: The Birth of the Papal State, 680–825.* 1984

Kenneth Pennington. *Pope and Bishops: The Papal Monarchy in the Twelfth and Thirteenth Centuries.* 1984

Patrick J. Geary. *Aristocracy in Provence: The Rhône Basin at the Dawn of the Carolingian Age.* 1985

C. Stephen Jaeger. *The Origins of Courtliness: Civilizing Trends and the Formation of Courtly Ideals, 939–1210.* 1985

J. N. Hillgarth, ed. *Christianity and Paganism, 350–750: The Conversion of Western Europe.* 1986

William Chester Jordan. *From Servitude to Freedom: Manumission in the Sénonais in the Thirteenth Century.* 1986

James William Brodman. *Ransoming Captives in Crusader Spain: The Order of Merced on the Christian-Islamic Frontier.* 1986

Frank Tobin. *Meister Eckhart: Thought and Language.* 1986

Daniel Bornstein, trans. *Dino Compagni's Chronicle of Florence.* 1986

James M. Powell. *Anatomy of a Crusade, 1213–1221.* 1986

Jonathan Riley-Smith. *The First Crusade and the Idea of Crusading.* 1986

Susan Mosher Stuard, ed. *Women in Medieval History and Historiography.* 1987

Avril Henry, ed. *The Mirour of Mans Saluacioune.* 1987

María Rosa Menocal. *The Arabic Role in Medieval Literary History.* 1987

Margaret J. Ehrhart. *The Judgment of the Trojan Prince Paris in Medieval Literature.* 1987

Betsy Bowden. *Chaucer Aloud: The Varieties of Textual Interpretation.* 1987

Felipe Fernández-Armesto. *Before Columbus: Exploration and Colonization from the Mediterranean to the Atlantic, 1229–1492.* 1987

Michael Resler, trans. *EREC by Hartmann von Aue.* 1987

A. J. Minnis. *Medieval Theory of Authorship.* 1987

Uta-Renate Blumenthal. *The Investiture Controversy: Church and Monarchy from the Ninth to the Twelfth Century.* 1988

Robert Hollander. *Boccaccio's Last Fiction: "Il Corbaccio."* 1988

Ralph Turner. *Men Raised from the Dust: Administrative Service and Upward Mobility in Angevin England.* 1988

David Anderson. *Before the Knight's Tale: Imitation of Classical Epic in Boccaccio's* Teseida. 1988

Charlotte A. Newman. *The Anglo-Norman Nobility in the Reign of Henry I: The Second Generation.* 1988

Joseph F. O'Callaghan. *The Cortes of Castile-León, 1188–1350.* 1989

William D. Paden. *The Voice of the Trobairitz: Essays on the Women Troubadours.* 1989

William Chester Jordan. *The French Monarchy and the Jews: From Philip Augustus to the Last Capetians.* 1989

Edward B. Irving, Jr. *Rereading* Beowulf. 1989

David Burr. *Olivi and Franciscan Poverty: The Origins of the* Usus Pauper *Controversy.* 1989